FOR ENGLISH LANGUAGE TEACHERS

英 语 教 师 专 业 素 养 丛 书

丛书主编

顾永琦（新西兰）
Peter Yongqi Gu

余国兴
Guoxing Yu

Principles for Language Teaching

外语教学的原则

Jack C. Richards（新西兰） 著

外语教学与研究出版社
FOREIGN LANGUAGE TEACHING AND RESEARCH PRESS
北京 BEIJING

京权图字：01-2023-0271

图书在版编目（CIP）数据

外语教学的原则 ＝ Principles for Language Teaching ：英文 ／（新西兰）
杰克·C.理查兹（Jack C. Richards）著. —— 北京 ：外语教学与研究出版社，
2023.3
　（英语教师专业素养丛书 ／ 余国兴等主编）
　ISBN 978-7-5213-4293-2

　Ⅰ. ①外… Ⅱ. ①杰… Ⅲ. ①英语-教学研究-英文 Ⅳ. ①H319.3

中国国家版本馆 CIP 数据核字 (2023) 第 035250 号

出 版 人　王　芳
项目策划　姚　虹
责任编辑　都楠楠
责任校对　徐　宁
装帧设计　郭　莹
出版发行　外语教学与研究出版社
社　　址　北京市西三环北路 19 号（100089）
网　　址　https://www.fltrp.com
印　　刷　三河市北燕印装有限公司
开　　本　650×980　1/16
印　　张　24
版　　次　2023 年 4 月第 1 版 2023 年 4 月第 1 次印刷
书　　号　ISBN 978-7-5213-4293-2
定　　价　55.00 元

如有图书采购需求，图书内容或印刷装订等问题，侵权、盗版书籍等线索，请拨打以下电话或关注官方服务号：
客服电话：400 898 7008
官方服务号：微信搜索并关注公众号"外研社官方服务号"
外研社购书网址：https://fltrp.tmall.com

物料号：342930001

SERIES EDITORS' PREFACE

Pedagogical content knowledge for English language teachers is a series that aims to provide a comprehensive knowledge base for busy classroom teachers. As the name suggests, the series covers issues related to the nature of language competence and how this competence is best taught, learned and assessed. It is hoped that, armed with this broad range of pedagogical content knowledge, ESL/EFL teachers will be able to meaningfully interpret the targets of teaching, learning and assessment, diagnose and solve problems in the teaching process, and grow professionally in the meantime.

The series includes the following seven broad areas:
1) Principles of language teaching
2) Curriculum and targets of teaching
3) Teaching language skills and knowledge
4) Teaching methodology and teaching tools
5) Testing and assessment
6) Language learning
7) Teacher as researcher

Unlike other books that aim for a similar knowledge base, this series attempts to be a digest version that bridges the gap between theories and practices. It also aims to offer easy reading and inexpensive texts that teachers will find easily accessible and applicable. To achieve these aims, all books in this series are written in simple English or Chinese. Each book in this series is authored by an acknowledged authority on the topic. It includes a brief introduction to theories plus a brief review of major research findings. The main text, however, focuses on how the theories and research can be applied to the ESL/EFL classroom.

In addition to the print copy for each book, an e-book version will also be available. Short video clips may also be made available at the publisher's website where some authors introduce their books.

Besides English language teachers who teach ESL/EFL at secondary and primary schools, target readership of this series also includes trainee teachers on short and intensive training programmes. Pre-service teachers who are studying for the MA in TESOL/Applied Linguistics and Year 3/4 English majors who aspire to be English language teachers should find the series very useful as well.

In second language teacher education, in addition to the "how to teach ..." questions, we often hear about central issues such as form vs. meaning, the place of the mother tongue, and the balance point among different skills of the target language. The real tasks inside the classroom, however, are rarely separated into these issues. When teacher educators visit schools, one common request is a list of high-level principles and guidelines. So long as these principles are followed, teachers can improvise, as it were, and wouldn't wander too far off track.

The book *Principles for Language Teaching* is meant to do exactly this. Arguably, there is rarely a more appropriate author than Professor Jack C. Richards to offer such advice. With more than five decades of teacher education experience, Professor Richards crystalises scholarly research into 17 chapters grouped under eight areas:

1) Foundations of teaching English

2) The role of teaching principles

3) The nature of language lessons

4) Dynamics of the language classroom

5) Features of classroom activities

6) Achieving functional language development

7) Creative practice in teaching

8) The nature of teacher change

We hope readers will benefit from this book as much as we have.

Peter Yongqi Gu and Guoxing Yu
Series Editors

CONTENTS

PART 1 FOUNDATIONS OF TEACHING ENGLISH

PART 2   THE ROLE OF TEACHING PRINCIPLES

PART 3   THE NATURE OF LANGUAGE LESSONS

Chapter 6   Understand the nature of lesson structures and activities

Chapter 7   Develop learner-centered lessons

PART 4   DYNAMICS OF THE LANGUAGE CLASSROOM

Chapter 8   Manage your classroom as an effective learning space

Chapter 9   Create an emotionally supportive classroom

PART 5   FEATURES OF CLASSROOM ACTIVITIES

Chapter 10   Use skill-getting and skill-using activities

Chapter 11   Showcase your creativity

PART 6 ACHIEVING FUNCTIONAL LANGUAGE DEVELOPMENT

Chapter 12 Focus on learning outcomes

Chapter 13 Teach grammar as a communicative resource

PART 7   CREATIVE PRACTICE IN TEACHING

Chapter 14   Use your textbook as a sourcebook

PART 8   THE NATURE OF TEACHER CHANGE

Chapter 17   Plan your professional development

Glossary   359

PART 1

FOUNDATIONS OF TEACHING ENGLISH

Chapter 1 Recognize the nature of English as an international language

Introduction

The community of English language teachers worldwide includes countries where English may have different roles and functions. In some contexts, English is a medium of instruction and is widely used in the community alongside other local languages, while in other contexts English may have the status of a school subject with limited functions elsewhere. In addition, English is spoken in many different ways around the world, raising the issue for both teachers and students of which variety of English students should be taught or aim to master. Should they be taught to speak like native speakers of English in English-speaking (Anglophone) countries such as the USA or Australia? But this would not be a suitable goal in countries such as Singapore or India where there are rich local varieties of English. And in other situations is it acceptable for a student to speak English with an accent that reflects his or her mother tongue which might be French, Spanish or Korean? An awareness of the role English plays in today's world and particularly the issues raised by the spread of English as an international language (EIL) is an important part of the professional knowledge required of English teachers today and has an impact on many decisions teachers need to make (Sharifian, 2009). These issues are the focus of this chapter.

1.1 Dialects, accents, and varieties of English

For many people "English" refers to the nature of English as a mother tongue or first language for people in Anglophone countries such as Australia, Canada, New Zealand, the United Kingdom, and the USA. However, even within the so-called English-speaking or Anglophone countries, "English" means different things. There is great variety in the ways in which English is spoken, as is reflected in differences in the use of some vocabulary items, and of grammar and pronunciation (Galloway & Rose, 2015). Varieties of English with their own distinctive features are often referred to as *dialects*. In the United Kingdom four kinds of main dialects are often identified: *Southern English dialects*, *West Country dialects*, *East and West Midlands English dialects* and *Northern English dialects*. In the United States linguists estimate the number of US dialects could range from a basic three – *New England English*, *Southern American English* and *Western/General American English* – to 24 or more. Different varieties of spoken English are found in every Anglophone country, since they serve to mark important differences among people, such as the regions in which they live (regional dialects), their social classes (social dialects or sociolects) and their culture. A dialect is often associated with a particular *accent* (how a dialect is pronounced). With its accent, sometimes a dialect gains status and becomes the standard variety of English in a country and is the variety used to teach those learning English. The variety of English used in this way in the UK is referred to as *Received Pronunciation* (RP), which is only spoken by about 15% of the population. Dialects and accents are a culture-based aspect of language and accents differ in every country and even territories within a country. In the US, people from other regions say that Texans speak with a "twang", southerners are said to speak with a "drawl" by people from other parts of the US, and those in the northeast are said to speak faster than their southern neighbors. A person's region is often recognized through his or her speech patterns and accents.

Choose a country that you are familiar with and one that has a national language. Is the language spoken with a particular accent? If so, what is the source of this accent?

1.2 Kachru's Inner Circle and Outer Circle territories

Today English is no longer primarily associated with the ways in which it is used in Anglophone countries or by "native speakers". English has spread beyond its original boundaries and there are now greater numbers of users of English beyond its original territories. Many different factors account for the spread of English beyond its traditional status as a "mother tongue". In order to clarify the distinction between what was traditionally referred to as English as a *first language, second language,* and *foreign language,* the Indian linguist Kachru (1985) has introduced the terms *Inner Circle, Outer Circle,* and *Expanding Circle* using the image of three concentric circles to describe the status of English around the world – a distinction that is less clear-cut today though still a useful reference. The **Inner Circle** refers to Anglophone countries, where English is the primary language and the native language or mother tongue of the majority of the population, such as in the United Kingdom, the United States, Australia, New Zealand, Ireland and Anglophone Canada. The **Outer Circle** of English refers to countries where English has become established as a legacy of colonialism such as in India, Nigeria, Bangladesh, Pakistan, Malaysia, Tanzania, Kenya, South Africa and the Philippines and where local varieties of English have developed, a process sometimes described as indigenization. These indigenized or localized varieties of English developed because of the widespread use of English within colonial administrations and particularly through the use of English medium instruction. Populations within these territories were typically multicultural and multilingual and used English across a variety of domains since English was often the only language people from different cultural and linguistic groups in a community had in common. Some interaction required a minimal level of fluency and ability in English (such as communication with traders, merchants, domestic workers, and laborers, and where code-switching or translanguaging may have been a feature of transactional interaction when possible). Other settings for the use of English (such as in education, the law, and administration) would have required a much higher level of ability in English.

In Outer Circle contexts English plays an important part in people's sense of their personal, cultural, and national identities and their using of English to express their identities, such as Nigerians, Indians, or Singaporeans. They are not simply speakers of English, but speakers of Nigerian, Indian, or Singapore English, sometimes referred to as "world Englishes". Commenting on the indigenization or "Indianization" of English in India, Monfared and Khatib (2018) quote:

> These processes of Indianization go beyond the surface linguistic levels, and involve the underlying cultural presuppositions and their linguistic realizations. India's multilingualism and ethnic pluralism have added further levels

> of complexity. In 'mixing' words, phrases, clauses and idioms from the Indian languages into English, or in 'switching' from one language into another, one is not just using a code, one is also expressing an identity, a linguistic 'belonging'. Such mixing and switching take for granted, for example, the multilingual and multicultural competence of the interlocutors. In such interactions, naturally, the 'native' speaker becomes peripheral: Indian English thus has become a code of local culture and local cultural presuppositions. (pp. 60–61)

Linguists describe the differences in the communicative functions of English in Outer Circle settings as reflecting differences in these varieties of English: the *basilect*, *mesolect*, and *acrolect*. The uses of English reflect a continuum from one variety of English to another. The subvariety used by those with high levels of English medium education – the acrolect – is usually described as the local standard for the use of English (e.g. Standard Malaysian English and Standard Nigerian English). The basilect is the subvariety often used by those with lower levels of education or by people in informal settings (known in Singapore as "Singlish"). And the mesolect refers to any subvariety between them, although there are no clear boundaries between these "lects". Educated speakers of English in these settings (e.g. in Singapore, Malaysia and Nigeria) may sometimes use the acrolect or an upper mesolect in more formal situations, and something closer to the basilect in a more informal context (Platt & Weber, 1980).

What are some differences in the ways a language is used in formal and informal situations? Can you give some examples with the use of English?

1.3 English in the Expanding Circle

Kachru has used the term *Expanding Circle* to refer to countries where English has no official role but is widely used as a medium for accessing knowledge and information and for international communication, such as in China, Poland, Russia, Japan, Egypt, the Netherlands and the Nordic countries where English has usually been referred to as a foreign language. Today, speakers of English in the Outer Circle and Expanding Circle countries are said to make up the majority of the total number of speakers of English worldwide. Traditionally in the Expanding Circle countries, English was one of several foreign languages that students could choose to study in public education and for most people had restricted uses beyond the school setting. School-leavers' proficiency in English was often quite restricted since learning opportunities were largely confined to the classroom and use of the textbook. Today, however, in many Expanding Circle countries, English is now much more widely understood and used and is no longer regarded as a foreign language since for many people it may be the language they use for much of their higher education and also in the workplace. This is a consequence of its role in globalization, commerce, trade, tourism, popular culture, English medium education (Richards & Pun, 2022) and the use of English as a lingua franca. In addition, the Internet, technology and the media, and the use of English in face-to-face as well as virtual social networks provide greater opportunities for learners and users of English to engage in meaningful and authentic language use than were previously available in the classroom. Consequently in countries where English once had little impact beyond education, today's students often graduate from high school with considerable fluency in English. For them, English is no longer a "foreign language" and the property of native speakers but one which forms an important part of their identities and communicative competence as citizens of the world and as users of English as an international language as these comments from students in Finland and Denmark reveal:

> English has gained a particularly prominent role in Finnish homes through various media technologies. Films and television programs, for example, are not usually dubbed. Internet sources are abundant and available, as are console games, computer games and music. Many children also seem to be fearless in looking for solutions in various manuals, instructions, tutorials and "walk-throughs" in the English language.

> You can hear English all the time in Denmark – on television, on the radio, on the Internet, in newspapers, etc. I'm sure you learn something even from a passive language situation like this; at least the language starts to sound familiar. Above all you understand how ubiquitous and important a language like English is.

Do you think people make greater use of English today in China than they did in earlier times? If so, what accounts for this increase in the use of English? In what situations and for what purposes is English now being used?

As the examples above illustrate, attitudes towards English will depend on where the learner is located, and what his or her goals are in learning English. In a study of Indonesian learners of English, Lamb (2004: 3) has found:

> In the minds of learners, English may not be associated with particular geographical or cultural communities but with a spreading international culture incorporating (inter alia) business, technological innovation, consumer values, democracy, world travel and the multifarious icons of fashion, sport and music.

1.4 Targets and standards for the use of English

The spread of English and the emergence of its role as an international language raise important questions in determining policies and practices for the teaching of English (Rose & Galloway, 2019). What kind of English should students aim to acquire? Should the target be British English, Australian English, Singapore English or some other variety of English? The question should really be restated as follows: What variety of spoken English should be the target and used to determine the standard that will be used as the basis for teaching and assessment? This restatement of the issue reflects the fact that when people speak of British English or American English, they are primarily referring to a particular group of speakers' accent. Although there are minor differences in written English and in spelling conventions between, for example, British English and American English, when a language school identifies itself as teaching "American English" or when a textbook states that it teaches "British English", it usually means that a standard British accent (Received Pronunciation) or standard American accent (General American English) will be provided as the model for speaking activities in the materials; or in the case of Outer Circle countries, production models will be in the standard or local acrolectal variety of English, such as Standard Filipino English. Listening input (e.g. through audio and video resources) may provide examples of many different kinds of English, but if examples are provided as a basis for repetition and practice, they will normally provide a standard Inner or Outer Circle model. Much of the world's teaching of English outside of public education takes place through private language institutes and some organizations (such as the British Council). In Europe, the stated variety of English taught is mostly identified as British English. English teachers in many countries in Europe would traditionally have sought to learn and teach the use of Received Pronunciation – the accent that carries greater social prestige than a regional British accent, as seen in a Croatian student's comments on a teacher's pronunciation:

> Some of the professors here speak a sort of very snobbish English, like X. I mean, terribly posh ... So, obviously, they'd internalized some sort of model in their stays in England which carries a slightly old-fashioned sense of prestige. (Vodopija-Krstanovic, 2011: 216)

In many other parts of the world (e.g. Japan, Mexico, South America), language institutes generally advertise themselves as teaching American English, as do the international textbooks that they make use of. An American (or North American) accent is often preferred by younger learners today since English spoken with an American accent is the one most often used in popular culture, though sometimes an institute might seek to distinguish itself from others by offering to teach British English and to use British English teaching materials, as is sometimes the case in Mexico and Brazil. In Chile and Argentina where there is often a historical association with Europe and with British and European culture, institutes offering British rather than American English are more common than in other parts of Latin America.

> *What targets do your students typically set for themselves when learning English? How useful do they think these targets will be for them? Do they express a preference for a particular variety of English?*

1.5 Exonormative and endonormative standards

In the contexts above where for many learners the standard or prestige variety of English spoken in an Anglophone country is seen as the ideal learning target, the focus on an external standard is referred to as an *exonormative* orientation to spoken English. The target for learning is "native-speaker English" – a variety which is believed to reflect prestige and legitimacy (Kirkpatrick, 2007) and which is codified in dictionaries and grammar and used as the basis for textbooks and teaching materials. Reflecting on the attitudes of many Europeans, Mackenzie (2014: 120) has argued that "many multilinguals clearly do feel that they have some kind of obligation to learn languages 'properly,' by which they generally mean as the natives speak them … few people espouse the 'imperfect learning' of French, Spanish, Arabic, Russian or Chinese as a pedagogical goal". This is presumably a common attitude from learners in Expanding Circle contexts despite the fact that at the practical level an exonormative target represents an unattainable (and most often unnecessary) goal for most learners. Even though learners may invest considerable time and effort in trying to master a native-speaker accent, most English language users are unlikely to be able to speak English without an accent that is influenced by the pronunciation features of the first language – one that is referred to colloquially as a "foreign accent".

> *What are some features of spoken English that account for differences between British and American English?*

In countries where English is widely used as part of the local linguistic landscape, a focus on external norms as the standard for spoken English has been replaced by an *endonormative* orientation as noted with the example of local "Englishes" used as models in Inner Circle contexts, which Mozaheb and Monfared (2020: 29), following Kirkpatrick (2007) and Schneider (2011), characterize as:

> An endonormative model ... is one where "a localised version of the language has become socially acceptable" (Kirkpatrick, 2007, p.189). In this model, a codified endonormative model (Kirkpatrick, 2007; Schneider, 2011) based on the acrolect of the local variety (i.e. spoken by local educated speakers) could be used in local ELT [i.e. English language teaching] classrooms. In this model, the multilingualism of teachers is considered an asset because the teachers provide a model of English that seems attainable by the learners and the teachers are more familiar with social norms ...

Instructional materials in these cases (e.g. in India, Malaysia, and the Philippines) might provide examples of people speaking with a variety of accents (e.g. British, Australian, Indian, Mexican, or American accent), but exercises which provide models for spoken practice will use the local standard variety of English, i.e. the acrolect. However, research on teachers' and students' attitudes towards different varieties of English often reports mixed results and in many cases teachers and learners are generally oriented towards Inner Circle norms as targets for pronunciation (Ahn, 2014; Derwing & Munro, 2005; Murphy, 2014; Sifakis & Sougari, 2005; Üresin & Karakaş, 2019), presumably reflecting the emphasis on native-speaker norms in their textbooks and learning resources.

1.6 Standards for written English

The different "Englishes" above, such as American, Australian, Indian or Nigerian English, are largely identifiable by features of spoken English rather than written English. It is through the spoken language that people realize their national and cultural identities, as either Britons, South Africans, Australians, Ghanaians or Jamaicans. What we can refer to as standard written English (the variety used in writing for academia, international commerce, publishing, the media, etc.), apart from minor differences in spelling, vocabulary and sometimes grammar, is usually the same, whether a text is written in Norway, China, Hungary or Russia. When writing for an international readership, a good writer in English generally aims to write in a neutral, internationally accepted style, and not in a way that highlights the part of the world in which he or she lives or works. This standard for writing is sometimes referred to as "written international English", which is the standard for written English used in professional, educational, institutional, scientific and academic contexts. This is the model presented in numerous handbooks and guides for both native and international English writers, such as Weiss (2005).

What purposes do you use written English for? How do you decide whether something you have written in English reflects international standards of written English?

1.7 The role of culture in learning English as an international language: Big C culture and Small c culture

Many of the world's languages are restricted in their use to a particular region or location. These include Asian languages such as Korean, Japanese, Thai and Khmer and European languages such as Polish, Finnish, Czech or Basque. Other languages such as Chinese, German, and Spanish are spoken in several different countries but none of these languages are used in the diversity of contexts in which English is used. Learners learning any of these languages will normally aim to learn to use them in the way they are used by native speakers, and textbooks and resources will provide models of native-speaker usage. If you wish to learn Japanese, Thai or Finnish your aim will usually be to learn how to use it in the way it is spoken by native speakers in Japan, Thailand, or Finland. If you wish to learn Spanish you will need to decide which variety of Spanish you want to master: Spanish as spoken by native speakers of Spanish in Spain, Mexico, or Chile, for example.

When a language is limited in its use to a particular country or territory, it is also assumed that language learning also includes understanding how the language reflects the world view or "culture" of its speakers. For example, prior to the spread of English as a global language, the teaching of English often included a literature component since it was assumed that a language could not be understood unless it was understood in relation to the culture in which it was embedded, typically the national culture of an Anglophone country. A course in American culture or British culture was often a part of the curriculum for language learners learning American English or British English. This understanding of culture is sometimes referred to as *Big C culture*, which is linked to the concept of a nation state: "speech communities were seen as grounded in the nation – the national context in which a national language was spoken by a homogeneous national citizenry" (Kramsch, 2013: 64). Achievements in art, architecture, music, and literature were highlighted to indicate the prestige and uniqueness of the nation. In the case of English, textbooks included information on the social customs and practices of people in English-speaking countries, particularly those of the middle class, whose social practices were presented in terms of home life, leisure activities, customary practices associated with events such as meals and weddings, as well as interpersonal relations. The textbooks also included words for culturally specific practices, such as local words for eating – *barbie* (Australia), *hangi* (New Zealand), *high tea* (UK), and *pot luck* (US). For this reason, native-speaker teachers were often preferred since they were assumed to have an understanding of the cultural contexts of Anglophone cultures. Seargeant (2009: 56) describes the consequence in Japan of prioritizing the role of culture in English language teaching, rather than mastery of spoken English:

> The language becomes not so much a tool for international communication, but a living artifact belonging to a foreign culture. Likewise, native speaker teachers become specimens of that foreign culture, their role as instructors of specialized knowledge overshadowed by their status as foreign nationals, so that it is the emblematic presence of a foreign culture in the classroom that is the defining factor in their appointment in schools.

> *For students learning Chinese as a foreign language, what are some examples of Big C culture that would be important for them to know?*

However, when English has the status of a global language, it has no necessary link with any particular national Big C culture. Furthermore, the Anglophone countries themselves are today increasingly multicultural, and to focus on the cultural achievements of the white middle class is seen as both racist and unrepresentative of the nature of contemporary Anglophone societies.

As a consequence of the issues raised by the idea of Big C culture in language teaching, two alternative notions emerged within applied linguistics: the notion of *Small c culture* – the culture of social interaction through language (Kramsch, 1993), and the notion of intercultural competence (Bok, 2009).

1.8 Intercultural competence

All uses of English as an international language are inevitably cross-cultural encounters and involve people from different cultures and backgrounds. The participants may have different understandings about how exchanges and interaction between people typically take place, and differences in conventions of language use can sometimes lead to misunderstanding. For example, an American professor may feel comfortable if students address him or her by the first name, whereas in many Asian cultures this would be considered disrespectful. The ability to interact and communicate appropriately with people from different cultural backgrounds is known as *intercultural competence*. Learning to use English as an international language involves not only reflecting on how your own language may reflect culturally specific conventions but also learning how to manage interaction among people from cultures who use language in ways that may be different from the norms you are familiar with in your own culture. This involves learning how speech acts such as requests, apologies, compliments, greetings, invitations, complaints and refusals are realized in cross-cultural communication and how transfer of speech act conventions from one language to another can lead to misunderstanding.

Can you give examples of the ways that speech acts such as greetings, introductions, and compliments may be expressed differently in your culture and another culture?

An important feature of many speech acts is how they express relations between participants. Some speech acts can be thought of as involving an imposition on the other person (e.g. requests and invitations), and some can involve a potential loss of face (e.g. criticisms, refusals and complaints). In this case, they may be performed indirectly, rather than directly, depending on how well the participants know each other. In the case of speech acts that involve impositions or threats of losing face, indirect expression of speech acts can be a form of politeness. Whether a speech act is performed directly or indirectly not only depends on the relationship between the two persons and reflects factors such as social distance, age, gender and power, but also depends on the conventions of a specific culture. What may be considered appropriate for a direct realization of a speech act (e.g. an opinion) in one culture may be considered suitable (i.e.

considered more polite) for indirect expression in another.

Another area where differences often occur is whether the favored style for interpersonal communication is one in which speakers reveal very little of themselves (their beliefs, wishes, opinions, likes, dislikes and things which may not be shared with others), or one in which there is generally a willingness to reveal details of one's inner self in interacting with others. Thus, if we compare two cultures, we may find that what is regarded as part of the private self in one may be part of the public self in another (LoCastro, 2012). Some topics such as one's religious beliefs, political beliefs, marital status or income may be considered private in one culture and hence are not considered suitable topics for discussion in public, but this may not be the same in another culture. Cultures may also be different in the degree that topics are expected to be developed in conversation, rather than be merely touched upon. Liddicoat and Crozet (2001) report that Australians and French speakers often handle such a simple exchange as a question about the weekend (*Did you have a pleasant weekend?*) quite differently. In Australian English, the question is part of a ritualistic exchange and is not intended to lead to a real discussion about the weekend.

There are several dimensions involved in developing intercultural competence in English as an international language:

Awareness: Developing awareness that what seems normal in one culture may not be true of other cultures.

Curiosity: Willingness to learn about the diverse ways in which interaction occurs in different cultures.

Tolerance: Accepting that cross-cultural communication may sometimes result in unintended misunderstanding.

Flexibility: Willingness to adjust and adapt one's use of English in order to maintain open channels of communication.
Risk-taking: Willingness to tolerate uncertainty and to use negotiation and communication strategies to achieve successful communication.

What are some ways in which watching movies can be used to help students develop intercultural competence?

1.9 Using English as an international language

1.9.1 English for Inner Circle and Outer Circle users

While the term "English as an international language" refers to a geographic or territorial account of the use of English as the world's global second language, it also refers to how English can be used in ways that enable it to serve as an international language – one that is not defined by the norms and practices of particular local contexts but functions as a flexible and dynamic resource that is shaped by its users and the circumstances of its use. This means when Inner and Outer Circle speakers (e.g. native speakers of British, Australian, Indian, or Nigerian English) use English as an international language, they need to use it in ways that may be different from the ways they use it in predominantly local contexts, i.e. within their own speech communities. "Local" or "insider" uses of English are characterized by the participants' shared expectations as to the functions of interaction and how they typically proceed. The participants have shared linguistic, cultural and schematic knowledge and familiarity with local social and discourse conventions. Citing Wray and Grace (2007), Mackenzie (2014: 38) argues that languages that are used predominantly for esoterica or intra-group communication "generally have features that are semantically and grammatically complex: 'much of what needs to be said can be said elliptically and formulaically, with huge reliance on shared knowledge, pragmatics and common practice' ". Sometimes much can be understood and there is no need to express verbally, and a lot of interaction may be conducted in an informal and colloquial speech style reflecting empathy and rapport.

When English is used as an international language, however, speakers need to adjust their speech to make it less reflective of local knowledge and discourse practices. They will need to use high-frequency vocabulary and to avoid colloquialisms, vague language, obscure syntax or a marked regional accent or dialect – particularly when communicating with people who have limited proficiency in English. Some have termed this use of English as *Globish* (Nerrière, 2004), a concept that is not without its critics. In Europe, meetings of the European Union are increasingly carried on in English, since it is argued that English is the language that excludes the fewest people present. However, this comes at a cost, since many native speakers of English are notoriously hard for colleagues in Brussels to understand, and it is often observed that they talk too quickly and use obscure idioms. Consequently, some language schools in the UK are now offering courses in "offshore English" to help business people develop a more comprehensible way of using English when they work abroad. Offshore English is said to consist of 1,500 or so of the most common English words and a kind of syntax that is stripped of unnecessary complexity and vagueness.

In classes in offshore English, native speakers are taught to speak "core English", to avoid idioms (e.g. to say "make every effort" instead of "pull out all the stops"), to use Latin-based words instead of those with Germanic roots, to avoid colloquial usage and strong regional accents, and to use a slower rate of speaking. This reflects the ideas advocated by a movement known as *Plain Language*, which seeks to encourage people to use clear, straightforward and accessible language in official documents.

Plain language is defined as follows:

> A communication is in plain language if its wording, structure, and design are so clear that the intended audience can easily find what they need, understand what they find, and use that information. (see https://plainlanguagenetwork.org/)

In written English, features of plain language texts include:
- using concise sentences (15–20 words maximum)
- positive (not negative) clauses
- active (not passive) voice (using "if you break the law" instead of "if the law is broken")
- verbs rather than complex nouns (using "identify" instead of "identification")
- common words rather than jargon

How do you modify your spoken English when communicating with people who have restricted ability in English?

1.9.2 English for Expanding Circle users

The comments above refer to interaction in which one (or more) speaker has a native-speaker command of English (e.g. from an Inner or Outer Circle country) and other interlocutors draw on whatever communicative skills they may have acquired from formal instruction or from other contexts. However, English as an international language also refers to situations where English serves as a lingua franca and where none of the participants are native speakers of English (Mackenzie, 2014). In these situations, the speakers' primary goals may not be to mimic American English, British English or some other variety of English but rather to develop the ability to use both spoken and written English as a communicative resource which will serve their purposes. For example:

- using English to communicate in situations where it is the only language the participants have in common (e.g. between Chinese and Japanese people or between Norwegians and Brazilians)
- using English online with international contacts from the Expanding Circle, for example in video games or on social media
- using English for transactional purposes with other speakers of English as an international language, such as purchasing items online or making travel arrangements by phone
- using English with others who may have limited proficiency in English, for example while traveling in countries where many local people may not be fluent in English

The functions and the circumstances for which English might be needed as in the examples above are often unpredictable, dynamic, and multidimensional, involving both linguistic and paralinguistic means of communication – both making use of language, gestures, eye movements as well as body movements, and reflect a great deal of linguistic variability. And since participants are bilingual or multilingual, "interactions are likely to include borrowing, code-switching, and other types of crosslinguistic interaction" (Mackenzie, 2014: 4). The nature of today's world means that occasions for the use of English in this way are becoming increasingly common. Young people in particular are very mobile and the workforce in many occupations are increasingly multicultural and multilingual. In circumstances such as these, as Breeze and Guinda (2021: 10) comment:

> When it comes to spoken English, there is a consensus that what matters most is comprehensibility and good communication skills, and that pronunciation should be clear – but the issue of accent is now regarded as having only secondary importance.

What advice do you give your students about the kind of pronunciation they should aim to achieve in English?

Participants in these settings are no longer viewed as second language learners but as *multicompetence language users* (Zacharias, 2010); they are not being considered "as eternal 'learners' on an interminable journey toward perfection in a target language. Speakers may opt out of the role of learner at any stage, and take on the identity of language users, who successfully manage demanding discourses despite imperfections in the code" (Mauranen, 2006: 147). They make use of their skills in using English as an "international" or somewhat hybrid variety of English (sometimes referred to as *cosmopolitan English*) which draws on many sources, including school-based learning, words, idioms and expressions that they may have observed in movies or television programs, first language patterns and ways of expressing meaning, as well as creative ways of using English that they have arrived at through practice. While both fluent and intelligible it would not necessarily contain the same phonological distinctions that are found in native-speaker "Englishes" such as Received Pronunciation of British English (Derwing & Munro, 2005; Jenkins, 2000; Monfared & Khatib, 2018), or the same grammatical resources employed by native speakers in Inner and Outer Circle contexts. Unlike English used in Inner and Outer Circle contexts, English as a lingua franca has no native speakers. It does not draw on a core of stable features but varies according to the contexts of its use. Its speakers come from diverse language backgrounds and the extent of mutual comprehensibility found in EIL contexts will vary from situation to situation. As Mackenzie (2014: 2) comments, unlike nativized world "Englishes", English as a lingua franca "is not, and will almost certainly never become, a stable variety, because of the range of participants in the international use of English".

Mozaheb and Monfared (2020: 28) comment:

> ... the goal of teaching English today from an EIL perspective is to prepare the learners to use English to become part of the globalised world, which is linguistically and culturally various, and thus both teachers and EIL courses should prepare learners for such diversity and to represent English as a pluralistic and dynamic component rather than a monolithic and static one.

Communicating in English as an international language may be more demanding for interlocutors than communicating in the L1 (first language), as Mauranen (2012: 7) observes:

> The cognitive load in EFL is usually heavy on account of the variety and unpredictability of language parameters: interlocutors' accents, transfer features, and proficiency levels.

Hence Mackenzie (2014) has cautioned against overly positive accounts of interaction in English as an international language, noting that reports of such interaction are generally based on what he calls "angelic" (i.e. idealized) interpretations from a very limited and selective data base and that a lot of such interaction may sometimes be problematic. Interlocutors may not be successful in trying to express what they want to say due to limitations in proficiency, i.e. of vocabulary, conversational routines, fixed expressions and grammar, resulting at times in inarticulate or incomprehensible attempts at communication with participants needing to make use of code-switching, requests for assistance, clarification requests, simplifications of form and meaning, prompting, paraphrasing, repetition, self- or other-initiated repairs, silence, topic change or topic abandonment, and a variety of communication and pragmatic strategies that may or may not always lead to successful understanding. Although many participants in using English as a lingua franca may indeed be users of English, they may still be learning how to use English for communicative purposes.

Conclusion

Recognition of the status and functions of English as an international language has implications for teachers of English, for learners, and for those involved in developing materials and resources for the teaching of English in international contexts. Understanding the nature of English as an international language – one that is owned by its users rather than only by those in the Anglosphere, i.e. the Inner Circle and the Outer Circle – requires a rethinking of the "idea" of English, a change in the mindset for both teachers and learners. It requires moving beyond the traditional idea of English that links it to the language and cultures of the Anglosphere and recognizing that there are many different "Englishes", each with its own validity and a part of the identities of both native speakers and people who use English alongside other languages in their linguistic repertoires. The English language curriculum should expand students' knowledge of the complex, varied, and fascinating roles English fulfills as an international language.

Learning a language involves arriving at a stage where the learner is no longer a *language learner* but a *user of English*. Reaching this threshold marks a milestone in the learning trajectory of a successful language learner. The ability to count to 50 in a language, to recite the names of the days of a week and to turn a sentence from the present tense to the past tense may be regarded as examples of language learning, but they are not examples of knowing how to use English for communication, which is the essential nature of English as an international language. Once a learner is able to use English as a communicative resource no matter what its limitations may initially be, this ability should be celebrated as an accomplishment and a sign that English is or is now becoming an aspect of his or her communicative competence and language repertoire.

Follow-up

Develop and administer a short questionnaire to find out what your students' attitudes towards learning English are.

References and further reading

* I am grateful to Nicola Galloway for comments on this chapter.

Ahn, H. (2014). Teachers' Attitudes towards Korean English in South Korea. *World Englishes, 33*(2), 195–222.

Bok, D. (2009). Foreword. In D. K. Deardorff (Ed.), *The Sage Handbook of Intercultural Competence* (pp. ix–x). Thousand Oaks: Sage Publications.

Breeze, R. & Guinda, C. S. (2021). *Teaching English-Medium Instruction Courses in Higher Education: A Guide for Non-Native Speakers.* London: Bloomsbury Academic.

Deardorff, D. K. (Ed.). (2009). *The Sage Handbook of Intercultural Competence.* Thousand Oaks: Sage Publications.

Derwing, T. M. & Munro, M. J. (1997). Accent, Intelligibility, and Comprehensibility: Evidence from Four L1s. *Studies in Second Language Acquisition, 19*(1), 1–16.

Derwing, T. M. & Munro, M. J. (2005). Second Language Accent and Pronunciation Teaching: A Research-Based Approach. *TESOL Quarterly, 39*(3), 379–397.

Galloway, N. & Rose, H. (2015). *Introducing Global Englishes.* Abingdon: Routledge.

Jenkins, J. (2000). *The Phonology of English as an International Language: New Models, New Norms, New Goals.* Oxford: Oxford University Press.

Kachru, B. B. (1985). Standards, Codification and Sociolinguistic Realism: The English Language in the Outer Circle. In R. Quirk & H. G.

Widdowson (Eds.), *English in the World: Teaching and Learning the Language and Literatures* (pp. 11–30). Cambridge: Cambridge University Press.

Kirkpatrick, A. (2007). *World Englishes: Implications for International Communication and English Language Teaching.* Cambridge: Cambridge University Press.

Kramsch, C. (1993). *Context and Culture in Language Teaching.* Oxford: Oxford University Press.

Kramsch, C. (2013). Culture in Foreign Language Teaching. *Iranian Journal of Language Teaching Research, 1*(1), 57–78.

Lamb, M. (2004). Integrative Motivation in a Globalizing World. *System, 32*(1), 3–19.

Liddicoat, A. J. & Crozet, C. (2001). Acquiring French Interactional Norms through Instruction. In K. R. Rose & G. Kasper (Eds.), *Pragmatics in Language Teaching* (pp. 125–144). New York: Cambridge University Press.

LoCastro, V. (2012). *Pragmatics for Language Educators: A Sociolinguistic Perspective.* New York: Routledge.

Mackenzie, I. (2014). *English as a Lingua Franca: Theorizing and Teaching English.* New York: Routledge.

Mauranen, A. (2006). Signaling and Preventing Misunderstanding in English as Lingua Franca Communication. *International Journal of the Sociology of Language, 177*, 123–150.

Mauranen, A. (2012). *Exploring ELF: Academic English Shaped by Non-Native Speakers.* Cambridge: Cambridge University Press.

Monfared, A. & Khatib, M. (2018). English or Englishes? Outer and Expanding Circle Teachers' Awareness of and Attitudes towards Their Own Variants of English in ESL/EFL Teaching Contexts. *Australian Journal of Teacher Education, 43*(2), 56–75.

Mozaheb, M. A. & Monfared, A. (2020). *Exonormativity, Endonormativity or Multilingualism: Teachers' Attitudes towards Pronunciation Issues in Three Kachruian Circles* (Dissertation presented to the project of

World Englishes). Imam Sadiq University.

Murphy, J. M. (2014). Intelligible, Comprehensible, Non-Native Models in ESL/EFL Pronunciation Teaching. *System, 42*, 258–269.

Nerrière, J.-P. (2004). *Parlez Globish: Don't Speak English.* Paris: Eyrolles.

Platt, J. & Weber, H. (1980). *English in Singapore and Malaysia: Status, Features, Functions.* Kuala Lumpur: Oxford University Press.

Richards, J. C. & Pun, J. (2022). *Teaching and Learning in English Medium Instruction: An Introduction.* New York: Routledge.

Rose, H. & Galloway, N. (2019). *Global Englishes for Language Teaching.* Cambridge: Cambridge University Press.

Seargeant, P. (2009). *The Idea of English in Japan: Ideology and the Evolution of a Global Language.* Bristol: Multilingual Matters.

Schneider, E. W. (2011). *English around the World: An Introduction.* Cambridge: Cambridge University Press.

Sharifian, F. (Ed.). (2009). *English as an International Language: Perspectives and Pedagogical Issues.* Bristol: Multilingual Matters.

Sifakis, N. C. & Sougari, A.-M. (2005). Pronunciation Issues and EIL Pedagogy in the Periphery: A Survey of Greek State School Teachers' Beliefs. *TESOL Quarterly, 39*(3), 467–488.

Tsang, A. (2020). Why English Accents and Pronunciation 'Still' Matter for Teachers Nowadays: A Mixed-Methods Study on Learners' Perceptions. *Journal of Multilingual and Multicultural Development, 41*(2), 140–156.

Üresin, F. & Karakaş, A. (2019). Investigation of Turkish EFL Teachers' Views about Standard Languages, Dialects and Language Varieties through the Lenses of English and Turkish. *The Literacy Trek, 5*(2), 1–24.

Vodopija-Krstanovic, I. (2011). NESTs versus Non-NESTs: Rethinking English-Language Teacher Identities. In J. Hüttner, B. Mehlmauer-Larcher, S. Reichl & B. Schiftner (Eds.), *Theory and Practice in EFL Teacher Education: Bridging the Gap* (pp. 207–227). Bristol: Multilingual Matters.

Weiss, E. H. (2005). *The Elements of International English Style: A Guide to Writing Correspondence, Reports, Technical Documents, and Internet Pages for a Global Audience.* New York: Routledge.

Wray, A. & Grace, G. W. (2007). The Consequences of Talking to Strangers: Evolutionary Corollaries of Socio-Cultural Influences on Linguistic Form. *Lingua, 117*(3): 543–578.

Zacharias, N. T. (2010). *The Evolving Teacher Identities of 12 South/East Asian Teachers in US Graduate Programs* (PhD dissertation). Indiana University of Pennsylvania.

Chapter 2 Develop your professional knowledge and skills

Introduction

In Chapter 1 we have described the status of English today as an international language, reflecting the fact that it has become the world's second language. As a consequence of globalization, the World Wide Web and the spread of English on a global scale, English has become not only the language of international communication, commerce, trade, travel, media, and pop culture, but also in some countries a medium of instruction for some or all subjects in schools, colleges, and universities. The role of English as an international language means that in many countries, effective programs for the teaching of English are increasingly seen as important for national development. Mastery of English by at least a significant segment of the population is also increasingly viewed as a key factor in the progress in education, business, industry, trade and commerce, and for membership of the international community. There is consequently a growing demand for innovative approaches to the teaching of English and for teachers who have a high level of professional knowledge and skills. In this chapter we will describe the kinds of professional knowledge and skills needed by today's English language teachers.

What are some ways in which approaches to the teaching of English changed in your experience? How have these changes affected you?

2.1 Teaching English as a profession

Teaching English is not something that anyone who can speak English can do. It is a profession, which means that it is a career in a field of educational specialization and requires a specialized knowledge base obtained through both academic study and practical experience. As a profession the teaching of English is also a field of work where membership is based on entry requirements and standards. The professionalism of English teaching is seen in the growth industry devoted to providing language teachers with professional training and qualifications – a recognition of the fact that employers and institutions have come to realize that effective language teaching programs depend on the quality of their teachers. This professionalism is reflected in continuous attempts to develop standards for English language teaching and teachers and in the proliferation of professional journals and teacher magazines, conferences and professional organizations. This professionalism is also reflected in requirements for English teachers to demonstrate their levels of proficiency in English as a component of certification or as a hiring prerequisite, in the demand for professional qualifications for native-speaker teachers, and in the greater level of sophisticated knowledge of language teaching required of all English teachers.

Do you belong to any professional language teaching organizations? If so, what value do they have for you?

But what do the specialized knowledge and skills that language teachers need consist of? Next in this chapter we will explore four issues that are central to the professional knowledge and practice of teachers of English: *disciplinary knowledge, proficiency in English, pedagogical content knowledge*, and *practical teaching skills*.

2.2 Disciplinary knowledge

Disciplinary knowledge (also known as subject or content knowledge) refers to what a teacher knows about his or her teaching subject. The notion of English as an international language is an important aspect of disciplinary knowledge for teachers of English. Teachers of any subject in an institution are expected to have specialized knowledge about their discipline that is not shared with teachers of other subjects. In the case of English, this includes a variety of kinds of language-related knowledge deriving from those disciplines in which language and language learning are the objects of study, such as linguistics, applied linguistics, second language acquisition, sociolinguistics, and discourse analysis. From these and other sources, as part of our professional education we acquire a body of knowledge about our teaching subject – English. The TESOL International Association (formerly known as Teachers of English to Speakers of Other Languages and often referred to as TESOL) has described five areas of knowledge and skills required of TESOL teachers teaching from kindergarten through to the 12th grade. These include:

1) knowledge about language
2) knowledge about the sociocultural context
3) planning and implementing instruction
4) assessment and evaluation
5) professionalism and leadership

Knowledge about language includes:
- Knowledge of English language structures in different discourse contexts to promote acquisition of reading, writing, speaking, and listening skills across content areas. Teachers serve as language models for ELLs (English language learners).
- Knowledge of second language acquisition theory and developmental process of language to set expectations for and facilitate language learning.
- Knowledge of language processes (e.g. interlanguage and language progressions) to facilitate and monitor ELLs' language learning in English.
- Knowledge of functions, learning domains, content-specific language and discourse structures, and vocabulary of academic English to promote ELLs' academic achievement across content areas.

Where and how did you develop your knowledge of English of the kinds described above? What are some ways of expanding your knowledge in these areas?

An aspect of studying the subject matter of a discipline such as language teaching also involves learning to understand the concepts and specialized terms that are used in the language teaching profession. This means learning how to be able to "talk the talk" and understand terms such as *top-down processing, alternative assessment, CLIL (content and language integrated learning), competence, text-based teaching,* and so on. However, there is no general consensus in the TESOL profession as to what the essential knowledge base required of TESOL teachers should consist of since this depends on the type of the program, the students it serves and their backgrounds and goals. For example, the core courses in the Master of Education (TESOL) degree at the University of Sydney are *Discourse and Language Teaching, Second Language Acquisition, Methodology and Language Teaching, Grammar and the Language Classroom, Literacy and Language Teaching*, and *Developments in English Language Teaching*, while those in the Master of Arts in English Studies (TESOL) degree at City University of Hong Kong are *Language in Its Social Context, Survey of Literary Genres, Dissertation* or *Capstone Project*. While some of these courses may not have immediate practical application, they form part of the essential subject or disciplinary knowledge that language teachers are expected to know. An instructor (Bartels, 2005: 75) on such a course has commented that "there is a body of encyclopaedic knowledge that an ES graduate must know, even though … it is of very little practical use".

Language-related knowledge of this kind has sometimes been referred to as "language awareness" (Andrews, 2001) and this has traditionally referred to a teacher's knowledge of language systems, particularly grammar. Students expect their teachers to be knowledgeable about the subject and knowing how to teach and communicate this expectation is important if you are to gain your students' trust, respect, and confidence. A foundation in the subject knowledge of TESOL can serve as a valuable reference and can also lead to a rethinking of some of our beliefs as is seen in these teachers' comments:

> The course on phonology was a real eye-opener for me. When the instructor explained the difference between stress-timed and syllable-timed languages I finally understood what makes the accent of some of my Spanish-speaking students so distinctive. Also fascinating were Jenkins' idea

of the phonological core and her idea that some features of Standard English pronunciation (such as aspiration on initial plosive consonants) don't necessarily need to be mastered by L2 (second language) speakers since omitting them does not impede communication. (Sylvia)

I didn't really enjoy the course on English syntax and grammar at the time, but now that I have been teaching for a while I realize that knowing quite a lot about how English works has made me more confident as a teacher. It also help[s] when I get asked tricky questions about grammar from my students. They really expect me to know all the answers. (Joon)

The course on English as an international language changed my understanding of myself. It prompted me to stop thinking of myself as someone who was not a native speaker but to make it clear to my classmates that unlike most of them, I spoke three languages and that my English was a marker of a variety of world English. Once I had understood this I became more comfortable participating in class and being a little more assertive. (Karen)

- *What are some of the ways in which a subject such as linguistics of English can be important for teachers?*
- *How do you think study of the following areas of language study could be of value to language teachers?*
    - *discourse analysis*
    - *sociolinguistics*
    - *pragmatics*
    - *psycholinguistics*
    - *second language acquisition*

2.3 Proficiency in English

The ability to teach a language obviously requires a good command of the language. However, for teachers of English as an international language this does not necessarily refer to native-speaker ability in English. Many of the world's English teachers may not have native-speaker ability in English yet they are still excellent teachers. In fact, they may be able to teach more effectively than many native speakers of English since non-native-speaker teachers can draw on their own experiences in learning and in many cases their knowledge of the learners' first languages. And consequently they can view language learning from the viewpoints of both teachers and learners. English teachers need to be able to use their ability in English in a special way – *as a pedagogical resource*, and this is not simply the same as fluency in English. The ability to teach English through English requires the use of specialized communicative skills rather than simply higher levels of "general language proficiency".

> *Are there any aspects of using English to teach English that you find difficult? How do you resolve these difficulties?*

As a teacher your use of language in your teaching is not only influenced by your own language proficiency and discourse skills but also by your learners' overall proficiency level. We generally adapt the complexity of our language to facilitate understanding and communication with our learners, hence when we teach low-proficiency learners there may be fewer opportunities to improvise or engage in language-rich input than when we teach students with higher levels of proficiency. If you are a teacher who feels your English needs to be improved, taking a course in English conversation at a local language center is not likely to be of much benefit since what is required is not more "general English" but rather further development of the specialized communicative skills that are necessary for teaching through English. Watching other teachers teaching (either through peer observation or online) as well as peer teaching and microteaching are ways in which these skills can be developed. The teacher's proficiency in English is further discussed in Chapter 3.

Have you taken any initiatives to maintain and develop your knowledge and fluency in English? If so, what are they?

2.4 Pedagogical content knowledge

Pedagogical content knowledge refers to the specialized knowledge that teachers draw on to provide a basis for language teaching. It is knowledge that draws on subject knowledge and teachers apply it in different ways to the practical tasks of language teaching. In addition to issues that a teacher of any subject faces such as classroom management and effective communication skills, an English teacher's knowledge base includes familiarity with one or more teaching methods such as task-based teaching and content-based teaching, teaching the four skills, knowledge of approaches to the teaching of grammar and pronunciation, curriculum design, teaching materials, assessment, and the use of technology in teaching. It also includes knowledge of the teaching context (learners, class size, course goals, etc.) and the impact it will have on teaching and learning. The TESOL standards in the domain of "Planning and Implementing Instruction" describe a few requirements for teachers of English as a second language (ESL) (https://www.tesol.org/docs/default-source/books/2018-tesol-teacher-prep-standards-final.pdf?sfvrsn=23f3ffdc_6), which can be summed up as follows:

- To plan for culturally and linguistically relevant, supportive environments that promote ELLs' learning and to design scaffolded instruction of language and literacies to support standards and curricular objectives for ELLs' learning in the content areas.
- To teach using evidence-based, student-centered, developmentally appropriate interactive approaches.
- To adjust instructional decisions after critical reflection on individual ELLs' learning outcomes in both language and content.
- To plan strategies to collaborate with other educators, school personnel, and families in order to support their ELLs' learning of language and literacies in the content areas.
- To use and adapt relevant materials and resources, including digital resources, to plan lessons for ELLs, to support communication with other educators, school personnel, and ELLs and to foster student learning of language and literacies in the content areas.

The ability to plan lessons is one of the core cognitive skills referred to in accounts such as those above. One of the differences between teachers and people not involved in the teaching profession is that teachers are able to see the potential of different resources for teaching and learning. These resources may include textbooks, technology, different kinds of *realia* (materials not developed for teaching purposes) as well as digital learning resources. A person with a teacher's mindset can envisage many ways of using different resources in his or her teaching. How does this person do this? Here is an example. An experienced teacher was given the following task:

A teacher has just called in sick. You are going to teach her 50-minute spoken English class (lower intermediate level) in five minutes. Your only teaching aid is an empty glass. What will your lesson look like? How do you think you would teach the lesson?

The teacher thought about it for less than a minute and then elaborated her idea for the lesson:

1) I would start by showing the glass and asking students to form groups and brainstorm for 5 minutes, to come up with the names of as many different kinds of containers as possible. They would then group them, according to their functions. For example, things that contain food, things that are used to carry things, things that are used to store things, and so on. I would model how they should do this and suggest the kind of language they could use. (10 minutes)

2) Students would present their findings to the class to see who had come up with the longest list. (10 minutes)

3) For a change of pace and to practice functional language, I would do some dialog work, practicing asking to borrow a container from a neighbor. First, I would model the kind of exchange I want them to practice. Then students would plan their dialogs following this outline:

a. Apologize for bothering your neighbor.

b. Explain what you want and why you need it.

c. Your neighbor offers to lend you what you want.

d. Thank your neighbor and promise to return it on the weekend.

4) Students would then perform their dialogs.

This example demonstrates the specialized pedagogical content knowledge that teachers make use of when they plan and teach their lessons. This knowledge is used to make decisions of the following kinds:
- To analyze potential lesson content (e.g. as in the example above, a piece of realia – a text, an advertisement, a poem, a photo, etc.) and identify ways in which it could be used as a teaching resource.
- To identify specific linguistic goals (e.g. in the areas of speaking, vocabulary, reading, writing, etc.) that could be developed from the chosen content.
- To anticipate any problems that might occur and ways of resolving them.
- To make appropriate decisions about time, sequencing and grouping arrangements.

Shulman (1987) has described this ability as a process of transformation in which the teacher turns the subject matter of instruction into forms that are pedagogically powerful and that are appropriate to the level and ability of the students. Experienced teachers use the skills of this ability every day when they plan their lessons, when they decide how to adapt lessons from their coursebooks and when they search the Internet and other sources for materials and content that they can use in their classes. Textbook writers make use of the same skills when they plan the development of a textbook. The ability to use knowledge and skills of this kind is one of the most fundamental dimensions of teaching, one that is acquired through experience, through accessing subject knowledge and through knowing what learners need to know and how to help them acquire it.

Experienced teachers are usually able to make these decisions very quickly not only because they are knowledgeable about the teaching subject and their learners but also because they can draw on a wide repertoire of activities and exercises and how they can be used.

Andrews (2001: 76) has discussed the concerns of a teacher who has good subject knowledge (e.g. knowledge of the uses of *shall* and *will*) but lacks the ability to present the distinction in a way that is comprehensible to her learners, i.e. she lacks pedagogical content knowledge.

> It's easy if you ask them to rewrite the sentences, because they find it easy to follow. However ... they just don't know when we are supposed to use passive voice and when we are supposed to use active voice. And one of the students even asked me 'Miss Wong, why do we have to use passive voice in our daily life?' and I find this question difficult to answer, ha, and I 'Oh, I'll tell you next time' ... and then I asked my colleagues 'Why do we use and teach passive voice?' and no one can give me the correct answer. And then I go home and think about it. But even now I really don't know how to handle that student's questions. I finish the worksheets with them and they know how to rewrite the sentences. But I don't know how to explain to them.

Shared lesson planning is one way to expand your pedagogical content knowledge, in which you share and compare how to deal with issues that a lesson plan needs to address. What are some other ways that can also be used to develop your pedagogical content knowledge?

2.5 Practical teaching skills

The teaching of any subject requires the mastery of a core set of basic skills or competencies that teachers make regular use of in the classroom. For language teachers, many of these skills have to do with managing different aspects of lessons. They include:

- choosing goals and outcomes for lessons
- planning and delivering lessons to address specific language skills and systems (e.g. grammar, vocabulary, reading, speaking and writing)
- using effective learning arrangements (e.g. whole class, group work and pair work)
- giving learners feedback on their learning
- checking learners' understanding
- guiding learners' practice
- monitoring learners' language use
- making transitions from one task to another
- using teaching resources effectively (e.g. textbooks, DVDs, whiteboards and computer software)

Becoming an English teacher means learning the basic classroom skills needed to present and navigate lessons, and to be able to access and implement such skills confidently and fluently. These skills or competencies are usually the focus of short certificate courses for novice teachers, who may later go on to take academic courses in subject knowledge and pedagogical content knowledge. Teaching from this perspective can be understood as an act of skilled performance, and in order to be able to carry yourself through a lesson, you need to be able to draw on a repertoire of techniques and routines. What we normally mean by the term "teacher training" generally refers to instruction in these basic classroom skills, often linked to a specific teaching context. During training, this repertoire of teaching skills can be acquired through observing experienced teachers and often through practice teaching in a controlled setting, using activities such as microteaching or peer teaching. Good teaching from a training perspective is viewed as the mastery of this set of skills or competencies. A repertoire of basic teaching skills can be acquired through experiencing teaching in a variety of different situations, with different kinds of learners and different kinds of content. Initially skills such as these may require conscious attention, but teachers often make use of them without awareness as they gain experience.

What are some aspects of teaching that can be learned from experience? What are some that you think are not easy to learn from experience alone?

Here is one teacher's account of how he developed his basic teaching skills:

Perhaps, it was because I was born and raised in a family of a primary school teacher that I had a teaching spirit inside me. I started teaching English when I was in my second year [of my BA in teaching English], just about three years after I first started learning, even though I had not had any formal training on teaching methodology, at all. I learned to teach by observing the way I was taught and by concentrating on what I thought to be "effective ways of teaching". I first started as a part-time teacher, teaching a one-hour class, every day, of 15 students at a beginner's level. The instruction was almost all in Khmer – my mother tongue – except for an occasional English phrase. I was so scared of my class getting out of control, since my students were all young teenagers; no one was above 15. And I did not remember using any handouts or extra activities, since I had to bear my own cost of the photocopies if I wanted to use any materials. Therefore, I chose to stick totally to the coursebook. However, I started reflecting on my teaching, and how I could make my class more fun and more beneficial for my students. Eventually, even though it was not a great teaching situation, I did learn how to become a better teacher while working there.

However, it was not until I was in my final year of my BA in teaching English, in which teaching pedagogy and teaching practice were heavily focused on, that I realized how different my teaching was from what were considered best practices. I started to do less talking; instead, I paid more attention to my instructions. Rather than just being obsessive with absolute control of my class, I started working more as a facilitator and a guide for language learning. Most of the time, I also tried to emphasize study skills, as part of my teaching. I am now more confident in adding extra resources to my lessons, localizing some part of the coursebook and rearranging the order of the content of the coursebook.

Adapting new techniques or skills into my teaching was not easy at first. I normally gave up during the first try if it did not work out. I was basically so scared of applying new ideas into my teaching. However, I started going to English teaching conferences in Cambodia, talking to my colleagues about techniques that had been successful in their classes, attending professional development workshops and observing other instructors teaching. All of these activities gave me more confidence and helped to shape a new teaching methodology. Now I understand that if I apply the new technique for the first time and it is not completely successful, I will adapt my strategy and try again.

(Virak)

As teachers like Virak accumulate experience and knowledge, there is a move towards a degree of flexibility in teaching and the development of the ability to improvise (see Chapters 7 and 11). Berliner (cited in Wright, 2005: 279) describes these stages in the development of expertise in teaching:

Stage 1 (novice): Teacher labels and learns each element of the classroom task. Set of context-free rules of performance acquired. Performance is rational, inflexible and needs purposeful concentration.

Stage 2 (advanced beginner): Similarities across contexts are recognised and episodic knowledge acquired. Strategic knowledge gained; knows when to ignore or break 'rules'. Prior classroom experiences begin to guide behaviour.

Stage 3 (competent): Teacher able to make conscious choices about actions, to set priorities and plan. Teacher knows, from experience, what is important and not important. Teacher now knows about dealing with errors.

Stage 4 (proficient): Intuition and knowledge begin to guide performance. Recognition of similarities across contexts acquired. Teacher picks up information from classroom and can predict events with some precision.

Stage 5 (expert): Has an intuitive grasp of situations and non-analytic sense of appropriate behaviour. Teaching apparently effortless and fluid. Automatic, standardised routines for management and instruction now operate. Teacher is likely to have difficulty in describing their thinking. (NB: not all teachers reach this stage.)

So while learning to teach from the perspective of skill development can be thought of as the mastery of specific teaching competencies, at the same time, these skills reflect complex levels of thinking and decision-making. Teaching is not simply the application of knowledge and learned skills. It is viewed as a much more complex process, affected by the classroom context, the teacher's general and specific instructional goals, the teacher's beliefs and values, the learners' motivations and reactions to the lesson and the teacher's management of critical moments during the lesson and the teacher's act of asking questions such as these (Borg, 2006, 2009):

- Do the students understand this? Are my instructions clear?
- Do I need to increase student involvement in this activity?
- Is this too difficult or not sufficiently challenging for the students?
- Should I try teaching this in a different way?
- Is this taking too much time?
- Is this activity going as planned?
- How can I get the students' attention?
- Do I need to improve accuracy on the task?
- Is this relevant to the aims of the lesson?
- Do the students need more vocabulary or grammatical support for the activity?
- Am I providing too much support and guidance, rather than letting the students have more responsibility for their learning?

What kinds of lessons proceed so smoothly for you that you seldom need to stop and address issues that arise in class? Are there any kinds of lessons that can be more problematic at times?

Conclusion

Language teaching is a field that is constantly revising its knowledge base, and while it is not possible or necessary to keep up with every new issue or development to date, it is important to be well informed about issues directly relevant to your teaching situation. The focus of this chapter has been four areas of professional knowledge and skills that we draw on in teaching English. Skills and expertise in English teaching can be developed through training, experience, filling out gaps in our knowledge by observing other teachers, and participating in workshops or courses, and through the many opportunities for independent study that are available on the Internet. However, there are other dimensions to teaching that reflect less visible features of our role as teachers, including issues that relate to our teacher identity and the ways in which we address the emotional side of teaching and learning. These are the focus of other chapters in this book.

Follow-up

Are there aspects of your professional knowledge and skills that you would like to further develop in the future? How would you go about doing so? Give examples below, and then compare them with examples given by your colleagues.

Areas	Goals for further development	Strategies to use
disciplinary knowledge		
proficiency in English		

(to be continued)

(*continued*)

Areas	Goals for further development	Strategies to use
pedagogical content knowledge		
practical teaching skills		

References and further reading

* For a useful framework of teaching knowledge and skills, see Cambridge English Teaching Framework (https://www.cambridgeenglish.org/images/167095-cambridge-english-teaching-framework.pdf).

Andrews, S. (2001). The Language Awareness of the L2 Teacher: Its Impact upon Pedagogical Practice. *Language Awareness, 10*(2 & 3), 75–90.

Bartels, N. (Ed.). (2005). *Applied Linguistics and Language Teacher Education.* New York: Springer.

Borg, S. (2006). *Teacher Cognition and Language Education: Research and Practice.* London: Continuum.

Borg, S. (2009). Language Teacher Cognition. In A. Burns & J. C. Richards (Eds.), *The Cambridge Guide to Second Language Teacher Education* (pp. 163–171). Cambridge: Cambridge University Press.

Richards, J. C. (2017). Teaching English through English: Proficiency, Pedagogy and Performance. *RELC Journal, 48*(1), 7–30.

Shulman, L. S. (1987). Knowledge and Teaching: Foundations of the New Reform. *Harvard Educational Review, 57*(1), 1–22.

Tsui, A. B. M. (2009). Teaching Expertise: Approaches, Perspectives, and Characterizations. In A. Burns & J. C. Richards (Eds.), *The Cambridge Guide to Second Language Teacher Education* (pp. 190–197). Cambridge: Cambridge University Press.

Wright, T. (2005). *Classroom Management in Language Education.* New York: Palgrave Macmillan.

Chapter 3 Review your use of English in teaching

Introduction

One of the features of an English lesson is that during the lesson, English is both the *target* of learning and the *means* of learning. Input and exposure to English may be from the resources you use, including the textbook, audio and video recordings and the Internet, but much of the English the learners hear and work on is provided by your use of both spoken and written English. Many teachers of English as an international language are native speakers of English – either in Inner Circle or Outer Circle contexts. Many others are competent and confident users of English, perhaps at an "upper intermediate" level, yet they are competent and successful teachers of English because they know how to use their English as an effective teaching resource. In this chapter we will consider your use of spoken English and the nature of your use of English when you teach, and how your use of English can be used effectively to support students' learning of English.

3.1 What kind of proficiency in English does an English teacher need?

While knowledge of English is a key aspect of teachers' professional competence, it is only one aspect of it. As we will see throughout this book, many other factors play a role in how well you can teach, such as your professional knowledge and teaching skills as well as your interest and enthusiasm for teaching. Knowledge of English is of course also important, but the issue is: How much and what kind of English does the teacher need? And how does the teacher's use of English in teaching help students develop their knowledge and proficiency in English? Although language is an important aspect of how language teachers view their ability to teach English, the kind of proficiency needed to teach English is not so easy to characterize. The language teaching profession has traditionally advocated that the better a teacher speaks English, the better he or she will be as an English teacher. Hence it is commonly assumed that a language teacher who is a native speaker of English is at an advantage compared to one who is not a native speaker – an assumption that Freeman (2016: 182) has described as the legacy in language teaching "of the valuing of 'nativeness' as a criterion for being a 'good' language teacher", another aspect of what has been referred to as "native-speakerism".

> *If English is not your first language, how would you describe your proficiency in English? Does it affect your teaching in any way?*

3.2 NESTs and NNESTs

A teacher for whom English is not his or her first language is sometimes known as a non-native English-speaking teacher or NNEST, while one for whom English is a first language is referred to as a NEST (native English-speaking teacher). The majority of the world's English teachers (80% according to some sources) are NNESTs, many of whom are expert users of

English. Some, however, may not be and their English may have these characteristics:

> These teachers may have only a basic command of general English – most are likely at the Common European Framework of Reference [for Languages] (CEFR) A1 or A2 levels (Council of Europe, 2001). They may use the local first language (L1) for a considerable proportion of the class period, either because of the limitations of their own English proficiency (they are more comfortable and less embarrassed speaking in L1) or because they feel their students may not understand them if they use English. (Young et al., 2014: 3)

- *In view of the role of English as an international language, do you think the distinction between NESTs and NNESTs is still useful?*
- *In what ways do you think a lesson taught by a teacher whose English is at Level B1 of the CEFR might differ from one taught by a teacher whose English is at Level C1?*

In the language teaching literature, the teacher's command of English has been described as impacting several dimensions of teaching:

> A teacher with a poor or hesitant command of spoken English will have difficulty with essential classroom teaching procedures such as giving instructions, asking questions on text, explaining the meaning of a word or replying to a student's question or remark. ... A teacher without the requisite language skills will crucially lack authority and self-confidence in the classroom, and this will affect all aspects of his or her performance. (Cullen, 2002: 220)

Mitchell (1988: 166) has viewed language proficiency as the basis for the teacher's ability to engage in improvisational teaching:

> No functional syllabus, 'authentic' materials, or micro-computer program can replace the capacity of the live, fluent speaker to hit upon topics of interest to particular individuals, continually adjust his/her speech to an appropriate level of difficulty and solve unpredictable communication problems from moment to moment, or to 'scaffold' the learner's attempts at FL speech. In all this the teacher and his/her interactive skills are decisive.

The comments above are true of my own experience. I speak Indonesian and French but with limited ability in both. I could teach either language to beginners, but due to my limited proficiency, my teaching would be heavily dependent on the textbook, especially the audio and video components of the textbook. In a lesson following the P-P-P format (a model used to describe typical phases of a presentation of new language – presentation, practice and production), I could handle the presentation and practice phases of the lesson but would have difficulty with the production phase and could not engage in improvisational teaching.

Language ability has also been linked to a teacher's sense of his or her professional identity: "for non-native English teachers, language proficiency will always represent the bedrock of their professional confidence" (Murdoch, 1994: 254). Hence, language teachers often see improvement in their language proficiency as central to their professional development and to their identity as knowledgeable professionals. A teacher comments:

> As a non-native English speaker I was worried about my language skills at first when I started to teach English. ... As the lessons progressed, I became more confident in my teaching and I actually forgot that I was a non-native speaker of English while I was teaching because I became so engrossed and interested in delivering my lessons. (Soo Jin)

How do you think about learners' views of their teachers' use of English? What do you think their expectations are for how their teachers use English?

Comments such as those above reflect the viewpoint that language proficiency (ideally referenced to that of a native speaker) is key to a teacher's ability to teach in a second or foreign language. Yet the present reality is that, as noted above, most of the world's English teachers do not have or need "nativelike" ability in their English to teach well: they need to be able to teach *with* the language, which is the focus of this chapter.

3.3 Teaching English through English

The issue central to a teacher's use of English is what the threshold of communicative ability is; the teacher must reach this threshold to be able to teach English effectively. And does this require a special kind of proficiency different from that which a second language user of English would need for other purposes? As Elder (2001: 149) comments: "How does one define the domain of teacher proficiency and is it distinguishable from other areas of professional competence or, indeed, from what is often referred to as 'general' language proficiency?" Measures of general language proficiency such as the levels described in the CEFR or in the frameworks such as the Cambridge proficiency exams are insufficient to measure the kinds of specialized communicative skills needed to teach English through English (Elder, 1994), which consist of:

1) the ability to use the target language as both the medium and target of instruction
2) the ability to modify target language input to render it comprehensible to learners
3) the ability to produce well-formed input for learners
4) the ability to draw learners' attention to features of the formal language

The knowledge and ability referred to by Elder would play a crucial role in how you manage and direct the progress of lessons. Language has been described as having two primary functions in the classroom: the *regulative function*, which refers to how language is used to manage the social space of the classroom, that is, for classroom management (see Chapter 8), and the *instructional function*, which refers to how language is used to develop the knowledge and skills that are the focus of a lesson.

Examples of these functions are seen below:

- explaining the goals of a lesson
- explaining task requirements
- giving instructions
- using formulaic expressions and phrases for classroom routines and procedures
- using English for classroom management
- explaining the procedures for an activity
- modeling the pronunciation of words and sentences
- reading aloud from a text or passage in the textbook
- asking questions
- answering students' questions
- using terminology related to language (e.g. *clause* and *function word*)
- giving explanations
- using metaphors and synonyms in explaining meanings
- guiding and monitoring students' work
- providing corrective feedback
- using transition words and phrases to mark the closure of one activity and the start of another activity
- monitoring your own language use and adjusting it for accuracy or difficulty
- paraphrasing and summarizing information in a text
- giving praise and encouragement for students' attempts to communicate
- explaining meanings of words or sentences
- expanding students' responses to questions
- providing examples of how words and other items are used
- building on and developing students' responses
- managing classroom talk towards specific lesson goals
- reviewing a lesson
- providing spoken preparation for written and other tasks
- checking students' understanding
- leading discussion activities
- giving feedback on the accuracy and appropriacy of students' language

Which of the functions above do you find most difficult to carry out in English? Choose five functions from this list and compare with a colleague.

3.4 Using English to support scaffolded and dialogic learning

The instructional functions in the list above play a role in what are referred to as *scaffolded learning* and *dialogic learning*. "Scaffolding" describes language learning as a social process of guided participation, mediated through the guidance of another more knowledgeable person. Through repeated participation in a variety of joint activities, a novice learner develops new knowledge and skills. In the classroom, scaffolding is the process of interaction between two (or more) people as they carry out a classroom activity where one person (e.g. the teacher or one learner) has more advanced knowledge than the other. During the process, discourse is jointly created through the process of assisted or mediated performance, and interaction proceeds as a kind of joint problem-solving between teacher and student. Throughout, the teacher provides opportunities for noticing how language is used, experimenting with language use, practicing new modes of discourse and restructuring existing language knowledge. Language proficiency can be presumed to play an important role in determining the effectiveness with which the teacher can provide support for scaffolded learning of this kind. A teacher has given an example of how he uses scaffolding in his teaching:

Student failure to produce as expected is many times the result of lack of, or ineffective, scaffolding. Take writing for example. With effective scaffolding, students can produce texts that they would never be able to produce by themselves. In the ELT institute I work for, writing assignments typically follow this structure:

1) Students are presented a model that they read, discuss and subsequently analyze so as to identify relevant rhetorical features, such as what genre or type of text it is, the types of discourse markers used, and how the text is organized into introduction, development and conclusion, etc.

2) Students are given a topic to develop in the same genre as the model text.

3) Students engage in activities to generate ideas, such as free writing, debating, etc.

4) Students organize the ideas generated in an outline or a diagram.

5) Students write their first drafts.

6) The teacher and/or peers give feedback on the content and form of the first drafts.

7) Students rewrite their texts. The end products are the results of the scaffolding provided and the social construction that took place among students and between the teacher and students.

(Geoff)

What kinds of scaffolding do you provide for your learners in your lessons? Can you give examples from a typical lesson that you have taught or from a skill-based lesson such as a reading or listening lesson?

Language use is also crucial in facilitating a mode of teaching referred to as dialogic talk, which Alexander (2008: 30) describes as talk which achieves "common understanding through structured, cumulative questioning and discussion that guide and prompt, reduce choices, minimise risk and error, and expedite the 'handover' of concepts and principles". We can see this in this example of interaction between a teacher and the students as the teacher explains an exercise in the students' textbook:

Teacher: Have you finished yet? Have you completed the questions at the bottom of the page?

Student 1: Not yet.

Teacher: (to another student) Where are you up to, Juan? Are you finished yet?

Student 2: No, not yet.

Teacher: Try to finish up to here (points to the book). Write your answers on a separate piece of paper. (to another student) Akito, why are you writing it in your book?

Student 3: Sorry.

Teacher: Why don't you work in pairs and check your answers together?

Student 3: OK. Check answers?

Teacher: Yes, check your answers. You and Akito can check your answers together.

We'll discuss the use of questions later in this chapter.

3.5 Using English as a teaching resource to support incidental language learning

An important functional skill in the list mentioned earlier is how the teacher provides feedback on learning. Two kinds of learning can take place during an English lesson – *incidental language learning* as well as learning through corrective feedback that the teacher provides.

Incidental language learning refers to language learning that takes place incidentally as students use English to negotiate understanding and to complete exercises and activities during their English lessons. Learning to use English as a teaching resource involves learning how to use it to support incidental language learning, which can take place in several ways:

1) Through your use of questions: effective questioning techniques can promote the students' use of more complex language. Examples of questions of this kind include:
   - What do you mean by …?
   - Why do you think that …?
   - Are you saying that …?

2) Through providing corrective feedback: when elaborating or clarifying a student's answer you may provide more complex or appropriate language. Examples of feedback of this kind include:
   Student: *I not understand the diagram on Page 46.
   Teacher: You can't understand the diagram?
   Student: No I can't.

3) Through elaborating and developing students' responses: in this way you can provide examples of how language is used to develop concepts. Examples of elaboration of this kind include:
   Teacher: What does "environment" mean?
   Student: Natural things around a place.
   Teacher: Yes, it's the natural world around us, such as the land, the air, plants and animals, especially when we are

thinking of things that are affected by human activity.

4) Through repeating students' answers: through repeating and expanding students' answers you can provide examples of new vocabulary and academic language.

Examples of repetition of this kind include:

Teacher: What is rust?

Student: From iron, it's oxide.

Teacher: Yes, it's a kind of iron oxide formed by the reaction of iron and oxygen when iron is in contact with water or moisture in the air.

5) Through explaining the nature of an activity: through clarifying the nature, goals and procedures of an activity, you are able to provide examples of how language is used for describing relations such as sequence and cause and effect.

Examples of explanation of this kind include:

Teacher: What you have to do for this activity is first of all to plot all of the information you have found on a graph that shows the temperature changes in the region over the last century. When you have completed that you should then …

6) Through checking understanding: when you ask students to summarize, explain, or provide examples, students develop the ability to produce extended discourse.

Examples of the act of checking include:

Teacher: You said you would go to classify and analyze the information you found. Can you say how you are going to do that?

Student: First we are going to arrange the information we found in the lists according to frequency, then we will use some statistical measure to compare the information in the two lists.

7) Through using student presentations: through listening to other students presenting reports, students can compare their language with the language used by other students.

The ability to use English this way when you teach is an important aspect of the teacher's professional competence.

> *Can you give examples of how you provide incidental feedback to your learners?*

3.6 Providing corrective feedback

Corrective feedback is feedback that serves to draw the students' attention to incorrect pronunciation and use of words or grammar, and to correct their errors. The following are commonly used feedback strategies:

1) Explicit correction: you indicate an error and provide the correct form.

   For example:

   Student: *Not goed ...

   Teacher: Went.

2) Recasting: you reformulate the student's language use and give the correct form.

   For example:

   Student: *I didn't understood ...

   Teacher: You didn't understand?

3) Clarification requests: you show a lack of understanding to prompt the student to try again.

   For example:

   Teacher: Sorry?

4) Grammar prompts: you comment on the grammar used.
   For example:
   Teacher: Say it again using the past tense.
5) Elicitation: you try to elicit the correct form, for example, by providing the first part of a sentence that the student is attempting to say.
6) Repetition: you repeat the error, highlighting the incorrect word or form.

Interaction between you and your students of this kind can provide opportunities for students to receive input that contains more grammatically and lexically complex features than they can currently use. The same is true of the interaction that takes place among students themselves, since in any group activity there are typically students with different levels of language ability.

However, in order to make sure that the language students experience in input would lead to learning, researchers suggest that two things need to occur. First, the student has to notice the features of the language in input. This is known as the noticing hypothesis that will be further discussed in Chapter 10. Second, opportunities need to be provided for students to have repeated opportunities to practice using the new language features over time.

Read the following dialog and think what kind of corrective feedback the teacher has made use of in this example:
   ***Teacher**: When did you start studying here?*
   ***Student 1**: *I start here since 11th of January.*

Teacher: *When did you arrive? You arrived on the 11th of January. Did you? You must have started the next day. Did you?*
Student 1: *The 11th of January.*
Student 2: **No, we start at 13th.*
Teacher: *On the 13th of January. When did you start studying here again (points to another student)?*
Student 3: **I start study on the 13th of January.*
Teacher: *Again.*
Student 3: **I start study on the 13th of January.*
Teacher: *I started ...*
Student 3: **I stotted ...*
Teacher: *I started ...*
Student 3: *I started ...*
Teacher: *I started studying here on the 13th of January. Everyone. I started studying here ...*
Students: *I started ...*
Teacher: *I started studying here on the 13th of January.*
Students: *I started studying here on the 13th of January.*

3.7 Use of questions in teaching

Questioning is another basic functional skill in teaching, including language teaching, and is an example of dialogic interaction discussed earlier. In some classrooms over half of the class time is taken up with questions. Questions are used to stimulate and maintain students' interest, to encourage students to think and focus on the content of the lesson, to clarify what a student has said, to elicit particular sentence patterns, grammar or vocabulary, to check students' understanding and to encourage students' participation in the lesson. Common question types are:

- managerial questions: questions that guide classroom activities and procedures
- rhetorical questions: questions used to emphasize a point or to reinforce an idea or a statement
- closed questions: questions used to check retention or to focus thinking on a particular point, which can be answered with "yes" or "no" or with a limited sense of possible answers such as a date or piece of information
- open questions: questions that can be answered freely and are used to promote discussion or student interaction

The skill with which we use questions in teaching accounts for many aspects of classroom dynamics and interaction. We too often overuse closed questions that require short answers and often do not require students to "stretch" their English or to try out different ways of saying things. Open questions on the other hand can be used to generate ideas and classroom communication. It is also important to provide as many opportunities as possible in a lesson for students to ask questions and to ensure that all students have a chance to ask questions, not simply those who are more outgoing or whose English may be more fluent. Therefore we need to monitor the "action zone", which will be further discussed in Chapter 8.

3.8 Using language to assist learning

In using English to teach English we need to ensure that the language we use in our lessons is neither too simple nor too complex to provide useful learning support for students with limited proficiency in English. In order to provide support and input that could be comprehensible to learners, i.e. at the level referred to as input+1 or i+1 (Krashen, 1985), English teachers – whether they are native speakers or second language users of English – need to learn how to modify and adapt their use of English. Experienced teachers who are non-native speakers of English have usually developed effective ways to do this since they have been learners of English themselves, whereas native speakers who are not trained as language teachers are often not aware of the complexity of the language they often use. In the classroom, both you and your students need to find ways of arriving at a common understanding of meaning. This involves making use of linguistic as well as non-verbal communication strategies such as adding extra stress to key words, saying things in different ways to make sure they are understood, and using gestures and hand movements to emphasize meaning.

What strategies do you use when there is a breakdown in communication between you and your students due to the students' limited language proficiency?

You can use a variety of ways to modify your English to enable it to provide support for understanding and learning. For example:

1) By speaking more slowly. Fluent English speakers are often not aware of how fast they speak or how fast it may appear to listeners. We often need to use a slower rate of speech when necessary in teaching than we would use in other situations.

2) By using more pauses. We tend to pause more and to use longer pauses when teaching, especially when teaching learners with lower levels of proficiency in English. These pauses give learners more time to process what we have said and hence make it easier to understand.

3) By modifying pronunciation. We may sometimes use clearer articulation or a more standard style of speech, containing fewer reductions and contractions that we would use outside of the classroom. For example, instead of saying "Could ya read Line 6 please?", we may more clearly articulate "Could you …". An English teacher who has a strong regional or local accent (e.g. from Australia, New Zealand, Jamaica, or Scotland) may also need to use a more standard or international accent which is different from the one he or she would use in his or her own country.

4) By modifying vocabulary. We often need to replace a difficult word with one that is more likely to be familiar to our learners. For example, instead of saying "What do you think this picture *depicts*?", we might say "What do you think this picture *shows*?".

5) By avoiding idioms. It may be necessary to avoid idioms and colloquialisms and replace them with more familiar words or expressions.

6) By increasing wait time. Wait time is the length of time that we wait after asking a question before calling on a student to answer it, rephrasing the question, directing the question to another student, or giving the answer. Providing longer wait time (e.g. five seconds) can increase student participation and give time for students to think about the language they need to use.

7) By modifying grammar. It may be necessary to simplify the grammatical complexity of our language in the classroom by using fewer subordinate clauses or complex tenses. For example, instead of saying "that would have been the best thing to do", we can say "that was probably the best thing to do".

8) By modifying discourse. You may sometimes need to repeat yourself or rearrange the topic of a sentence. For example, instead of saying "What was the name of the author that we studied last time?", we can say "The author we studied last time, what was her name?".

Modifying your talk in ways such as these is the result of trying to make yourself easy to understand and can provide essential support for learners' attempts at both understanding and producing output in English.

3.9 Code-switching

In situations where we and our students share the same L1 or a common language it is natural (though often not encouraged) for the shared language to be sometimes used alongside English during lessons, which is known as code-switching (or also as *translanguaging*). There are two contrasting opinions about code-switching in English classes. Those in favor of it see it as an acceptable strategy to use in a bilingual context that creates a supportive classroom climate. Opponents, however, argue that it inhibits the learning of English. Whether it is considered acceptable or not in a school may depend on several factors including school or institutional policy, attitudes of teachers and students towards the practice, their language proficiency, the lesson content, and the affective dimensions of classroom instruction. Teachers use a bilingual mode of communication primarily for explanatory purposes, but also for socializing and management functions. For example:

- to explain and clarify instructions
- to summarize parts of the lesson

- to highlight key points of the lesson
- to explain new concepts and terms
- to introduce a new topic
- to reinforce new information by repeating it in the L1
- to make the introduction of new content more efficient
- to increase learner motivation
- to establish rapport with students
- to achieve better classroom management
- to compensate for gaps in vocabulary knowledge
- to avoid saying something in English that requires complex syntax

- *Do you sometimes make use of code-switching during your lessons? If so, for which of the functions listed above do you sometimes feel code-switching is effective?*
- *What is the policy in your school towards the use of code-switching? Is code-switching felt to be generally appropriate when used appropriately or is it only used as a last resort?*

3.10 Monitoring the English you use when you teach

For students an important source of learning English is the English used by their teachers. Sešek (2007: 417) provides two examples of how limitations in a teacher's use of English could lead to misunderstanding on the part of the learners. In the first example the teacher confuses students by not using transition words between activities, while in the second example misunderstanding results from the teacher's pronunciation.

Sample 1: Novice teacher announces lesson topic and tries to elicit a key lexeme ('siblings'). '*Today we'll talk about brothers and sisters. What other word do we know that describes both?*' Students volunteer guesses, but it is clear that they did not understand the question. When the teacher gives the answer, we see that several students had known the word 'siblings'. Why did they not understand the teacher? There was a cohesion problem; the word 'other' is the only word referring to both brothers and sisters, and with the postmodifier used here it cannot refer back to the first sentence. The illusion of cohesion was all the more problematic since the teacher did not use any linguistic means to signal to the learners that she was moving from announcing the topic to eliciting vocabulary.

Sample 2: Novice teacher is discussing the topic of brand products with adult learners. After talking about other types of products, she says: 'What about watches?', mispronouncing the vowel sound in 'watch' by making it too narrow. The learners look puzzled and do not respond. Noticing this, the teacher repeats the word once or twice more, with more stress, but with the same pronunciation problem, learners still don't know what she means. Then she points to her own wristwatch, and the learners finally comprehend ('Oh, watches!').

Since for many teachers the classroom and interaction with students provide the main opportunities for them to use English, it is important to review your own use of English from time to time to make sure that it provides good models and examples of spoken English. Watching a video or listening to audio recordings of a lesson is a good way to do this. These are procedures that can be used:

Step 1: From time to time, make an audio or video recording of one of your lessons using a smartphone or other audio device. You could also have your students video the lesson or ask a colleague to make a recording.

Step 2: Choose a focus for the recording. Do you want to record the whole lesson or part of the lesson? Make sure the focus is on your use of English during the lesson.

Step 3: Play back the recording and assess your performance in terms of the quality of the English you used. Note both positive aspects of your use of English and anything you may wish to change or modify. You may also wish to share the recording with a colleague and explore questions such as these:

> *Pronunciation*: Were there any problematic sounds? Were important words pronounced correctly? How about consonant clusters and final sounds in words?
> *Vocabulary*: Was word choice appropriate? Were words pronounced with the correct stress?
> *Grammar*: Was the use of English accurate? Were tenses used correctly? How about distinctions between singular and plural nouns? Were there any recurring issues with sentence formation, linking words or other aspects of grammar?
> *Fluency*: Could you maintain successful communication in English? Was there frequent difficulty in finding the correct words or expressions? How clearly are you able to express your ideas in English?

Step 4: On the basis of what you learn from the lesson recording you can focus on specific language issues and pay more conscious attention to them when you teach, such as pronunciation of final sounds and consonants. In lesson preparation you can also anticipate any language issues the students might raise and consider ways of addressing these issues during the lesson. Observing other teachers' lessons can also provide examples of how teachers maintain a focus on the quality of the English they use in the classroom.

Conclusion

The focus of this chapter has not been on how well you speak English but on how well you can use English as a medium to teach English and the nature of the discourse that characterizes English lessons. For an English teacher, English has several functions. It provides a source of input to learning. It provides models and examples of spoken English, whose features are different from those of written English that teachers may be more familiar with. It is also the means teachers use to structure and develop their lessons, to guide and support learners in their learning and to give learners feedback on their performance. In using English as a medium of instruction fluency in English is not the only thing involved. Teachers need to use English in ways that are effective for learners at different stages in their learning and to develop awareness of how and how well they are able to use English as a teaching resource.

Follow-up

Microteaching is an activity that can be used to practice using English as a medium for teaching. Microteaching involves a teacher planning and teaching a short lesson (e.g. 10 minutes) to a group of fellow teachers.

Choose classroom activities that make demands on the teacher's use of English and that could be used as the basis for microteaching. You could choose functions from the list provided in this chapter as the basis for activities. In the group everyone takes a turn teaching the activities. Then reflect on each other's use of English with each activity.

References and further reading

Alexander, R. J. (2008). *Towards Dialogic Teaching: Rethinking Classroom Talk* (4th edition). Thirsk: Dialogos.

Cullen, R. (2002). The Use of Lesson Transcripts for Developing Teachers' Classroom Language. In H. Trappes-Lomax & G. Ferguson (Eds.), *Language in Language Teacher Education* (pp. 219–235). Amsterdam: John Benjamins Publishing Company.

Elder, C. (1994). Performance Testing as Benchmark for Foreign Language Teacher Education. *Babel: Journal of the Australian Federation of Modern Language Teachers Associations, 29*(2), 9–19.

Elder, C. (2001). Assessing the Language Proficiency of Teachers: Are There Any Border Controls? *Language Testing, 18*(2), 149–170.

Freeman, D. (2002). The Hidden Side of the Work: Teacher Knowledge and Learning to Teach. *Language Teaching, 35*(1), 1–13.

Freeman, D. (2016). *Educating Second Language Teachers*. Oxford: Oxford University Press.

Freeman, D., Katz, A., Gomez, P. G. & Burns, A. (2015). English-for-Teaching: Rethinking Teacher Proficiency in the Classroom. *ELT Journal, 69*(2), 129–139.

Freeman, D., Katz, A., Le Dréan, L., Burns, A. & King, S. (2016). *ELTeach: Global Implementation Report*. Boston: National Geographic Learning.

Hedge, T. (2000). *Teaching and Learning in the Language Classroom*. Oxford: Oxford University Press.

Johnson, K. E. (1995). *Understanding Communication in Second Language Classrooms*. New York: Cambridge University Press.

Krashen. S. D. (1985). *The Input Hypothesis: Issues and Implications.* London: Longman.

Mitchell, R. (1988). *Communicative Language Teaching in Practice.* London: CILT.

Murdoch, G. (1994). Language Development Provision in Teacher Training Curricula. *ELT Journal, 48*(3), 253–265.

Richards, J. C. (2017). Teaching English through English: Proficiency, Pedagogy and Performance. *RELC Journal, 48*(1), 7–30.

Sešek, U. (2007). English for Teachers of EFL – Toward a Holistic Description. *English for Specific Purposes, 26*, 411–425.

Tedick, D. J. & Lyster, R. (2020). *Scaffolding Language Development in Immersion and Dual Language Classrooms.* New York: Routledge.

Young, J. W., Freeman, D., Hauck, M. C., Gomez, P. G. & Papageorgiou, S. (2014). *A Design Framework for the ELTeach Program Assessments* (ETS RR–14-36). Princeton: Educational Testing Service.

PART 2

THE ROLE OF TEACHING PRINCIPLES

Chapter 4 Apply principles from approaches and methods

Introduction

Millions of people around the world study English and other foreign languages. The teaching of English provides a profession for thousands of teacher educators and teachers who share the commitment to finding effective ways to help learners develop their ability in English. In language teaching, the choice of activities and exercises teachers make use of may be based on the textbook, on the teaching methods prescribed in the school, or on the teacher's preferred repertoire of activities and exercises. However, whatever kinds of teaching activities you make use of, they are not simply a set of procedures that have been selected at random. Teachers' choices of activities and techniques are based on several factors such as the goals of the lesson, the learners' current level of language proficiency and their needs and interests. But above all, teaching reflects our beliefs and understanding about the nature of language and second language learning and these beliefs serve as a basis for the principles we try to realize in our classroom practices – principles such as: *learning starts with understanding*; *to develop accuracy as well as fluency*; *practice should always be meaningful*. One source of teachers' principles in language teaching can be those principles that are based on particular philosophies of teaching, which in language teaching are referred to as teaching *approaches* and *methods*. The nature of these and the role they play in teachers' classroom practices are the issues we explore in this chapter.

4.1 Approaches and methods

All proposals for the teaching of a second language draw on: 1) *a theory of language* – an account of what the essential components of language are and what proficiency or competence in a language entails; 2) *a theory of learning* – an account of the psycholinguistic, cognitive and social processes involved in learning a language. The theory of language and language learning underlying an instructional design provides the basis for *principles* that can serve to guide the processes of teaching and learning. Different instructional designs in language teaching often reflect very different understandings of the nature of language and of language learning. The particular theory of language and language learning underlying an instructional design, in turn, leads to further levels of specification in the form of *learning objectives* (the goals of teaching and learning), *the syllabus* (the primary units of organization for a language course), *teacher and learner roles* (the roles teachers and learners are expected to play in learning), and *classroom activities* (the kinds of activities and exercises that are recommended).

When an instructional design reflects a theory of language and language learning that can be applied in many different ways at the level of learning objectives, the syllabus, teacher and learner roles, or classroom activities, it is usually referred to as an *approach* (Darian, 1972; Richards & Rodgers, 2014). *Communicative Language Teaching* is described as an approach because the principles it makes use of can be applied in many different ways and can be used as the basis for different teaching methods and course designs. Teachers adopting a communicative approach have considerable flexibility in how they apply the principles in their own contexts. However, when an instructional design advocates specific syllabus, objectives, teacher and learner roles and classroom activities, it is referred to as a *method*. As for a method, there is little flexibility for teachers in how the method is used. The teacher's role is to implement the method. *Grammar Translation Method* and *Audiolingualism* are examples of methods in this sense.

> *What approaches and methods have you experienced in learning English? How did they differ in terms of the classroom activities and exercises they made use of?*

In this chapter we will consider how teachers sometimes make use of principles that are derived from particular teaching methods such as the *Direct Method* and the *Audiolingual Method* as well as course designs based on the communicative approach such as function-based, skill-based, and content-based course designs in language teaching.

4.2 Applying principles from methods
Let us visit some teachers' classes to find out how they make use of principles that are associated with different methods.

4.2.1 Using the Grammar Translation Method
Teresa teaches in a context where English is largely a school subject that students must study to past tests at high school or university. She believes that the best way to teach a language

is to first give students a detailed understanding of its grammar rules, followed by exercises that involve translating texts from the students' mother tongue into English and in reverse. She uses the students' first language as the medium of instruction much of the time, using it to explain new grammar items and to make comparisons between the students' mother tongue and English. Her class has 50 students. In her class we see students focusing mainly on reading and writing and they pay little attention to listening or speaking in English. She places a strong emphasis on vocabulary, and words are taught by using bilingual word lists, dictionary study and memorization. Teresa follows the principles of the Grammar Translation Method, some of which are:

- Emphasize the learning and use of correct grammar at all times.
- Use activities that involve comparing English grammar and sentence patterns with those used in the students' first language.
- Give priority to reading and writing.
- Memorization is the key to language learning.

> *Have you studied a language using the Grammar Translation Method? Do you sometimes use translation in your teaching (which in itself does not necessarily mean you use the Grammar Translation Method – it might just be an occasional technique that you use)?*

4.2.2 Using the Direct Method

The next class we visit is in a private language institute where teachers teach following what is known as the Direct Method. (The name reflects the belief that learners can understand meaning *directly* without the need for translation.) Teacher Carlos uses only English as the medium of instruction in his classes. He builds up spoken communication skills by using a carefully graded progression of exercises organized around question-and-answer exchanges between the students and himself in intensive classes of five or six students. Practical everyday vocabulary is taught through demonstration of objects and pictures. Some of the principles of the Direct Method Carlos has been taught to use are:

- Let students infer the meaning of grammar from the way English is used in speaking and writing.
- Get the most speaking practice out of each lesson.
- Emphasize the use of correct pronunciation and grammar.
- Only English should be used in class.

What do you think some of the difficulties might be in using the Direct Method?

4.2.3 Using the Audiolingual Method

The next teacher, Lionel, teaches English using the Audiolingual Method which places a strong emphasis on listening (the audio component) and repeating (the lingual component). Each lesson focuses on one or more patterns or structures that are first introduced through a dialog, which students practice first as a whole class and then in pairs. Lionel emphasizes accurate pronunciation and correct grammar at all times. Following the dialog practice, Lionel introduces a series of drills that focus on repetition of the key sentence patterns in the dialog and that becomes the focus of various kinds of drills and pattern practice exercises. Some of the principles Lionel tries to realize in his class are:

- Focus on developing accuracy first and then practice fluency.
- The ability to speak provides the foundation for reading and writing.
- Teach the language – not *about* the language.

> *Do you sometimes use drills in your lessons? If so, what kind of drills do you use and for what purposes?*

4.2.4 Using the P-P-P Method

Now we visit a class where the teacher, Anna, makes use of what is sometimes called the Structural Method, but that is perhaps better known as the P-P-P Method. In this method, teaching is organized around a structural or grammatical syllabus that provides a graded introduction to the basic structures and sentence patterns of English. A word list of some 2,000 common and useful words is also used. Anna recently attended a workshop where she was introduced to the P-P-P Method. This method builds lessons around three phases – *presentation*, *practice* and *production*:

Presentation: A text, an audio clip or a video is used by the teacher to present the grammar in a situation that requires the use of the new grammar. This could be a dialog or a short text.

Practice: A controlled practice activity is used focusing on the correct use of the new grammar. The teacher uses activities such as drills and transformations, gap-filling or cloze exercises, and multiple-choice questions.

Production: In this phase the learner practices using the new grammar in freer communication through dialogs, role-plays and other activities where there is less language control.

Anna's lesson moves from controlled to freer practice of grammatical structures and from oral practice of sentence patterns to their fluent use in speech, reading and writing. In the lesson we observe Anna starts with presentation of new vocabulary and sentence patterns followed by pronunciation practice. She then goes on to drill the students using substitution tables. The lesson ends with students reading short passages containing the new structures and vocabulary followed by a written exercise.

Anna's lesson draws on these principles:
- Accurate use of grammar provides the foundation for all language skills.
- Use situations and contexts to communicate the meaning of new language.
- Use demonstration and examples rather than translation to teach the meaning of vocabulary.

What is a common feature of the methods discussed above?

4.3 Assumptions behind the methods

The methods above all have in common a view that language learning starts with mastering the grammar of a language. Language development involves gradually building up a basic repertoire of grammatical structures and vocabulary and practice in using them in different situations. This leads to the development of "grammatical" or "linguistic" competence. Grammatical competence refers to the knowledge we have that accounts for our ability to produce and understand sentences in the language. It refers to knowledge of the building blocks of sentences (e.g. parts of speech, tenses, phrases, clauses, and sentence patterns) and how sentences are formed. It is our grammatical competence that enables us to recognize that a sentence such as "to the movies I yesterday goes" is not grammatical and should be corrected as "I went to the movies yesterday". Grammatical competence is the focus of many grammar practice books, which typically present a rule of grammar on one page and provide sentence-based exercises to practice using the rule on the other page. The approach to the teaching of grammar is a *deductive* one: students are presented with grammar rules and then given opportunities to practice them, as opposed to an *inductive* approach in which students are given examples of sentences containing a grammar rule and asked to work out the rule for themselves. With the oral-based methods such as the Audiolingual Method and the Direct Method, once a basic command of the language is established through oral drilling and controlled practice, the four skills are introduced, usually in the sequence of speaking, listening, reading, and writing (Rivers, 1981; Williams & Burden, 1997).

4.4 The communicative approach in language teaching

Let us now visit some classrooms where teachers draw on a theory of language known as "communicative competence" (explained below), rather than the theory of grammatical competence, as the basis for how they plan and teach their classes. The lessons we will observe are all examples of an approach referred to as *Communicative Language Teaching*, or the *communicative approach*, which can be applied in different ways to the design of language courses and teaching materials (Littlewood, 1981; Richards & Rodgers, 2014). First, we will visit a speaking class.

4.4.1 Function-based course design

In Celine's speaking course she begins by considering the purposes and situations her students would need English for. Most are interested in learning English for tourism and travel, so she plans her course around two kinds of activities: English for social interaction such as *greetings*, *meeting people* and *making small talk*, and English for transactional purposes such as *checking in at a guest house, eating in a restaurant* and *buying things in a pharmacy*. She then develops a course that focuses on the grammar, vocabulary, and other skills needed to use English for these purposes.

In this lesson that we observe Celine first gives students situations to think about where they might run into a colleague or friends (e.g. at the cinema). How would they greet them? What questions might they ask? How would they close the conversation?

Students work on this in pairs, and then they compare answers around the class. Then Celine plays short video clips from TV series which show people in the situations the students have practiced. The class study the language that is used, and later Celine gives them scripts of the exchanges with some words and expressions blocked out and asks the students to try to complete them. After checking their responses, the students practice the exchanges. Then Celine gives them new situations to think about and they create dialogs in pairs before practicing them in front of the class. At the end of the lesson Celine gives some time to address the grammatical and other points that have come up during the students' practice.

Celine's function-based course makes use of the following principles:

- Plan lessons around communicative functions (such as *requests*, *offers*, *introductions*, *greetings* and *small talk*).
- Practice the expressions and strategies speakers use for social interactional functions and for transactional functions.
- Move from controlled to freer practice of functions.
- Deal with grammar as a follow-up to lessons rather than the starting point for lessons.

How different is this from the Direct Method?

4.4.2 Skill-based course design

Tom is a teacher in a university language center in an Anglophone country. The university has many international students and Tom teaches a course on "listening to academic lectures in English". Rather than make "advanced English" the focus of the course – whatever that is – Tom makes use of a skill-based source for teaching listening. To do this Tom first develops a list of some of the essential listening and note-taking skills his students will need to learn. These include:

1) identifying the scope and focus of a lecture
2) listening for main ideas
3) identifying supporting ideas and examples
4) listening for details
5) identifying the speaker's viewpoint
6) distinguishing facts from opinions
7) summarizing while listening
8) following a sequence of information
9) processing information in real time

In the lesson we observe Tom focuses on recognizing cues a speaker gives during a lecture to signal the flow of information throughout the lecture. He gives out a list which contains examples of discourse signals and expressions used to indicate main ideas and supporting details such as those used to highlight main ideas, examples, anecdotes etc. as well as the use of repetition, rhetoric, questions and summaries. He then gives out copies of the transcript of a lecture and asks students to listen to the audio of the lecture without looking at the transcript. The students then work in pairs to circle and label the discourse features. Tom then discusses their responses with them and reminds them to listen for similar discourse signals when they attend lectures.

Some of the principles that guide Tom in developing his course are:
- Focus on the listening skills specific to lectures, seminars and other instructional genres.
- Develop a graded introduction to academic listening skills.
- Avoid teaching too many skills at the same time.

> *What are some of the skills that could be included in a reading course?*

4.4.3 Content-based course design

Now we visit Carmen's class for second-year university students majoring in English. Carmen decides to replace the language-based course she has inherited from the previous course coordinator with a content-based course in which topics and themes are used as the basis for the curriculum rather than grammar. These topics provide a framework around which language skills, vocabulary and grammar could be developed in parallel. The topics covered in the course are:

1) drugs
2) persuasion
3) advertising
4) pandemics
5) immigration
6) Native Americans
7) modern architecture
8) microchip technology
9) ecology
10) alternative energy
11) nuclear energy
12) crime in novels and films
13) business ethics

Each lesson begins with reading and discussion related to the topic of the lesson. Then students work in groups; each group chooses a small group project related to the topic that requires the group members to go online to research information. They also have to decide what form the outcome of the project would be (an essay, a class presentation, a debate, etc.) and Carmen guides them through the language requirements of whatever project they select. Once they have planned their project, they review it with other groups and consult Carmen for any support they need. Carmen bases her planning on these criteria:

1) Planning decisions should be based on content factors rather than linguistic criteria.

2) Rather than have separate strands in the course for reading, writing, listening and speaking, she uses an integrated skill-based approach. The topic of the texts selected for each lesson would determine the language skills (reading, speaking, etc.) as well as study skills (e.g. reading and summarizing) that would be addressed in the lesson.

3) An effort would be made to maximize the use of authentic materials related to the content of the lesson.

4) Content would be chosen based on the students' academic

goals as well as their interests and concerns (e.g. current social and cultural issues).
5) Language development would depend on features of the texts used in the lesson.

Among the principles Carmen makes use of in her content-based course are:
- Use content rather than language as the basis for organizing learning, instead of learning English for its own sake.
- Choose content that reflects students' interests and needs.
- Use content as the basis for integrating the learning of the four skills (reading, writing, listening and speaking).
- Use content to provide authentic and meaningful use of language.

If you were using content as the basis for a course for your students, what kinds of content would they be most interested in?

4.4.4 Task-based course design
Ricardo, another teacher in the same university has adopted a different approach to the organization of his second-year course. He chooses a task-based way of organizing the course tasks rather than use linguistic or other criteria. Ricardo bases his choice of tasks on the following criteria:
1) A task is something that a learner does or carries out using his or her existing language resources.
2) It has an outcome which is not simply linked to learning language, though language acquisition may occur as the learner carries out the task.

3) It involves a focus on meaning.

4) In the case of tasks involving two or more learners, it calls upon the learners to use communication strategies and interactional skills.

Examples of tasks of this kind are:

1) ordering a product on the Internet

2) assembling a piece of furniture with a friend following the instructions provided by the manufacturer

3) working with a partner to make a map of your school campus

4) following a video demonstration to prepare a French chicken dish

5) planning a trip to Europe with a friend

Ricardo believes that students can develop their language skills and other dimensions of communicative competence as a by-product of their engagement in interactive tasks. Of course, teachers make use of many different kinds of tasks as part of their regular teaching, but teachers such as Ricardo believe that tasks can be used as the primary unit both in planning teaching (i.e. in developing a syllabus) and in classroom teaching. The starting point for planning his course is therefore to select tasks that are related to issues and activities in the students' lives, both on campus and beyond the campus.

Ricardo's lessons typically follow a three-phase sequence:

1) Introducing the task. This motivates the students to perform the task and prepares them for carrying out the task by providing clear instructions on what the purpose of the task is and how it should be performed.

2) Guiding performance of the task. He observes students' progress and provides necessary language support.

3) Post-task feedback. He gives feedback on the task and provides follow-up language support and development.

Ricardo seeks to apply the principles of task-based course design in his lessons. These include:
- Focus on the process as well as product.
- Use purposeful and meaningful tasks appropriate to the learners' proficiency level.
- Use tasks that involve authentic and meaningful communication and interaction.

What kind of tasks do you think would be motivating and useful for your students?

4.4.5 Text-based course design

Finally, we will observe a teacher who makes use of texts as the basis for organizing her course. This is known as *text-based language teaching*. Rosa teaches university students in an EFL (English as a foreign language) context and believes that language learning for her students involves the mastery of the different types of texts that they will encounter in their university studies. The word "text" here is used in a special sense to refer to structured sequences of language that are used in specific contexts in specific ways. For example, in a day a speaker of English may use spoken English in many ways including the following:

1) a casual conversational exchange with a friend
2) a conversational exchange with a stranger in an elevator
3) a telephone call to arrange an appointment at a hair salon
4) an account to friends of an unusual experience
5) discussion of a personal problem with a friend to seek advice

Each of these uses of language can be regarded as a text in that it consists of a unified whole with a beginning, a middle part, and an end, it conforms to norms of organization and content, and it draws on appropriate grammar and vocabulary. Language learning from this perspective involves being able to use different kinds of spoken and written texts in the specific contexts of their use. Text-based teaching involves:

1) teaching explicitly about the structures and grammatical features of spoken and written texts
2) linking spoken and written texts to the cultural contexts of their use
3) designing units of work which focus on developing skills in relation to whole texts
4) providing students with guided practice as they develop language skills for meaningful communication through whole texts

According to this view, learners in different contexts must master the use of the text types occurring most frequently in specific contexts. These contexts might include studying in an English medium university, studying in an English medium primary or secondary school, working in a restaurant, working in an office, working in a store, and socializing with neighbors in a housing complex. The following are common text types:

Exchanges: simple exchanges relating to information about goods and services

complex or problematic exchanges

casual conversation

Forms: simple formatted texts

complex formatted texts

Procedures: instructions

protocols

Information texts: descriptions
explanations
reports
directives
texts which combine one or more of these
text types
Story texts: recounts
narratives
Persuasive texts: opinion texts
expositions
discussions

As its name implies, the core units of course planning with a text-based approach are text types. So, in planning her course Rosa has to identify the text types her students will need and what the language demands of the texts are. In her lessons she generally follows a sequence of four stages as in this example of her teaching of *recounts* (personal stories):

Stage 1: She introduces the notion of recounts and students discuss when they might encounter them as well as what kinds of information they might expect in them and in what order. They then receive an example as a model and discuss it.

Stage 2: Rosa leads the students through a discussion of the text and its linguistic features. They compare it with other kinds of texts.

Stage 3: As a class activity the students propose a topic for a recount and jointly plan what it would say and how it would be organized.

Stage 4: Students prepare their own texts, compare their drafts with others, and then take turns to read them to each other in groups.

Some of the principles Rosa seeks to reflect in her teaching are:
- Use texts to integrate the learning of different language skills.
- Use authentic models of texts to guide students' learning.
- Develop students' awareness of the linguistic and rhetorical features of texts.

4.5 Assumptions behind the different course designs

The five kinds of course design discussed above – function-based, skill-based, content-based, task-based and text-based – reflect a different view of the nature of language learning from that seen in the Grammar Translation Method, the Audiolingual Method and the Structural Method, one based on the concept of communicative competence rather than grammatical competence. While the focus of grammatical competence is the production of grammatically correct sentences, communicative competence describes the knowledge and skills needed to use English for communicative purposes. Communicative competence includes the following aspects of language ability:

- knowing how to use language for a range of different purposes and functions
- knowing how to vary use of language according to the setting and the participants (e.g. knowing when to use formal and informal speech or when to use language appropriately for written as opposed to spoken communication)
- knowing how to produce and understand different types of texts (e.g. narratives, reports, interviews and conversations)
- knowing how to maintain communication despite having limitations in one's language knowledge (e.g. through using different kinds of communication strategies)

To develop the learners' communicative competence, the starting point is to determine the learners' communicative needs. What are their purposes in learning English, in what situations will they use it, what kinds of events and activities will they take part in, and what kinds of language skills and knowledge will be required? While the nature of the learners' communicative needs is a priority in the communicative approach to language teaching, communicative course designs such as those discussed above also reflect a different understanding of the nature of second language learning. Rather than view second language learning as dependent upon learning and practicing the grammatical and other systems of English through drills and other techniques that involve memorization and rote learning, communicative course designs draw on other principles of teaching and learning. These can be summarized as follows:

1) Second language learning is facilitated when learners are engaged in interaction and meaningful communication.

2) Effective classroom learning tasks and exercises provide opportunities for students to negotiate meaning, expand their language resources, notice how language is used, and take part in meaningful intrapersonal exchange.

3) Meaningful communication results from students' processing of content that is relevant, purposeful, interesting, and engaging.

4) Communication is a holistic process that often calls for the use of several language skills or modalities.

5) Language learning is facilitated both by activities that involve inductive or discovery learning of underlying rules of language use and organization, and by those involving language analysis and reflection.

6) Language learning is a gradual process that involves creative use of language and trial and error. Although an error is a normal product of learning, the goal of learning is to be able

to use the new language both accurately and fluently.

7) Learners develop their own routes to language learning, progress at different rates, and have different needs and motivations for language learning.

8) Successful language learning involves the use of effective learning and communication strategies.

9) The role of the teacher in the language classroom is that of a facilitator, who creates a classroom climate conducive to language learning and provides opportunities for students to use and practice English and to reflect on language use and language learning.

10) The classroom is a community where learners learn through collaboration and sharing.

We will see these principles referred to throughout this book.

Conclusion

All the methods and approaches discussed in this chapter share a common assumption about the role of the teacher in language teaching, namely that adopting one of the methods or approaches and its associated principles will bring about successful learning. The teacher's task is to study the method or approach and its principles and then apply the principles to his or her own teaching. As one teacher comments:

> I studied French from a teacher who was using a French version of Audiolingualism. The advice we were told was to "just follow the teacher". There was a strong emphasis on dialog repetition and pronunciation and no pair work or group work and after three weeks I didn't really have any communicative skills in French. (Claude)

Many training programs for novice teachers assume that a core domain of pedagogical content knowledge for teachers is understanding the principles and practices of one or more teaching approaches or methods and learning to teach according to the core principles. During their training, teachers study the principles and their associated procedures, apply them in their lessons, and receive feedback on their performance from the trainer and other trainees. Assessment may be based on how well the teacher can use the principles and procedures of the approach, method, or course design. Although perhaps there is more flexibility in the practice of using communicative course designs rather than older methods such as the Direct Method, they still provide maps for teachers to learn and follow. Hence methods (and approaches) are often criticized as reflecting a top-down view of teaching – one in which the teacher is an implementer of methods designed by others. However, in order for teachers to achieve their potential it is important for them to be able to use approaches and methods flexibly and creatively, based on their own beliefs, judgment and experiences. This means that teachers should be encouraged to transform and adapt the methods they use to make them their own, that is, to personalize and individualize them. Learning to use the techniques and procedures of a specific method is probably essential for teachers when they first start teaching, because doing this provides them with the confidence needed to face learners and with tried and tested techniques and strategies for presenting their lessons. For novice teachers, in the early stages of their professional development, teaching often involves applying techniques and procedures developed by others. An approach or a predetermined method, with its associated activities, principles, and techniques, may be a useful starting point for an inexperienced teacher, but it should be seen only as that. As the teacher gains experience and knowledge, he or she will begin to develop an individual approach or personal method of teaching, one that draws on an established approach or method but that also uniquely reflects the teacher's individual beliefs, values, principles, and experience. This is the focus of Chapter 5.

Follow-up

Compare two or more different coursebooks available for teaching English in your locality. What kind of approach, method, or course design do you think they are based on? How is this reflected in the kinds of activities and exercises they contain?

References and further reading

Adamson, B. (2004). Fashions in Language Teaching Methodology. In A. Davies & C. Elder (Eds.), *The Handbook of Applied Linguistics* (pp. 604–622). Oxford: Blackwell Publishing.

Darian, S. G. (1972). *English as a Foreign Language: History, Development, and Methods of Teaching*. Norman: University of Oklahoma Press.

Howatt, A. P. R. & Widdowson, H. G. (2004). *A History of English Language Teaching* (2nd edition). Oxford: Oxford University Press.

Littlewood, W. (1981). *Communicative Language Teaching*. Cambridge: Cambridge University Press.

Richards, J. C. & Rodgers, T. S. (2014). *Approaches and Methods in Language Teaching* (3rd edition). Cambridge: Cambridge University Press.

Rivers, W. M. (1981). *Teaching Foreign-Language Skills* (2nd edition). Chicago: University of Chicago Press.

Williams, M. & Burden, R. L. (1997). *Psychology for Language Teachers: A Social Constructivist Approach*. Cambridge: Cambridge University Press.

Chapter 5 Develop your personal teaching principles

Introduction

In Chapter 4 we've looked at how teaching methods and approaches reflect different beliefs and assumptions about the nature of language and language learning; they serve as the source for different principles for the teaching of English. Principles for "best practice" may also be described in curriculum frameworks developed in the curriculum department of a ministry of education, in teaching organizations such as TESOL or in recommendations at the institute or school level. These often reflect educational philosophies and approaches at the time as well as culture-based beliefs about teachers, teaching, and learners. In addition, as teachers we also have our own beliefs and principles about how best to teach. Some of these may have been acquired during our professional education while others may have been formed from our teaching experience. In this chapter we will look at the nature of teacher beliefs and principles and how they influence the way we teach.

5.1 Beliefs and principles

Beliefs refer to our understanding or opinions about the truth of something. For example:

- Students learn in different ways.

- Memorization is the key to successful language learning.
- Language learning involves interaction with other learners.

Principles describe how beliefs provide guidelines for practices.

Teaching principles are the basic guidelines or foundation describing how teaching should be carried out. For example:
- Make learning fun.
- Teach to the whole class, not just to the best students.

The following table gives examples of beliefs and principles that can be derived from them:

Beliefs	Principles
Students learn in different ways.	Provide different options for completing tasks.
Memorization is the key to successful language learning.	Include memorization activities in every lesson.
Language learning involves interaction with other learners.	Make regular use of group activities.

Practices are the practical ways in which teachers apply or draw on their principles in teaching. For example, in applying the principle of making regular use of group activities, the teacher may make use of a variety of group-based activities such as ranking activities and information gap activities. In this chapter we will explore teachers' beliefs and principles and how they influence teachers' classroom practices.

5.2 The influence of school-based learning on beliefs, principles and practices

Apart from principles that are derived from approaches and methods which are the focus of Chapter 4, what are other sources of teachers' principles? One source of how we teach is our previous experiences as learners. What we know and believe about teaching English is often influenced by English lessons that we have experienced and teachers who have made an impression on us by the way they teach. These experiences may be the source of some of the principles that we seek to realize in our teaching. For example, if we experienced grammar-dominated and test-dominated teaching at school when we were learning English, we may develop the same understanding of teaching. Our teaching may be dominated by principles such as "to teach to the tests", "to start every lesson with grammar practice" or the principle that "errors are the enemies of learning". Sitting in the classroom for hundreds of hours throughout our education provides socialization into established traditions of what is understood by the concept of "a good teacher" or of "good teaching". These views of teaching may also reflect culture-based teaching practices. For example, teacher roles may be related to culture-specific assumptions about power and authority in the classroom which can be reflected in features of classroom interaction. Cortazzi and Jin (2013: 1) describe culture-based approaches to teaching and learning:

> Members of different cultural communities may have different preferences, expectations, interpretations, values and beliefs about how to learn or how to teach. ... Cultural ideas of learning, often subconscious and taken for granted,

are absorbed in early learning in the absence of contrasting ideas and are not normally articulated; they are built up in interaction in families and through early and later schooling as cultures transmit ways of learning and children are socialized into education and then, through education, into so much else in the wider world.

Chakrakodi (2022: 134–135) comments on the nature of school learning in India:

An examination of the government schools in India shows that the teacher plays the traditional role of an authority figure in the classroom. Classes are kept rigidly under the teacher's control. Rules such as maintaining silence in classrooms and answering only if you know the right answer may discourage processes that are integral to SLA.

Children are not active participants even in the first language acquisition process. They are passive recipients of the input given by the teacher. It is the teacher who initiates a talk, usually by way of asking display questions and students answer his/her questions. Conversation in the classroom is, hence, limited only to questions and answers. If at all there is any peer-to-peer interaction in the classroom, it happens in L1. Teachers translate and explain texts before dictating answers.

Quieti and Nanni (2022) similarly observe:

In Thailand, the culture, and therefore the culture of education, is quite different from the west. Due to the immigration of Chinese to Thailand, certain Confucian traditions have been adopted within the education system (Nguyen et al., 2006; Wang & King, 2008), and one element of this is a ... structure where the teacher is a highly respected figure of authority within the class, and the students are mainly listeners (Kainzbauer & Hunt, 2016), which has led to a predominantly teacher-centered classroom ...

What principles about the roles of teachers and learners are reflected in the accounts above? Do you share these principles? Why or why not?

5.3 Beliefs about English

In Chapter 1 we've discussed the nature of English as an international language and some of the implications of rethinking the nature of English from the EIL perspective. Teachers' or learners' beliefs and understanding about English can influence the targets they set for the teaching or learning of English. Here are some examples of beliefs that people may have about English:

- English is the world's most important second language.
- It's important to learn to speak like a speaker from an English-speaking country, such as the US or the UK.
- English spoken with a British accent sounds better than when spoken with an American accent.
- You shouldn't speak English with an accent that reflects your first language.
- English grammar is not very systematic.
- English contains more idioms than other languages.
- English is more difficult to learn than other languages.
- English has more grammar than other languages.
- You need to study the culture of English-speaking countries when you study English.

> *Do you agree or disagree with the statements above? Can you add three other beliefs about English to the list? Compare your responses with a colleague.*

Your beliefs about English and the role of English as an international language will influence the principles you seek to apply in your teaching. These will be reflected in the emphasis you give to factors such as mastery of English grammar, nativelike pronunciation, and the values associated with English that you communicate to your students.

As one teacher comments:

> I emphasize that English does not belong to any one country or culture and belongs to anyone who needs it. I talk about "cosmopolitan English", that is, English used by people as a common language and not based on any native-speaker variety of English.

We can represent the relation between beliefs about English and the principles and practices that relate to them in the following table:

Beliefs	Principles	Practices
English is an international language.	Develop skills in using English for cross-cultural communication.	Teach communication strategies for using English as a lingua franca.

(to be continued)

(*continued*)

Beliefs	Principles	Practices
Stress and rhythm should be the basis for a good accent in English.	Make stress-timed rhythm a focus of pronunciation teaching.	Use transcripts of dialogs to practice using "targetlike" rhythm and stress in English.
Grammar provides the foundation for communication.	Teach students to understand the difference between Chinese grammar and English grammar.	Use grammar translation exercises.

Can you suggest a principle related to each of the following issues?
- *the teacher's use of English in teaching*
- *correcting students' grammatical errors in a speaking activity*
- *the role of pair and group work in a language lesson*

5.4 Beliefs about second language learning

Our beliefs about learning a second language may also be influenced by how we have learned English and other languages and by our teaching experience and can lead to different opinions about how best to learn English. For example, do you agree or disagree with the following statements?

- Girls are better at learning English than boys.

- Memorizing word lists is a useful way to improve your English.
- You need to understand grammar to learn a language well.
- Children learn languages differently from adults.
- Drills are a useful way to learn grammar.
- Practice is the only way to learn a language.
- Translation exercises are good to practice writing.
- Watching movies in English is a good way to improve your English.
- Speaking well in English is more difficult to learn than reading or writing.

In the following example, a teacher describes how her teaching principles are influenced both by her beliefs about English and by the goals of second language learning:

> Even though I have been an English teacher for more than 10 years I still used to think of myself as a language learner. I think this was because when I was learning English we were often told we should aim to speak like a native speaker of English, even though that was a very unrealistic target. Gradually my ideas about English began to change when people started talking about English as an international language and people wouldn't need to try to mimic native speakers when using English. I began to think of myself not as a language learner but as a multi-competent language user, meaning that my ability to speak English and other languages was something I should celebrate. I try to pass this message on to my learners. I emphasize that they should set their goal as learning to be a successful user of English. So I build into my lessons lots of activities that enable students to use what they know of English and to consider themselves successful if they have

made themselves understood rather than consider themselves unsuccessful because they can't always use the correct grammar or pronunciation. (Kari)

What core principles does Kari seek to realize in her teaching?

Teachers' beliefs may sometimes be very different from those of our learners. Let's consider the statements below which reflect the beliefs of many of today's language teachers and support learner-centered principles about language teaching:

- Learning involves acquiring organizing principles based on people's experiences with different kinds of learning.
- The teacher is a resource person who provides input for learners to work on.
- Language input can be found everywhere – in the community, in the media, on the Internet as well as in the classroom and the textbook.
- It is the role of the teacher to help learners manage their own learning by helping them find resources they can make use of.
- Success in learning depends on the learners forming hypotheses about language from their encounters with it. Errors are a sign of the learners' developing hypotheses.

The following table illustrates how beliefs about learning and language use influence both principles and teaching practices.

Beliefs	Principles	Teaching practices
Students should aim to speak like native speakers of English.	Errors should be corrected before they become habits.	Make use of drills and repetition exercises.
Fluency is more important than accuracy in language use.	Treat errors as evidence of learning.	Use tasks and group-based activities.

Our learners, however, may have different beliefs about language learning, leading to a potential clash between our teaching principles and the expectations of our learners, as reflected in these learner comments:

- I don't know what I need to learn. It's the teacher's job to know that.
- Without knowing the grammar you will never learn.
- Pair work and group work are not useful because you end up learning bad English from your classmates.
- A British accent is the best one to learn.

Do you sometimes feel that you need to change some of your learners' beliefs about learning English? Which ones? Why?

5.5 Principles that reflect learner differences

A major source of our beliefs and principles is our teaching experience. Experience tells us what to expect with the kind of students we are most familiar with, which may be young learners, teenagers, university students or adults. We soon become familiar with the interests of each group of learners, what their goals may be for learning English, typical difficulties to anticipate and the kinds of activities that work well with them. Young learners, teenagers and adults bring very different approaches and understandings to language learning. They have very different needs, goals and interests; they bring different beliefs, attitudes and motivations to second language learning and make use of different learning approaches. Principles that work well with one age group may not be successful with learners from a different age group as we see in the following examples.

5.5.1 Teaching young learners

Teacher Gina's experience has mainly been teaching young learners, that is, those in grade school and up to the age of 12. She comments:

> My young learners have lively imagination. They are curious about the world about them. They learn fast from their peers, their siblings, their parents and the media. They are talkative. They enjoy play and games. They watch and imitate what the classmates do.
>
> I find they learn best through the experience of using English rather than through studying rules and practicing them. So I make use of activities and using language that is linked to behavior, actions and the classroom context. They learn language as it occurs, as a part of doing things. But they have short attention spans. Their attention spans are closely linked to their interests in things around them. They enjoy short activities and tasks that reinforce new language. These activities and tasks need to be repeated and reinforced often in enjoyable, yet challenging, learning environments. They

also are often physically active, learning through play, through manipulating objects or through playing with toys and other objects that may keep them occupied for hours. And they learn through interacting and using language in context, rather than through learning abstract language. They are not interested in studying language as a system, but rather in using it as a means of communicating and interacting with others. What this means is that they want to see results here and now – something that they can demonstrate or show to their parents when they go home. Above all they want to have fun in the English class.

Through many years of teaching young learners, Gina has developed a set of principles that serve as the basis for her teaching:
1) Build teaching around activities and physical movement.
2) Build lessons around linked activities.
3) Build lessons around tasks.
4) Provide support and guidance for tasks.
5) Involve students in creating resources that support their learning.
6) Build lessons around themes.
7) Choose content children are familiar with.
8) Use activities that involve collaboration.
9) Create a supportive learning community in the classroom.
10) Use enjoyable activities that children can accomplish without frustration.
11) Provide rich language support.
12) Give clear goals and feedback.
13) Use English for classroom management.
14) Use the mother tongue when it is needed.
15) Bring speakers of English to class.
16) Choose appropriate forms of assessment.

Can you give examples of two activities that work well with young learners? What principles do they reflect?

5.5.2 Teaching teenagers

Teacher David teaches classes of teenagers (learners between the ages of 12 and 17) at a secondary school. He enjoys teaching teenagers and understands that the teenage years are a period of time when young people are maturing and forming their own identities – identities that sometimes clash with the roles expected of them by adults and teachers. He comments:

Teenagers are often difficult to teach. They are going through physical changes that may affect their appearance, as well as their emotions. They may be sensitive about how they appear and how people perceive them and many of the issues they are facing are played out in secondary school. This means they prefer interacting with peers during learning activities; they have a strong need for approval; they need regular activity because of increased energy levels. I find that they want to become increasingly independent, but at the same time they have a strong need to belong to a group and seek peer approval. Also they are often very sensitive to ridicule or embarrassment. One good thing is that they have usually had wide out-of-school exposure to English, but this can mean you have a class with very mixed levels. Of course they have grown up with computers, the Internet, multimedia and social networking and they know how to explore the Internet to find things they need. So they generally expect their language classes and their language learning experiences to reflect the kinds of technology they are familiar with. They also have many opportunities for learning English outside of the classroom.

The biggest difficulty I faced when I started teaching teenagers was to shift from a style of teaching where I made most of the decisions to one where I gave as much autonomy as possible to my learners. This meant the maximum use of group activities and techniques, drawn from the repertoire of cooperative learning. I find it essential to build on opportunities for teenagers to showcase their talents. It's also important to let them take responsibility for what and how they learn, whenever possible. Sometimes this means leaving the classroom entirely for activities that take place elsewhere in the school or neighborhood.

The following principles underlie David's approach to teaching teenagers:

1) Choose activities that motivate learners.
2) Create a positive classroom climate.
3) Establish appropriate rules for classroom behavior.
4) Personalize the students' learning.
5) Give students choices of what to learn.
6) Allow students to showcase their talents.
7) Choose appropriate forms of assessment.

> *What are some typical problems you have to deal with when you are teaching teenagers?*

5.5.3 Teaching adults

The next example is from Sara, who teaches adult English courses in an Anglophone country. She comments:

Teaching English to adults is very different from teaching younger learners. My typical adult class consists of people with a wide variety of knowledge and previous learning experiences that may include work-related experiences, as well as family responsibilities if they are parents. So a class often contains people of very different educational, linguistic and cultural backgrounds. There may be great differences in life experiences, education and social backgrounds. This can often provide a rich resource to draw upon in teaching. Generally I find that they like to be involved in managing their own learning. For example, they may want to decide what topics and skills they want to study in class, and what kinds of materials they wish to use. They will have opinions about what works best for them. And they prefer me to be a facilitator, rather than a manager or controller of their learning. They are able to take responsibility for many aspects of the class, such as deciding on grouping arrangements. Also, usually they are in class for a specific reason. They know what they want from a course and expect a course to be well planned, with clear learning outcomes. They may have preferences for particular aspects of language that they wish to study. They often have busy lives and are strongly motivated to acquire skills and knowledge that will empower their lives and in which they see immediate relevance. They expect to see a good reason for completing activities that I assign them and want to see clear practical results, especially results that they can apply in their lives – at work and in daily life.

Sara makes use of the following principles in designing English courses for adult learners:

1) Start with needs analysis.

2) Develop clear statements of learning outcomes.

3) Prepare students to use English in real-life situations.

4) Use materials from the learners' world.

5) Provide a safe learning environment.

6) Use the learners' first language as a resource.

7) Encourage learning outside of class time.

8) Be prepared for mixed ability levels.

9) Choose appropriate forms of assessment.

Which group do you think you would enjoy teaching more: young learners, teenagers, or adults? Why?

5.6 Beliefs and principles about the nature of effective teaching

Teaching is a very personal activity. A teacher brings his or her own philosophy and understanding of teaching to his or her classes, reflecting some of the influences discussed above. This is seen in the way two teachers in the same institution – Belinda and Brian – describe their approaches to teaching and their different understandings of how to achieve effective lessons.

Belinda has eight years' teaching experience. She is a quiet, soft-spoken teacher who is always polite and pleasant with her students. Her students do well academically and are always quiet and attentive in class. The students sit in single rows. When the teacher enters the room, students stand up and greet her. They raise their hands when they want to speak, and they stand when they answer the teacher's questions. Belinda follows the textbook closely in her teaching. She tends to be teacher-centered in her teaching because a core belief for her is that students come to class to learn. One of her principles is to "keep the lesson focused on the learning activities".

Brian has three years' teaching experience. His class does not do as well academically as Belinda's class, although his students work hard and are enthusiastic. Brian has an excellent relationship with them, but his class is much less traditional in its organization. Students do not have to stand up when he enters the class or raise their hands to ask a question, or stand up when they answer the teacher's questions. The classroom atmosphere is very relaxed. Students can volunteer answers when they wish to do so and the class is sometimes quite noisy. Brian does not like the textbook and often uses his own teaching materials and activities.

What do you think one of Brian's principles is?

These examples illustrate that we may have different orientations towards teaching from other teachers and that our beliefs account for differences in the principles we seek to realize in our lessons. These differences reflect differences in how to see the teacher's role in the classroom, the role of the textbook, the teacher's approach to classroom management and the style of communication and interaction that takes place in class.

5.7 Personal teaching principles

As we've seen in Chapter 4 and in the examples above, our teaching principles in language teaching may be derived from different sources, including method-based accounts of the nature of second language teaching and learning, our initial training and experience and our understanding of ourselves and our role as teachers. During our initial teacher training, we will be introduced to the principles and practices recommended in our schools or institutions and taught how to use them in our teaching. The history of language teaching is an account of many principles that have come and gone. As the comedian Julius "Groucho" Marx once commented: "Those are my principles, and if you don't like them … well, I have others."

Teaching is a thinking and cognitively driven process and as we develop experience and expertise in our teaching contexts, we also develop personal principles that we draw on in our teaching (Borg, 2006). These principles reflect our teaching situations, beliefs, experience, training and sense of professional identity and guide many of the decisions we make when we teach. They are a bottom-up source of principles that complement the principles we may have developed from other sources and reflect our evolving understanding of teaching. For example, Anna, a teacher of adults, describes her teaching philosophy:

> I think it's important to be positive as a personality. The teacher has to be a positive person. You have to show a tremendous amount of patience. And I think if you have a good attitude you can project this to the students and establish a relaxed atmosphere in your classroom. … And although I think a lesson plan is useful, what is more important for me is to find the easiest way for students to understand what they need to learn.

The teacher's philosophy emphasizes her attitude and the need to create a positive environment for learning in the classroom. Her justification for lesson planning is based on helping the students rather than helping the teacher.

Another teacher describes how her view of teaching has changed over the years. Her earlier view of herself as a teacher was very teacher-led and reflected a tightly planned and executed approach to teaching. Her current approach, however, reflects her view of herself as more of a guide or facilitator – she tries to create lessons which enhance communication and cooperation between learners and in which the teacher takes a back seat:

> I know it's a business lesson, but I really like to activate their knowledge. My beliefs are very much humanitarian in that they will learn if they feel a warm cooperative atmosphere in the classroom, so I'm very concerned that they build up a trust among themselves.

She has developed a student-based approach to teaching that is dependent on establishing trust between the students and the teacher. In order to conduct a student-centered lesson she spends most of her class time on small group activities with students working on tasks in pairs or groups and carrying out many of the functions that the teacher might perform in a more teacher-fronted class.

Teachers such as these suggest how our belief systems lead to the development of rational principles that serve as a source of how we carry out our teaching. As we teach, we monitor our teaching to see if our principles are being realized and make modifications or changes to our lessons to ensure that our principles are being realized. Examples of principles of this kind are:

- Follow the learners' interests to maintain their involvement.

- Always teach to the whole class – not just to the best students.
- Seek ways to encourage independent student learning.
- Make learning fun.
- Every student is a winner.
- Build takeaway value in every lesson.
- Address learners' mental processing capacities.
- Facilitate learner responsibility or autonomy.

And here are examples of how teachers' personal principles have influenced decisions they made during teaching:

Principles	Impact on teaching
Follow the learners' interests to maintain their involvement.	The teacher diverted the lesson to a new topic that the students had raised and built the lesson around the topic rather than the one in the book.
Seek ways to encourage independent student learning.	The teacher stopped the lesson to change the seating arrangement because he realized the students would become more actively involved with a group-based rather than whole-class activity.
Help students to be engaged meaningfully with a reading text.	The teacher realized that the text was too difficult for many of the students; so rather than have the students work independently on the text she switched to a teacher-directed activity in which she created a scaffold or propositional structure for the text through questions and answers with the students.

(to be continued)

(continued)

Principles	Impact on teaching
Make sure that every student has an opportunity to learn at his or her pace.	The teacher recognized that some students in the class were less proficient than others and included an activity in the lesson that weaker students can perform well.
Create a receptive attitude for learning.	When the teacher sensed that the lesson was dragging or not engaging the students, she switched to an activity that would boost the students' interest, such as a short game, a song or an activity involving physical movement and action.

Consider a particular class you teach and a typical group of learners in that class. What are some of the principles you try to realize when you teach the class? How might these be observable to a visitor observing your class?

Conclusion

As we have seen in this chapter and in Chapter 4, our teaching principles are derived from different sources and reflect factors related to our teaching contexts, our experience, our beliefs about the nature of language teaching and learning and the individual qualities we have as teachers. They are also specific to the kinds of students we teach, since principles that work well for us with young learners, for example, may not necessarily be equally effective with older learners. It is important to develop an awareness and understanding of our teaching principles and to reflect on whether they are always the most appropriate basis for our teaching. As we acquire more knowledge and experience as teachers we may sometimes need to modify or replace our principles to ensure that they serve as the best possible basis for our teaching.

Follow-up

Write a short account of your teaching context and focus on one of the classes you typically teach or are familiar with. What is the nature of the class? Who are the learners and what challenges do they face in learning English? What are two personal teaching principles that you make use of in your teaching? Give examples of how these influence your teaching. Then share your account with a colleague and compare it with his or her account.

References and further reading

Borg, S. (2006). *Teacher Cognition and Language Education: Research and Practice.* London: Continuum.

Chakrakodi, R. (2022). Socio-Cultural Factors and Second Language Acquisition. https://www.riesi.ac.in/wp-content/uploads/2022/02/09-CRN-LanguagingSocio-culturalfactors.pdf

Clark, C. M. & Peterson, P. L. (1986). Teachers' Thought Processes. In M. C. Wittrock (Ed.), *Handbook of Research on Teaching* (3rd edition, pp. 255–296). New York: Macmillan.

Cortazzi, M. & Jin, L. (2013). Introduction: Researching Cultures of Learning. In M. Cortazzi & L. Jin (Eds.), *Researching Cultures of Learning: International Perspectives on Language Learning and Education* (pp. 1–17). Basingstoke: Palgrave Macmillan.

Crookes, G. (2009). *Values, Philosophies, and Beliefs in TESOL: Making a Statement.* New York: Cambridge University Press.

Golombek, P. (2009). Personal Practical Knowledge in L2 Teacher Education. In A. Burns & J. C. Richards (Eds.), *The Cambridge Guide to Second Language Teacher Education* (pp. 155–162). Cambridge: Cambridge University Press.

Jin, L. & Cortazzi, M. (2011). Re-Evaluating Traditional Approaches to Second Language Teaching and Learning. In E. Hinkel (Ed.), *Handbook of Research in Second Language Teaching and Learning* (Vol. 2, pp. 558–575). New York: Routledge.

Nguyen, P.-M., Terlouw, C. & Pilot, A. (2006). Culturally Appropriate Pedagogy: The Case of Group Learning in a Confucian Heritage Culture Context. *Intercultural Education, 17*(1), 1–19.

Quieti, A. & Nanni, A. (2022). Characteristics of Effective English Language Teachers: Student and Teacher Perspectives at a Thai University. *SAGE Open, 12*(2).

Woods, D. (1996). *Teacher Cognition in Language Teaching: Beliefs, Decision-Making and Classroom Practice.* Cambridge: Cambridge University Press.

PART 3

THE NATURE OF LANGUAGE LESSONS

Chapter 6 Understand the nature of lesson structures and activities

Introduction

Today's learners can make use of many opportunities to learn English beyond classroom-based lessons. For many younger learners in particular, the Internet, the media and face-to-face as well as virtual social networks provide greater opportunities for meaningful and authentic language use than are generally available in the classroom. These learning opportunities are more likely to be interactive, social, and multimodal. Learners can interact using English with people in almost every part of the world. They can download apps that support many aspects of language learning and can use these while waiting for the bus or train or traveling to school. And when they get home they may enter a chat room to interact with other language learners or speakers of English; they may enter game sites and play video games that require them to understand and use English, or they may watch a TV program or movie in English, following the subtitles if necessary. However, despite the new opportunities and conveniences available in these ways for the majority of people, their language learning journeys begin in the classroom, where the foundation is laid for successful language learning in and beyond the classroom. The focus of this chapter is how teachers use their pedagogical content knowledge to develop coherent structures for their classroom lessons.

6.1 The nature of lesson structures

As we've observed in Chapter 5, a teacher of any subject comes to teaching with his or her own experience, accumulated during his or her time as a student in school or university. Much of what we know about teaching is the result of hundreds of hours of participation in lessons taught by teachers of different subjects. This is sometimes called the "apprenticeship of observation". From this experience teachers develop an awareness of what constitutes a lesson, which we can define as follows:

A lesson is a coherent sequence of instructional activities that are chosen to help achieve a learning goal or outcome.

A lesson is not a random set of activities; it reflects a series of linked phases or *moves*. Moves determine how a lesson progresses from an *opening* phase to a series of *instructional activities* and concludes with a *closing move*. How these stages are realized leads to typical lesson structures or formats for different kinds of lessons such as grammar lessons, reading lessons, or vocabulary lessons. Learning how language lessons can be structured is a priority in training courses for novice language teachers. It may involve *observing* different kinds of language lessons and *identifying* their overall structures and the moves that they are composed of, *studying* lesson transcripts to identify their components and how particular moves and the transitions between the moves are achieved, *planning* lessons using particular formats for lessons (such as the *presentation*, *controlled practice*, and *free practice* in a grammar lesson) and *practicing* the different phases of a lesson through microteaching.

The assumption behind a focus on the components of lessons

in this way is that novice teachers will be able to employ this knowledge base when they teach complete lessons in the classroom. It provides a way of bringing system and order to lessons (Kennedy, 2016). As Kavanagh et al. (2020) comment:

> This breaking down enables novices to cultivate a nuanced professional vision and language: through categorization, novices gain a better understanding of what to look for and how to describe and interpret what they see. By identifying and naming the component parts of practice, TEs [teacher educators] support novices to practice and use the language of their profession. The challenge remains that separating the part (a pedagogical move) from the whole (teaching practice writ large) can alternately illuminate and minimize the complex practice of experienced teachers.

In what follows we will examine the three primary moves in a lesson – the *opening*, the lesson's *instructional activities*, and the *closing move*. We will focus in detail on the core of any lesson – its instructional activities.

6.2 Lesson openings

The opening move of a lesson consists of the procedures the teacher uses to focus the students' attention on the learning aims of the lesson. The opening generally occupies the first few minutes of the lesson and can have an important influence on how much students learn from the lesson. It can serve a variety of purposes such as to arouse students' interest in the lesson, to give an overview of what is to come in order to mentally prepare the students for the lesson or to make connections to previous lessons.

Can you suggest other purposes for a lesson opening?

The way a lesson opens will depend upon the purpose of the lesson opening and the nature of the lesson. For example, in opening a lesson you could choose to describe the goals of the lesson by stating the information or skills the students will learn, to describe the relationship between the lesson or activities and the students' needs or to describe what the students are expected to do in the lesson. A teacher comments:

> I find that the right lead-in to a lesson gives the students confidence to know what the lesson will be about. I tend to give them an overview of the session before I start, without revealing too many details which they don't need to know at that stage. Sometimes I may outline what I will expect from them at the end of the session. At other times, it is better to keep an element of surprise for an activity or a session to work. (Anna)

Suggest openings for lessons which include the following main activities:
- *writing a comparison/contrast essay*
- *reading a review of a movie*
- *listening to advice on how to deal with a health problem*
- *watching a video of a job interview*

6.3 A lesson's instructional activities

The core of a lesson consists of the instructional activities students take part in. These consist of a series of linked stages or moves that help achieve the lesson's goals and outcomes. The content of each stage of the lesson will be determined by the nature of the lesson and by general principles for the organization of lessons. For example:

- Activities should be sequenced in terms of difficulty.
- Receptive skills should precede productive skills.
- Content shouldn't be limited to the textbook; make use of learner-generated content rather than teacher-provided content.
- Controlled practice should be followed by freer practice.

Structures of language lessons reflect our pedagogical content knowledge, that is, our understanding of the processes involved in learning and using vocabulary, grammar, and reading, writing, speaking and listening skills.

6.3.1 Skill-based lessons

Skill-based lessons such as listening and reading lessons often contain three stages: a pre-listening/pre-reading stage, a while-listening/while-reading stage, and a post-listening/post-reading stage as seen in these typical stages in a listening lesson:

Stage 1: *Pre-listening*: Activities prepare the students for a listening activity by providing essential background information, by presenting any unknown vocabulary that is central to the listening activity and which cannot be guessed from the context, and by helping the students select suitable purposes and strategies for listening.

Stage 2: *While-listening*: Students process a text for meaning and respond in different ways, according to the type of the text they listen to and their purposes in listening. This activity provides an opportunity for intensive listening practice and also helps students develop strategies they can use to improve their listening, such as focusing on key parts of a text and guessing words from the context.

Stage 3: *Post-listening*: The teacher checks students' understanding of the text and where errors in understanding have occurred to explore what has caused them and what follow-ups are appropriate. This is also an opportunity for students to respond to the content of the text in different ways and to make links to other skills, such as writing or discussion.

Suggest pre-listening, while-listening, and post-listening activities to be used in listening lessons that contain the following listening texts:
- *a girl talking about tourist attractions in her city and giving suggestions for a two-day visit*
- *two persons discussing a recent movie they have watched – what it is about, and what they think of it*

Speaking lessons take many different forms but often make use of a seven-stage cycle of activities (Goh & Burns, 2012):

Stage 1: *Focus learners' attention on speaking.* Students think about a speaking activity – what it involves and what they can anticipate.

Stage 2: *Provide input and/or guide planning.* This may involve pre-teaching vocabulary, expressions or discourse features and planning for an activity they will carry out in class (e.g. a presentation or a transaction).

Stage 3: *Conduct speaking tasks.* Students practice a communicative speaking task (or a few such tasks) with a focus on fluency.

Stage 4: *Focus on language/skills/strategies.* Students examine their performance or look at other performance of the task, as well as transcripts of how the task can be carried out, and review different features of the task.

Stage 5: *Repeat speaking tasks*. The task is performed a second time.

Stage 6: *Direct learners' reflection on learning*. Students review and reflect on what they have learned and difficulties they have encountered.

Stage 7: *Facilitate feedback on learning*. The teacher provides feedback on their performance.

- *What activities do you usually use in a speaking lesson? Do you make use of procedures such as those above?*
- *What typical stages do you make use of for a writing lesson and for a pronunciation lesson?*

6.3.2 Method-based lessons

Teaching approaches and methods also provide formats for lesson structures. For example, in the sequence of activities typically found in lessons based on the P-P-P Method (discussed in Chapter 4) are:

1) Presentation. The new grammar structure is presented, often by means of a conversation or short text. The teacher explains the new structure and checks the students' understanding of it.

2) Controlled practice. The students are given intensive practice in the structure under the teacher's guidance and control. They practice using the new structure in a controlled context, through drills or substitution exercises.

3) Free practice. The students practice using the new structure without any control by the teacher. They practice using the

new structure in different contexts, often through using their own content or information, in order to develop fluency with the new structure.

4) Checking. The teacher elicits use of the new structure to check that it has been learned.

5) Further practice. The new structure is now practiced in new situations or in combination with other structures.

> *What sequence of activities would you use in a pronunciation lesson?*

6.3.3 Text-based lessons

A text-based lesson contains the following sequence of activities (Feez, 1998):

1) Building the context. This introduces the social context of the text type being studied and examples of the text type are presented, such as a personal report or a narrative text.

2) Modeling and deconstructing the text. Students investigate the structural pattern and language features of a model text and compare it with other examples of the same text type.

3) Joint construction of the text. Students begin to contribute to the construction of whole examples of the text type. The teacher gradually reduces the contribution to text construction, as the students move closer to being able to control the text type independently.

4) Independent construction of the text. Students work independently with the text. Learner performance is used for assessment.

5) Linking to related texts. Students investigate how what they have learned in this teaching/learning cycle can be related to other texts in the same or similar context.

In your teaching context, what sort of writing texts could you teach with the text-based approach described above?

6.4 Departing from conventional lesson structures

Lesson structures such as those above prioritize the visible and observable components of lessons rather than the thinking that underlies the choice and use of activities. They also overlook the fact that classroom life can be dynamic and unpredictable and often requires the teacher to rethink his or her intentions and to improvise responses to unanticipated classroom events. Furthermore, if teachers are overdependent on fixed formats and lesson structures they are less likely to think creatively and to look for novel ways of dealing with teaching incidents, i.e. to respond to these as opportunities for personal innovation and creative thinking.

An example is an approach Hamed (a teacher) sometimes uses in teaching grammar to his intermediate-level students. Rather than follow the sequence of *presentation, controlled practice* and *free practice* that could be regarded as a feature of the P-P-P Method, Hamed starts with *free practice*, then provides *controlled practice* and ends the lesson with *presentation*:

1) Free practice. Students are given a task (e.g. a role-play) to complete and they complete it as best as they can. Based on their performance, Hamed identifies some of the language they need for better performance of the task.

2) Controlled Practice. Students repeat the task one or more times and as they are trying to do this, the teacher gives them some of the words and expressions that they need.

3) Presentation. As a follow-up, the teacher and the students analyze the task and the difficulties that have arisen as they perform it. Hamed gives an explicit account of the language demands and features of the task and the "rules" that it reflects. Students may now be given another task of the same kind to practice.

Another teacher describes how she teach writing in different ways, rather than always rely on the same set of procedures:

> I have a repertoire of at least 20 different ways of dealing with a writing task depending on which stage of the process we are working on. Sometimes we work with brainstorming techniques like listing, cubing or using mind maps. Sometimes we do continuous writing on topics they generate, just to focus on fluency. At other times we work with the organization of a text, identifying the best sequence to present elements of the text and allocating different learners to generate the ideas and language for different parts. In this way we come up with a collaborative text. I also use reformulation in class a lot – this involves presenting two versions of a completed text: a learner's original text and then a version of it that I have reworked to make it communicate more effectively. The positive thing about reformulation is that it involves no "correction" of the learner's text but invites students to identify the changes that have been made and to discuss why they have been made. In this way it is developing their critical skills and helping them find ways of evaluating and improving their own texts. The key is to keep the activities fresh and to encourage learners to contribute the content. (Sarah)

6.5 Features of instructional activities

The core component of a lesson is referred to as the lesson's *instructional activities*. Doubtless the styles of teaching English that occur around the world vary considerably, however, for many students, the following approach to an English lesson, observed in English classes in Indonesia (Lamb, 2009: 240), would be familiar:

> My observation notes report teacher-dominated lessons based on a standard textbook with a grammatico-lexical syllabus and offering a set of traditional activities (cf. Lamb & Coleman, 2008), including teacher explanations of language, reading comprehension tasks, reading texts aloud, grammar and vocabulary exercises, and feedback sessions involving pupils writing their answers up on the blackboard. Oral work consisted mainly of teacher questions, plus some choral chanting.

Throughout our teaching careers we typically make use of a core set of basic activities and lesson formats that define the nature of the teaching and learning that we provide. The activities we choose as the main instructional stage of the lesson reflect what we know or understand about the nature of listening, speaking, reading and writing and how we believe these skills should be best taught. The choice of an activity will also depend on the learners' overall level. For example, in a low-level class, "writing" may consist of copying a model composition from the board and making minor additions to it, while in an advanced class it may refer to the process in which students choose a topic to write about, and then go through a cycle of drafting and revising to produce final products. The activities and tasks that we make use of hence define the nature of teaching and learning in our classrooms (Airey, 2011; Clegg, 2007; Doyle, 1983). Kennedy (2016: 10) comments:

> It should not be surprising to learn that teachers' lesson plans are developed around *activities* rather than *topics* (Shavelson, 1983). When teachers enter their classrooms, they have in mind a specific sequence of events that will unfold in a specific way. Clark and Peterson (1986) refer to these plans as "activity flows."

A teacher comments:

> I think about the students, what they need and what they are capable of and I decide the kinds of things I want them to do during the lesson, such as working with a text or drafting a piece of writing. Of course, I have to think about what I want the students to learn in the lesson and with that in mind, I choose the kinds of resources to use and the exercises I will ask the students to complete. (Rosemary)

We draw on our pedagogical content knowledge, our professional training and experience and our beliefs about the nature of effective teaching to make decisions about the kinds of activities to use in teaching grammar, vocabulary, reading, writing, listening and speaking. And students have to learn the nature and purposes of the different kinds of classroom activities we make use of, how they should be carried out and what the intended products or outcomes of these activities should be. Students may not always share our beliefs about the usefulness of some of the activities we make use of. For example, in a speaking lesson the teacher may believe in the value of group discussion activities, while the students may prefer more teacher-directed activities and not see the value of trying out their English with other learners.

The following are examples of activities that can be used in teaching speaking and reading and their purposes.

Speaking activities	Purposes
dialog work	• teach fixed expressions and routines • provide examples of transactions • provide examples of moves (e.g. openings and closings)
study transcriptions of spoken exchanges	• develop awareness of the nature of authentic interaction • develop awareness of spoken grammar • develop awareness of differences between casual and formal interaction
information gap activities	• develop communication strategies • practice conversational repairs
surveys and questionnaires	• develop questioning strategies • learn how to ask follow-up questions
role-plays	• practice turn-taking • develop fluency
group discussion	• practice agreeing and disagreeing • learn new vocabulary

Reading activities	Purposes
reorganize a scrambled text	develop awareness of text structure
write headings for paragraphs in a text	practice reading for main ideas
skimming activities	develop a general idea and the organization of a text
prepare questions to go with a text	develop intensive reading skills
take notes of a text	develop study skills
timed reading	encourage rapid reading

What are three typical speaking and three typical reading activities that you make use of? What are their purposes?

6.6 Mechanical, meaningful, and communicative activities

In describing the nature of learning activities, a useful distinction can be made between activities that are either *mechanical, meaningful,* or *communicative*. A *mechanical activity* is a controlled practice activity which students can successfully carry out without necessarily understanding the language they are using. Examples are repetition drills and substitution drills designed to practice the use of particular grammatical or pronunciation features, such as a minimal pair pronunciation exercise in which students practice recognizing the difference between similar sounds, in contrasts such as *grammar/glamor, royal/loyal, arrive/alive, ramp/lamp, rock/lock, light/right, grow/ glow*, and *collect/correct. Sentence combining* is another example of a mechanical activity that requires students to combine two or more sentences into a single sentence, as a way of learning more complex sentence patterns. For example, combine each of these pairs of sentences into a single sentence:

1) The girl drank lemonade. The girl was thirsty.
2) The book was good. The movie based on the book was not good.
3) The weather was perfect. The girls were playing soccer.
4) The scientists trained him well. They helped him find a job when his training was complete.
5) Mark told me not to come with him. He looked longingly at me as I left.

A *meaningful activity* refers to one where language control is still provided but students are required to make meaningful choices when they complete the activity. For example, to practice the grammatical structures *adjective + infinitive* and *noun + infinitive* the teacher might use a matching task such as the following:

Look at the health problems below. Choose several pieces of advice for each problem using these patterns:

- It's important to get some rest.
- It's sometimes helpful to drink garlic tea.
- It's a good idea to take some vitamin C.

Problems	Advice
1. a backache	a. drink lots of liquid
2. a bad headache	b. get some medicine
3. a burn	c. go to bed and rest
4. a cough	d. run it under cold water
5. a fever	e. put a heating pad on it
6. the flu	f. put some cream on it
7. a sore throat	g. see a dentist
8. a toothache	h. see a doctor
	i. take some painkillers
	j. take some vitamin C

This activity provides language control, but it also involves meaningful practice.

A *communicative activity* is one which involves practice in using language within a real communicative context, where real information is exchanged, and where the language used is not totally predictable. Exercise sequences in many communicative coursebooks take students from mechanical, to meaningful or communicative practice. For example, the following activity is found in Richards (2006):

Superlative adjectives
Superlative adjectives usually appear before the noun they modify.

The funniest person I know is my friend Bob.
The most caring individual in our school is the custodian.

(to be continued)

(*continued*)

They can also occur with the noun they modify.

Of all the people in my family, my Aunt Ruth is **the kindest**.
Of all my professors, Dr. Lopez is **the most inspiring**.

Superlatives are often followed by relative clauses in the present perfect.

My cousin Anita is **the most generous** person **I've ever met**.
The closest friend **I've ever had** is someone I met in elementary school.

A Complete these sentences with your own information, and add more details. Then compare with a partner.
  1. One of the most inspiring people I've ever known is ...
     One of the most inspiring people I've ever known is my math teacher. She encourages students to think rather than just memorize formulas and rules.

  2. The most successful individual I know is ...
  3. Of all the people I know ... is the least self-centered.
  4. The youngest person who I consider to be a hero is ...
  5. The most moving speaker I have ever heard is ...
  6. The most important role model I've ever had is ...
  7. Of all the friends I've ever had ... is the most understanding.

(*to be continued*)

(*continued*)

---

8. One of the bravest things I've ever done is ...

B Use the superlative form of these adjectives to describe people you know. Write at least five sentences.

brave   honest   interesting   smart   generous   inspiring   kind witty

C Group work

Discuss the sentences you wrote in Exercises A and B. Ask each other follow-up questions.

A. My next-door neighbor is the bravest person I've ever met.

B. What did your neighbor do, exactly?

A. She's a firefighter, and once she saved a child from a burning building ...

If students read and practice aloud the sentences in the grammar box above, this constitutes *mechanical practice*. Exercises A and B can be regarded as *meaningful practice* since students now complete the sentences with their own information. Exercise C is an example of *communicative practice* since it is an open-ended discussion activity.

Can you give an example of mechanical/meaningful/ communicative activities to practice questions/using the past tense in narratives?

6.7 Tasks

The activities that can provide opportunities for communicative use of language and language development and develop fluency in communication are known as *tasks*, which are core activities in task-based language teaching (see Chapter 4). The features of these tasks are:

- interaction between the learners and users of the language
- collaborative creation of meaning
- meaningful and purposeful interaction through language
- negotiation of meaning as the learners and their interlocutors arrive at understanding
- learning through attending to the feedback learners get when they use the language
- paying attention to the language one hears (the input) and trying to incorporate new forms into one's developing communicative competence
- trying out and experimenting with different ways of saying things

Commonly used task types in language teaching are:

Jigsaw tasks: Learners combine different pieces of information to form a whole. For example, three individuals or groups may have different parts of a story and have to piece the story together.

Information gap tasks: One student or group of students has one set of information and another student or group has a complementary set of information. They must negotiate and find out what the other party's information is in order to complete an activity.

Problem-solving tasks: Students are given a problem and a set of information. They must arrive at a solution to the problem. There is generally a single solution to the problem.

Decision-making tasks: Students are given a problem for which there are a number of possible outcomes, and they must choose one through negotiation and discussion.

Opinion-exchange tasks: Learners engage in discussion and exchange of ideas. They do not need to reach agreement.

> *Can you give other examples of the tasks above?*

One of the issues that arise with task-based activities is that they may develop fluency at the expense of accuracy since spoken tasks in particular can often be accomplished with little attention to language form. Where and how will the development of accurate grammar or pronunciation take place? Should it take place before students carry out the task, or after they have carried it through and received feedback on their language performance, or are both options recommended? There are no easy answers to questions such as these, since the response depends on the nature of the task and its linguistic and communicative characteristics.

6.8 Lesson closings

The third move in a lesson is known as the lesson closing. Procedures used to end the lesson can serve to reinforce what has been learned in the lesson, to integrate and review the content of the lesson and to prepare the students for further learning. Closing procedures include summarizing what has been covered in the lesson, reviewing the key points of the lesson or asking students to demonstrate something they have learned from the lesson. A teacher describes a closing activity she uses:

> One way that I often use to close a lesson is to ask my learners to scribble on a piece of paper at the end of a lesson, what they remember about the lesson. This can be very telling. Sometimes the learners refer to something that I didn't pay much attention to, and that makes me wonder why it was so salient for them and not for me. Sometimes after a writing lesson I realize that they are more focused on the content of what we are writing about than the strategies and skills and elements that contribute to effective written texts. This information is extremely valuable as it gives me an inkling of how the learners perceive what goes on in class and gives me the opportunity to adjust my practice where I think this is needed. (Sarah)

What purpose do you usually have in mind when you end a lesson and how do you achieve it?

Conclusion

We have described the structure of a language lesson in terms of a sequence of three moves: the one that serves as the *lesson opening*, the one that consists of the *instructional activities* used in the lesson and the one that functions as the *lesson closing*. We have also described two kinds of procedures that are often the core components of lessons – *activities* and *tasks*. How teachers structure their lessons in terms of moves and the kinds of activities and tasks they make use of in doing so can account for the content of lessons and the way they develop. Reviewing one's own lessons and observing lessons taught by other teachers can help raise awareness of the nature of different kinds of lessons, the formats or organizational structures that they make use of, and the nature and demands of the instructional activities that are the lessons' primary focus.

Follow-up

Examine the activities in one unit of a coursebook. Can you find examples of mechanical, meaningful, and communicative activities as well as tasks? What type of activities predominates?

References and further reading

Airey, J. (2011). The Disciplinary Literacy Discussion Matrix: A Heuristic Tool for Initiating Collaboration in Higher Education. *Across the Disciplines, 8*(3), 1–9. https://wac.colostate.edu/docs/atd/clil/airey.pdf

Clegg, J. (2007). Analysing the Language Demands of Lessons Taught in a Second Language. *Volumen Monográfico*, 113–128.

Doyle, W. (1983). Academic Work. *Review of Educational Research, 53*(2), 159–199.

Feez, S. (1998). *Text-Based Syllabus Design.* Sydney: National Centre for English Language Teaching and Research, Macquarie University.

Goh, C. C. M. & Burns, A. (2012). *Teaching Speaking: A Holistic Approach.* New York: Cambridge University Press.

Kavanagh, S. S., Conrad, J. & Dagogo-Jack, S. (2020). From Rote to Reasoned: Examining the Role of Pedagogical Reasoning in Practice-Based Teacher Education. *Teaching and Teacher Education, 89*, Article 102991. https://doi.org/10.1016/j.tate.2019.102991

Kennedy, M. (2016). Parsing the Practice of Teaching. *Journal of Teacher Education, 67*(1), 6–17.

Lamb, M. (2004). Integrative Motivation in a Globalizing World. *System, 32*(1), 3–19.

Lamb, M. (2009). Situating the L2 Self: Two Indonesian School Learners of English. In Z. Dörnyei & E. Ushioda (Eds.), *Motivation, Language Identity and the L2 Self* (pp. 229–247). Bristol: Multilingual Matters.

Lemov, D., Woolway, E. & Yezzi, K. (2012). *Practice Perfect: 42 Rules for Getting Better at Getting Better.* San Francisco: Jossey-Bass.

Pica, T., Kanagy, R. & Falodun, J. (1993). Choosing and Using Communicative Tasks for Second Language Instruction. In G. Crookes & S. M. Gass (Eds.), *Tasks and Language Learning: Integrating Theory and Practice* (pp. 9–34). Clevedon: Multilingual Matters.

Richards, J. C. (2006). *Communicative Language Teaching Today.* New York: Cambridge University Press.

Shavelson, R. J. (1983). Review of Research on Teachers' Pedagogical Judgments, Plans, and Decisions. *The Elementary School Journal, 83*(4), 392–413.

Chapter 7 Develop learner-centered lessons

Introduction

Teaching English, as with the teaching of other subjects, requires simultaneous attention to many different dimensions of teaching. During the lesson we monitor our teaching and ask ourselves: Am I making myself clear? Am I teaching well? Is this activity of interest to the students? Are they learning anything useful from this? Is it too difficult for them? One of the things we do when we evaluate our teaching is to ask how well a lesson has realized the principles we seek to realize during the lesson, such as "keeping to the lesson plan", "minimizing the amount of the teacher's talking time" or "making sure the lesson deals with items that will come up in the test". Depending on our teaching experience, the kind of skills we are teaching, the goals of the lesson and the nature of the class, we can think about lessons from several different perspectives: *a teacher-centered perspective, a curriculum-centered perspective*, or *a learner-centered perspective*. Sometimes each of these perspectives may be a reference point at some moment during a lesson. In this chapter we will consider how these different perspectives influence our approach to a lesson and our understanding of what makes for a successful lesson. And we'll pay more attention to learner-centered lessons.

7.1 Teacher-, curriculum-, and learner-centered perspectives

7.1.1 The teacher-centered perspective

This understanding of good teaching views the key features of a lesson primarily in terms of teacher factors such as classroom management, the teacher's explanations, the teacher's questioning skills, how well the teacher maintains the students' interest level, and the teacher's manner. The following comments on lessons reflect what we are calling a teacher-centered perspective:

> I feel my lesson didn't end very well. I don't think the students understood what I wanted them to do, and I didn't give myself enough time to do a better job on making things clear. I should also have used group work for most of the lesson, rather than pair work, I think. (Brian)
>
> I felt very confident and satisfied with the lesson and I'm glad the students seemed to enjoy it. They were paying attention and had no difficulty understanding me. I was pleased with the way the video activity worked. I managed to move around and monitor the students during group work and made some notes about things I would pick up for extra practice next time. (Jun Hong)

7.1.2 The curriculum-centered perspective

This view of a successful lesson sees the lesson in terms of how well it is planned and how the activities in the lesson are integrated to make a coherent sequence of activities. For example:

> I think the lesson went well. I think opening with a revision activity gave good preparation for the rest of the lesson and I managed to cover everything I had in mind in lesson plan. (Rosa)

> It's important to me that I achieve the goals I set for the lesson and don't skip things I planned to cover. I need to feel I did a good job on covering the different stages of the lesson – the presentation phase, the practice stage, and the free production stage, for example – and I managed this well in today's lesson, I think. (Amar)

7.1.3 The learner-centered perspective

A teacher with this perspective thinks of a lesson from the point of view of the learners and their reaction to it.

> I like the way the students responded to the activities. Everyone was participating actively. They were very expressive and put a lot of feeling into the role-play. (Simian)

> To me the most important thing is that the students enjoyed themselves and had useful practice, and that the lesson was at the right level for them – not too easy or too difficult so that they felt it was worthwhile coming to class today. (Susannah)

These different perspectives on lessons can be summarized as in the table below:

teacher-centered perspective	The teacher is the primary focus; factors include the teacher's role, classroom management skills, questioning skills, etc.

(to be continued)

(continued)

curriculum-centered perspective	The lesson as a coherent instructional unit is the primary focus; factors include lesson goals as well as the opening, structuring, task types, flow, development, and pacing.
learner-centered perspective	The learners are the primary focus; factors include the extent to which the lesson engages students, participation patterns, and the extent of language use.

When do you think each of these perspectives is appropriate? Do you sometimes use each perspective in the same lesson?

A teacher-centered teacher focuses on his or her control of the lesson, the ease with which the teacher is able to develop and manage the lesson and how effectively he or she is able to answer students' questions. For a curriculum-centered teacher, the teacher's priorities are the pre-planned curriculum and how well the lesson covers the lesson plan. A learner-centered view means decisions are primarily based on the factors related to the group of students in the class at that time, how motivated, challenged, and engaged they are with the lesson and the kinds of participation occurring during the lesson.

However, while sometimes teachers may teach a lesson from a particular perspective, as we have noted above, sometimes all three perspectives will be referred to at different stages during the lesson. A teacher may begin a lesson with a curriculum-centered perspective, using a carefully developed lesson plan. During the lesson, feedback from the way the lesson is progressing may prompt the teacher to change direction and to find ways to achieve a greater degree of learner participation. Unplanned decisions of this kind reflect the teacher's monitoring of his or her teaching. At the end of the lesson the teacher may review the lesson from the teacher-centered perspective, asking, "What was my role in the lesson? Did I teach to the whole class or just to the students in the front rows? Did I dominate the lesson or did I provide sufficient opportunities for student practice?" Decisions of this kind that we make during teaching seek to achieve our understanding of good teaching practice. We discuss teacher beliefs and perspectives in several chapters of this book. The focus of this chapter is on what we refer to above as the learner-centered perspective on teaching and how it is achieved.

7.2 Learner-centeredness in teaching

Learner-centeredness in a lesson is reflected in different ways, including the extent to which you understand and acknowledge your students' individual needs and concerns, the way you monitor your teaching to ensure that it allows all students to participate, promotes their self-confidence and self-esteem, and leads to the sense of a bonded class where students collaborate and support each other's efforts. This means asking questions such as these: Is there a learner-friendly classroom atmosphere? Is my primary focus on how well I teach or how I can help students learn? Or how can the lesson connect to the learners' lives and interests?

What are some other features of learner-centered lessons? What are some ways in which you keep your learners in focus when you teach?

Let's now consider some of the ways in which questions such as those above can be answered and learner-centeredness can be realized.

7.3 Developing a class profile

One of the first things you can do to develop an understanding of your learners is to develop a profile of the sort of students you have in your class. For example, you can develop a class profile by finding the answers to the following questions:

- Why are they learning English?
- What benefits do they expect to get from knowledge of English?
- Do the students have similar backgrounds and English learning experiences?
- Are they of a similar proficiency level?
- Do they have contact with English outside of class?
- What kind of classroom activities do they enjoy?
- Are there any classroom activities that they do not enjoy?
- What kinds of problems do they typically have with English?
- Would they like you to correct their English at times?

Here is what a teacher's profile of her class looks like:

> When I did a learner profile of my students, I was interested in finding out about their family backgrounds, their language backgrounds, their motivational cues, their learning preferences, their personal interests, and their overall perspective on learning English. When I put all of these together, I learned a lot about my students and the information helped me better prepare my lessons and understand their approach to learning. For example, for one

> student I've discovered he is from a rural area and his family
> all speak the local language at home. In fact, the only time
> he has ever spoken English is in the English class. He is not
> fully motivated to learn English and is only here because his
> parents want him to learn English. He likes activities that keep
> him active, like games. On the other hand, another student is
> very different. She is from a middle-class family in the capital
> and she and her parents are fluent in English. They often speak
> English at home to help her improve her English. She normally
> pays attention in class. She likes pair and group activities a lot.
> (Kim)

Finding information of this kind can be carried out informally during one of your earlier meetings with a class. For example, you could use a short questionnaire or activity that students could complete individually about their approaches to learning and the sort of activities they like to take part in during lessons. For example, would they like the teacher to spend time on explaining grammar rules, do they like working with others in pairs or groups, and how do they like to be corrected in class?

You might also like to find out what your students feel about English in itself as we have noted in Chapter 5. You may also try to find out what successful students attribute their success in English to, as this teacher describes:

> When I asked my students to write about the kinds of
> strategies they used to learn English, one thing I found was
> that successful students would look for different ways of
> practicing things they had studied in class. For example, one
> student said that she repeated exercises we had done in class,
> at home. She also practiced using English expressions with her

> friends. Another student described how he kept an electronic diary and recorded things he wanted to remember. And one said that she wrote sentences on Post-it notes and posted them on her bedroom wall. (Teresa)

You can also get a good understanding of your students by working with other colleagues to review the kind of work students produce. For example, you may be able to review video recordings of students carrying out different classroom activities, written work such as essays, student projects or assignments or records of students' chat room interaction.

The kind of information you collect from these activities can help you better understand the difference between successful and less successful learners and the difficulties some classroom activities pose for learners.

> *What procedures do you make use of to find out more about your learners and their expectations for your course?*

7.4 Developing the class as a community of learners

Although a class is made up of learners who may have different individual interests and needs, it can also be thought of as a community of people who have many things in common, as one student said: "I feel my class is like a family. We help each other try to understand and to learn together."

Developing a class that functions as a learning community rather than a group of people who want to learn on their own is a key factor in developing learner-centered teaching. It plays a part in influencing how engaged students are with learning and helps a class become a community with shared goals and where students care for each other. There are several ways by which you can achieve this, such as by using students' names, by setting up groups where students enjoy working together, by identifying key students who can play a role in promoting collaboration, and by the ways which will be introduced next.

What are some other ways in which you can help develop the class as a community of learners who collaborate and respect each other?

7.4.1 By showing your commitment to helping students achieve success

As a teacher it's important for you to communicate your wish for learners to succeed and to find out as much as you can about their learning to enable you to best cater to their needs. This means helping students develop their self-confidence.

> The more I know about my learners, the better I can help them learn. Self-assurance can inspire second language learners to pass through the door of the world of English, especially those who do not believe in themselves. Why is it important for a student to believe in oneself? I have to deal with this question when working with students. Learners who boost self-confidence, boost success in acquiring the knowledge of a foreign language. In other words, they awake their credence in learning English. (Efron)

This means listening to our learners and helping them find ways of taking responsibility for and control of their learning.

7.4.2 By connecting lessons with the students' life experiences

An important feature of a learner-centered lesson is the extent to which the lesson connects with the learners' life experiences. Personalized teaching means teaching that focuses on the students' lives, goals, experiences, and interests.

> As far as I can, I try to personalize my lessons. I involve my students in developing the content of lessons. For example, if I am teaching students to write narratives, while the textbook provides examples of what narratives and their features are, as soon as possible I shift the lesson focus to sharing personal stories. When students share accounts of their childhoods and write about important events or experiences in their lives, they become much more involved in their writing. (Fiona)

> Even though my students don't seem to like doing the writing exercises in our textbook in class, I realized that they do quite a bit of writing in their daily lives, in the form of tweets and Facebook updates, for example. I created a Twitter account and a Google+ page for our class and got students to start writing short messages in response to each other. Gradually I assigned them different roles and had everyone contribute different parts to a short story we wrote collaboratively. The students loved it as it made the activity more familiar to their out-of-class experiences. (Kumiko)

What are some ways in which you make connections to students' life experiences?

Students can also help choose content for lessons. For example, they can work in groups to choose topics for an essay. Or in a lesson on idioms, instead of using examples from the textbook, students might complete lists of idioms they have come across out of class and bring these to class to discuss. Or when a lesson deals with a certain aspect of grammar (such as the present perfect or the past perfect) students can try to find examples in news reports or other texts on the Internet or in the media and bring these to class to discuss.

> In my business writing course we have to work with lots of very routine texts such as email messages, blog posts and business letters. To make it more interesting I ask students at the start of the semester to invent their own company, logo, staff list and products so that they can use this material when they are developing their own scenarios and situations throughout the semester rather than have to stick rigidly to examples in the textbook. In this way, they create a kind of personal narrative throughout the semester, telling different stories about what has happened in the company and what they need to communicate about. (Sara)

Here teachers describe how they make use of student-selected content and initiatives in lessons:

> I ask my students to collect examples of interesting texts they encounter out of class and bring these to class. I use these as the basis for teaching them about different text types and styles. The texts they bring to class are often more interesting than the ones in the book because these are the texts THEY are interested in. (Jose)

Recently in my writing class I asked learners to find any website or blog that interested them and submit a question to that website or blog and see if they could get an answer. I was a bit nervous because learners might choose unsuitable sites but thought I'd give it a go anyway. As it happened only a few students completed the assignment, but one of them did report on a Tandem Language Learning website she had found that welcomed learners to join for free. She had been paired up with an Australian girl who was learning Spanish and they had already exchanged several emails and were planning to have a Skype meeting. Her report was completely unexpected but ended up motivating several other students to visit the same site and find their own partners. Whereas at first, I thought the activity had been unsuccessful because not everyone did it, in fact this one student's enthusiasm ended up influencing several others to follow her lead, which eventually provided lots of additional written communication practice in English. (Danial)

What kind of topics and content do your students find most interesting as a focus for lessons?

7.4.3 By inviting students to question the textbook

Textbooks are developed for large and diverse populations of students, and your students will often find instances where an activity in the textbook can be adapted or replaced with one that is more relevant to the students' needs and interests:

I have to work with a writing textbook which is rather prescriptive. It lays down a lot of rules about how things should be done in different types of texts and leaves very little to the imagination. At first, I found this rather limiting, but now I use it as a talking point at the start of each lesson. I actively encourage the students to comment on the extent to which they believe the approach recommended by the textbook would work in every context and whether it is possible to generalize about how to produce a particular kind of text in every situation. Of course, the learners realize that the textbook writer cannot anticipate every situation and they are very creative in these discussions, often mentioning aspects of their culture which would oblige writers to do something differently. In this way I believe that questioning the textbook "rules" ends up teaching them more about writing and gives them a more sophisticated understanding of the way that context affects writing. (Jian)

Do you sometimes find it necessary to supplement your textbook? In what ways?

7.4.4 By finding ways to motivate students

Students become involved in learning when it motivates them. An important question to ask after every lesson is: Was it worth my students' time to come to class today? There are several features of a lesson that can give students a positive feeling about the lesson. Was the lesson interesting? Did students enjoy it? Were students involved and engaged in the activities? Did the activities have a purpose? Did students come away with a feeling that they had learned something? Was the lesson at the right level? Did the lesson give the students a sense of success rather than failure?

Often you can motivate students by challenging them, by engaging their curiosity, by encouraging deep learning rather than surface learning, and by developing a classroom atmosphere that encourages and motivates students in their learning.

> One fun way in which I introduce motivation into writing classes is to ask students who have written a narrative which includes a lot of interaction, to turn it into a movie script. This provides really excellent language practice with a strong focus on interaction. The work can also be shared by two students so that they have fun improvising the dialog and then writing it down. (Vera)

> My students all play video games so I have found this a good way to motivate them. This year I introduced digital games in class for the teaching of writing. It sure raised some eyebrows among my colleagues at first! I linked this to our writing curriculum as closely as I could – for example, when discussing different ways to organize a piece of writing, I asked students to describe their favorite games and the way the stories within them are built up. I've also found some games that involve a great deal of language use. *Ace Attorney* is one in which players take the role of an attorney and have to develop a strong case, present it convincingly and so on. Students created their own cases as practice in argument writing and had to respond to each other's writing to practice writing rebuttals. (Helena)

> I decided to teach my writing class with activities that would get my students out of their seats. And so I asked each of them to go up to the board and pin up his or her storyline under the genre in which he or she had chosen to write as homework for the preceding class. I was hoping that under each genre there would be more than two students contributing so that they can share their ideas and have more storylines to write. This seemed to work well, and the students all seemed quite alive,

especially in the hot afternoon, because they were up and doing something rather than listening to me! (Joseph)

Students seemed to enjoy the reading activity in my reading lesson, and they seemed to be able to concentrate better when they worked in a group where peers took turns to read one paragraph aloud to the others, rather than when I read to the whole class. Many of them mentioned specifically that they preferred to do reading comprehension this way rather than have to read the whole passage by themselves. Indeed, after the group activity, most of them were able to provide the correct answers to the comprehension questions, which exemplified their understanding of the passage. (Denis)

What kinds of activities do your students enjoy and find motivating? Are there other activities that your students do not enjoy?

7.4.5 By getting feedback from learners

There are different ways of getting informal feedback from learners on how they are responding to your teaching. Perhaps there is a class representative whom you meet with from time to time to get a sense of how the students are doing and whether you can do anything to improve their engagement in the course. The following is a technique that one teacher finds helpful:

I invite students to keep a written or an electronic journal in which they track their learning progress and write about their responses to things we have been doing in class and how useful they find them. Also, things they would like me to spend more or less time on. (Sylvia)

7.4.6 By making learning outcomes learner-centered

An important feature of learner-centered lessons is that students leave class knowing something that they find a useful addition to their understanding of English and how it is used, and something that is personally relevant to them. This may be a few useful words or expressions, a better understanding of how to organize a paragraph, or an improvement in some aspect of their pronunciation. The outcome of a lesson is learner-centered when it is not only *about* something, but *how to do* something, which the learners can make use of. A teacher describes ways in which he achieves this:

> I always look for activities in which the students can present something they have learned to the rest of the class. For example, at the end of a speaking lesson, students might work in groups to plan a little role-play. The groups will act them out and vote on which one they like best. Or if we have been working on descriptive writing, at the end of the lesson I might have each group develop a short description together and put it on a poster. Then we will put the posters up around the walls of the classroom for everyone to read and compare. (Dino)

Learning outcomes are discussed in Chapter 12.

Conclusion

There are many benefits of making lessons more learner-centered. For learners, lessons become more meaningful, enjoyable, relevant, and motivating and this has benefits not only for them but also for the teacher. For the teacher, learner-centered teaching can help build a classroom climate where students collaborate and support each other's learning and see the teacher in a different light. Now your role is not simply that of an instructor who is teaching English, but someone who is working to make the classroom a supportive environment for learning and who seeks to make connections with the students' feelings, motivations, and interests.

Follow-up

Work with one or more colleagues to develop a short questionnaire that could be used with students at the beginning of a new course to find out what kinds of things the students do to improve their English, what they hope to learn from the course, and what kinds of classroom activities they find useful.

References and further reading

Benson, P. (2012). Learner-Centered Teaching. In A. Burns & J. C. Richards (Eds.), *The Cambridge Guide to Pedagogy and Practice in Second Language Teaching* (pp. 30–37). New York: Cambridge University Press.

Legutke, M. (2012). Teaching Teenagers. In A. Burns & J. C. Richards (Eds.), *The Cambridge Guide to Pedagogy and Practice in Second Language Teaching* (pp. 112–119). New York: Cambridge University Press.

Nunan, D. (1988). *The Learner-Centred Curriculum*. Cambridge: Cambridge University Press.

Nunan, D. (2010). *Teaching English to Young Learners*. Anaheim: Anaheim University Press.

Tudor, I. (1997). *Learner-Centredness as Language Education*. Cambridge: Cambridge University Press.

Van Gorp, K. & Bogaert, N. (2006). Developing Language Tasks for Primary and Secondary Education. In K. Van den Branden (Ed.), *Task-Based Language Education: From Theory to Practice* (pp. 76–105). Cambridge: Cambridge University Press.

PART 4

DYNAMICS OF THE LANGUAGE CLASSROOM

Chapter 8 Manage your classroom as an effective learning space

Introduction

The language classroom is in many ways not a natural environment for learning a language. Students are often arranged in rows where they do not make eye contact with other students. And due to student numbers in many classrooms there are limited opportunities for students to take part in interaction and practice – both of them are fundamental requirements for second language learning. Consequently, the teacher is typically the person who gets most of the opportunities for using English during a lesson. Yet there are still ways of making the classroom a conducive space for language learning. In this chapter we will look at several features of a classroom and of communication within the classroom that are necessary if it is to provide a good environment for language learning.

8.1 Classroom climate

"Classroom climate" refers to the atmosphere of a class – the feelings you sense when you enter the class that suggest either that the students are in a mood to learn, look forward to the lesson, and have positive expectations for the lesson, or alternatively that the students are bored, disinterested, unmotivated and not willing to participate actively in the lesson. Classes that are positively motivated to learn create few problems of classroom management compared to classes with unmotivated students where teachers will have challenges in keeping students' attention on tasks. In a class with an effective classroom climate, the class functions as a learning community in which the teacher and the students collaborate to achieve shared goals; students show respect to each other and to the teacher; the teacher is a resource person who guides the students, providing support and encouragement for learning, rather than a manager or controller; and there is a safe and non-threatening atmosphere.

What are some other features of a class in which there is a positive classroom climate?

8.2 Strategies for creating a supportive classroom climate

Teachers usually have their own ways of creating a supportive classroom climate. Dörnyei (2001) has suggested that a supportive classroom climate can be created by conveying personal concerns to your students; for example, by greeting students and smiling at them, by noticing interesting features of their appearance (e.g. a new haircut) or by learning something unique about each student, and occasionally mentioning it to him or her.

What are some other ways in which you can put your class into a good mood for learning?

You no doubt have different ways of establishing a suitable classroom climate and often set out to do so in your initial contact with a new group of students. This is when you have to build a rapport with students, to create a friendly classroom atmosphere, to show that you are friendly and approachable and to remind students that you too were once a student so you understand what concerns and issues they may have. Perhaps you use a little humor, share common interests and experiences (e.g. hobbies, entertainment and music) with your students and take time to find out a little about their lives and backgrounds. Here are some examples of strategies teachers use:

> I always start my lesson with a fun activity of some sort – a song, a game, a quiz or something to relax the students. (Rita)

> I let the students know that I am very approachable. I will never make them feel awkward if they don't understand something or want me to explain something again. (Pauline)

> With younger students I sometimes have students make up fun names for themselves that we will use in class, such as "Henry the magician" or "Suzie the rock star". (Steven)

At the same time, you need to establish that language learning is a serious activity requiring hard work and effort and that your students' efforts will be respected and encouraged. Remind them that they should not be afraid to make mistakes or be shy to try out what they know, and they should never ridicule or make fun of other students' efforts. This means establishing rules for classroom behavior and establishing expectations for how the class will be managed.

8.3 Classroom management

Classroom management refers to the ways in which the different dimensions of a lesson will be managed and arranged to provide support for both teaching and learning. Classroom management is not simply an issue of discipline (something likely to be an issue for teachers in primary or secondary schools rather than in universities) since it depends on how you and your students see your roles in the classroom and the kind of learning community that emerges in the class. Among the key aspects of classroom management are the role of human emotions and feelings in the classroom (discussed in Chapter 9), the kinds of interaction and participation needed for successful learning and the ways in which the physical space of the class is organized to support learning.

A challenge is to establish norms for appropriate student behavior in the classroom so that students develop a sense of responsibility and cooperative behavior during lessons. There are several ways in which this can be accomplished. For example, you can ask the students to discuss what they feel are appropriate rules for classroom behavior, you can give them some examples and ask them how they think the teacher and other students should respond, or you can propose different ways of dealing with classroom issues and ask students to discuss them.

One teacher says:

> My students really appreciate having a set of class rules and it's one of the first things we do when we are in a new class. We collaborate on what these rules are for both the teacher

and students. I would like them to draw up a class contract that is written on poster paper and put it on the wall. A simple and serious-looking contract is fine, but I do keep the discussion light-hearted. So after we all agree on the class rules, we then discuss and agree on what the consequences of breaking the rules will be, such as contributing a few coins to an end-of-class party. I try to avoid English as punishment, for example requiring a student to sing an English song if the student breaks a rule. What is important is that the teacher follows the contract fairly and consistently. (Brian)

Dörnyei (2001) has suggested some examples of class rules:

For the students:

- Let's not be late for class.
- Always complete your homework.
- Once a term you can "pass", i.e. say that you haven't prepared.
- In small group work, only English can be used.
- If you miss a class, make up for it and ask for the homework.

For the teacher:

- The class should finish on time.
- Homework and tests should be marked within a week.
- Always give advance notice of a test.

For everybody:

- Let's try and listen to each other.
- Let's help each other.
- Let's respect each other's ideas and values.
- It's OK to make mistakes.
- Let's not make fun of each other's weaknesses.
- We must avoid hurting each other, verbally or physically.

Do you sometimes have to deal with classroom management issues? What kind? How do you usually respond to them?

8.4 Arranging the class for learning

A key dimension of language learning is interaction. While some aspects of language learning can be accomplished through watching movies or using an app or learning resources on the Internet, face-to-face communication with others is essential for making progress in learning. How can this be achieved in the classroom? What kinds of classroom arrangements are useful in language teaching and what kinds of opportunities or limitations do they offer?

8.4.1 Whole-class teaching

A common teaching mode for most school subjects is with the teacher at the front of the class presenting his or her subject matter to students arranged in rows. Is this how you most often teach? While this may be an efficient way of teaching some subjects, unless the lesson involves listening to a lecture and taking notes, it is generally limited in its suitability for teaching other language skills, particularly those that involve active interaction and communication among students or between students and the teacher. However, sometimes whole-class teaching can be usefully used to model the skills or procedures students should use in carrying out an activity, such as a "think-aloud" procedure which you use to talk through how you would complete a task. For example:

> Well, everybody, the first thing I would do in reading this text is to decide how to read it. Shall I skim quickly through it and get the gist first and then come back and read it again more closely? So I need to decide what kind of text this is and why I am reading it. What is my purpose and what approach best suits my purpose? (Ali)

This strategy of thinking out loud – guiding students' participation and understanding through questions and accepting and expanding on students' comments – can provide opportunities for students who might be reluctant to participate in the lesson to become more actively involved. Teaching to the class as a group is also often an efficient way of introducing activities and demonstrating how to carry them out. It can also be regarded as a form of *scaffolding* – providing guidance and preparation for an activity that students will later perform individually or within a group. Although whole-class teaching may serve to introduce a lesson and to clarify the nature and procedural language demands of a learning activity, in many lessons it provides a lead-in to other more student-centered activities, where pair and group work may be more suitable. So when you plan a lesson, it is important to consider when whole-class teaching is appropriate and when the transition to other types of teaching will occur in order to promote student-to-student interaction and to allow students to work on tasks at their own pace.

> *In a typical lesson, what percentage of the lesson time involves whole-class teaching?*

8.4.2 Action zone

With whole-class activities, a question-and-answer type of interaction is common. This guides students' understanding through prompting, clarifying, and minimizing risk of errors. However, in using questioning in this way it is easy to interact more with some students than with others. Although you try to give everyone a chance to participate, this is often the case. This creates what is called your *action zone*. This is indicated by those students whom you make regular eye contact with, those students whom you address questions to, and those students whom you nominate to take an active part in the lesson.

These students are located within your action zone and are likely to participate more actively in the lesson than students who sit outside the action zone. In many classrooms, this zone includes the middle front row seats and the seats up the middle aisle. If you are teaching from the front of the class, students seated there are more likely to have the opportunity to participate actively in the lesson because they are sitting closer to you. However, you may unconsciously have your own action zone which may differ from one class to another. For example, you may look more often to the right-hand side of the class than to the left-hand side, call on girls more often than boys, and tend to call on students whose English is better than others, students whose names are easiest to remember, or students who seem more anxious to be called upon.

The challenge in whole-class teaching is to make use of a more inclusive action zone. Some ways in which this can be accomplished are:

- Rearrange the class seating (e.g. in a circle) to provide more opportunities for interaction.

- Change students' seating regularly so that the same students are not always at the front or back of the class.
- Teach lessons from different places, e.g. not always from the front of the class.
- Invite a colleague to observe your teaching from time to time to see how inclusive it is.

What strategies do you use to make sure that you interact with all the students in your class and give all of them an opportunity to actively participate in lessons?

8.4.3 Individual work

Whole-class teaching usually leads to individual work. Students will be asked to complete an activity on their own such as drafting a composition, reading a text or completing an activity from the textbook. Individual activities allow students to complete activities at their own pace and set their own targets for learning, and if the class size is not too large, allow you to give individual feedback and support. However, individual work requires careful preparation, clear guidelines and instructions, and providing any language or other support that students may need, as well as making sure that the tasks are appropriate for all of the students in the class.

What are some classroom activities that you think are best carried out individually rather than as whole-class work?

8.4.4 Pair work

Pair work activities provide opportunities for the kinds of

interaction and communication – both input and output – that are important for developing language abilities. The benefits of pair work include that it enables students to learn from others, particularly from those who are more advanced than they are, it can be motivating when students enjoy working with a partner and it provides more opportunities for student practice and participation than a whole-class activity. However, pair work can also promote fluency at the expense of accuracy and hence requires consideration of whether and how students will receive feedback on their performance. Good preparation is needed for pair work activities. For example, if students are practicing a dialog, any pronunciation problems in the dialog can be dealt with before students begin their practice. They can change roles to give more opportunities for practice, and also add their own extensions of the dialog introducing a fun element as they read out their adapted dialogs and compare them.

> *What is your experience with pair work activities? What advice would you give to a teacher who is concerned about the value of pair work activities?*

8.4.5 Group work

Group-based activities are also widely used in language teaching and can increase the opportunities students have for using their English and can also increase student motivation by providing a risk-free environment for language practice. However, group activities require careful planning. Issues you need to consider are:

Time: How much time will be needed to set up the groups?

Membership: How will the groups be formed – by the students or the teacher and by what criteria? Should friends always sit together? Students often seat themselves in cliques by age, language group, friendship, and so on.

Group size: Groups of four are easiest to organize and manage.

Language proficiency: Should groups consist of students with the same language level or of those with different proficiency levels? One way is to mix the groups with learners of different proficiency levels, as they can help each other with different tasks. Students of higher proficiency levels can be given more challenging tasks, such as doing the job of the group reporter, or they can be asked to take notes during the group's discussion. Students of lower proficiency levels may have difficulty participating in group work.

Control: Will group work create difficulty with classroom management?

Students' views: Will students see the value of group work or see it as time-filling work on the part of the teacher?

Unequal lengths of completion time: What will you do if some groups finish before others? One solution is to have a backup plan to limit the amount of disruption from groups who may finish early (e.g. an additional task for students to complete, or two groups who finish early could be asked to discuss their work together).

> *What is your experience in using group work? When have you found it works well? What strategies do you use to ensure that group activities are productive?*

When you use group work activities, it is important to make the purpose of the grouping arrangement clear to the students. Two kinds of useful group-based learning activities are project work and problem-based learning. There are many different kinds of projects and they can be used anywhere, lasting from 30 minutes to several class periods, or longer. A group investigation task can be regarded as project work, which involves the class choosing an overall theme, such as "the value of regular exercise", and each group deciding to study one particular form of exercise such as running, swimming, or lifting weights in the gym and how to promote this particular form of exercise. Members of groups carry out research and present their findings to the class. With problem-based learning, students focus on solving a real-world problem such as child obesity; they collect information or carry out research to investigate the problem, and give suggestions or an action plan to resolve the problem.

8.5 Managing time in a lesson

In any lesson a limited amount of time is available for teaching and learning. While students need to accept that the success of their learning will depend on how much time they devote to it out of the classroom, it is the teacher's responsibility to ensure that maximum use is made of the time allotted to English in the school timetable. Effective use of time in lessons is an important aspect of teaching and plays a role in ensuring that a lesson flows smoothly and also that you are able to complete the activities you have planned for the lesson and do not need to rush through them. A useful way of understanding the use of time in a lesson is by thinking of classroom time as consisting of four different categories:

Allocated time is the time allotted for teaching a class in the timetable, such as the typical 40- or 50-minute class period.

Instructional time is the time actually available for teaching after you have completed non-instructional activities, such as taking attendance, returning homework, and so on. Perhaps in a 40-minute class period, 30 minutes of instructional time might be available.

Engaged time is that portion of time in which the students are actively involved in learning activities (also known as *time on task*). Perhaps it takes some time for students to start assigned activities, since they spend some time chatting, organizing their desks or computers and so on. Perhaps 25 minutes of the instructional time can be actually engaged time.

Academic learning time is the amount of time during which students are actively engaged in an activity and learning successfully from it. If an activity is too difficult or not well set up, students may spend some time on ineffective learning routines and strategies before they finally find a successful way of completing the activity.

So as you can see there is often much less time available for effective learning than the time suggested by the length of the lesson in the timetable. Many teachers find that they do not manage to spend more than 80% of their allocated time on actual teaching, since non-curricular activities are often time-consuming. Effective management of time can be achieved in two main ways – through planning for the use of time in a lesson plan and through monitoring the use of time during the lesson itself. However, although teaching manuals which accompany textbooks normally suggest how much time should be allocated to particular activities in a lesson, so many things can happen during the lesson that timing decisions made prior to teaching can only be approximate. If you depart from your lesson plan and make use of improvisational teaching you may use time in unplanned and unpredictable ways. A teacher comments on how he conveys to his students the planned part of the lesson:

> Before each lesson, I usually note, on a corner of the whiteboard, the activities the lesson will involve and how much time will be spent on each activity. This not only sends a message to the students that I have planned my lesson, but also gives both the students and myself a sense of where the lesson is going and how time will be spent during the lesson. If a student arrives late to class, I can also point to the board and let him or her know where we are up to in the lesson. (David)

Timing decisions of course affect the speed or pace with which a lesson moves. But the pace of a lesson is a subjective issue, since what appears fast to some learners may appear to be slow to others. And while you are teaching it is often difficult to judge the pace of a lesson, since you may be occupied with other aspects of the lesson.

> *What strategies do you use to make sure that you make the best use of the time available in your lessons?*

Conclusion

In this chapter we have looked at lessons in terms of the different ways lessons can be organized, e.g. in terms of seating arrangements, grouping, and use of time. There is of course much more to be said about lessons than has been surveyed in this chapter, such as the affective, linguistic and pedagogic dimensions of lessons – issues that we will explore in subsequent chapters.

Follow-up

Ask a colleague to observe one of your typical lessons (or a part of a lesson), particularly one where you are working with the whole class, and to consider questions such as these:

• Compared to your own teaching, do you feel that my lesson moved faster or slower than your own lesson, or at the same pace as it?

• Can you name some parts of the lesson that seemed to be done faster than you would have done them yourself?

• Can you name some parts of the lesson that seemed to be done more slowly than you would have done them yourself?

References and further reading

Dörnyei, Z. (2001). *Motivational Strategies in the Language Classroom.* Cambridge: Cambridge University Press.

Dörnyei, Z. & Murphey, T. (2003). *Group Dynamics in the Language Classroom.* Cambridge: Cambridge University Press.

Harmer, J. (2007). *The Practice of English Language Teaching.* Harlow: Pearson Education Limited.

Scrivener, J. (2012). *Classroom Management Techniques.* Cambridge: Cambridge University Press.

Senior, R. (2006). *The Experience of Language Teaching.* Cambridge: Cambridge University Press.

Chapter 9 Create an emotionally supportive classroom

Introduction

Effective teaching is often described in terms of how well you can manage your lessons, keep the students engaged and on task and successfully guide and support their efforts to learn English. But there is another dimension to teaching and learning that is also crucial to both your success as a teacher and the success of your learners, namely the role that positive and negative emotions can play in the language classroom. Knowing how to address both your own emotions in teaching and those of your students depends on your awareness of both the positive and negative emotions that language learning can create and how to respond appropriately to the emotional demands of teaching English. In this chapter we will explore the emotional aspects of the second language classroom and what you as a teacher can do to understand and manage emotional aspects of language teaching and learning, that is, to develop your emotional competence as a language teacher.

9.1 The nature of emotions in language teaching

Emotions are temporary feelings that are a kind of response to situations or events we experience in our daily lives. Although they may be temporary, they can influence the dynamics of the class and provide either a support or a hindrance to teaching and learning. Stepping into a classroom, you can usually readily get a sense of how well the students are motivated to take part in the lesson, or conversely, you may have a sense that the students are not motivated to learn or have low expectations for what the lesson will be like and what they are likely to learn from it. A class with positive feelings about learning English will be much more receptive to and supportive of your efforts than one with negative feelings about learning English.

Look at the following list of emotions which both teachers and students may experience in the English class. Can you add others to the list? Which ones do you think are most commonly experienced by teachers/students?

Positive emotions	being calm/excited/confident/satisfied/impressed/relaxed/interested/pleased/amused
Negative emotions	being nervous/angry/frustrated/anxious/bored/stressed/disappointed/embarrassed/confused

Learning a language is sometimes an emotionally charged experience for both teachers and learners and can arouse both negative as well as positive emotions as is seen in these comments:

The students in my writing class are really nice and I love teaching them. A few weeks ago they discovered when my birthday was. On the day of my birthday when I came into class they sang happy birthday for me and they had even bought a cake for us to share. (Teresa)

Once I discovered that a student who I thought was doing well in class was actually getting his brother to do all of his homework assignments (one of the other students in the class told me about it), I felt really disappointed with him and it was very uncomfortable to have to talk to him about it. (Megan)

What are some positive emotions you sometimes experience when teaching English? Are there sometimes negative emotions as well?

9.2 The teacher's emotional competence

Emotions reflect interaction between you and your teaching context and may include feelings about yourself, your learners, your teaching materials, your colleagues, your success as a teacher and both positive and negative feelings you may have about the challenges and rewards of being a language teacher. Learners may have both positive and negative reactions to the experience of learning English, too. During your initial teacher training you would have been reminded that being a teacher requires certain standards of performance in the classroom. As a teacher you are expected to express positive emotions when you teach, reflecting the fact that you are *knowledgeable, passionate, pleased, satisfied* and *confident* in your performance as a teacher as well as emotions that show you are *pleased, satisfied* or *motivated* by the performance of your learners. You are expected to manage and sometimes hide your emotions during teaching and should try not to display negative emotions when you teach, such as *anger, frustration, tension* or *nervousness*, since these may lead students to think that you are not competent and are not in control of your class. One teacher comments:

> I get really irritated, annoyed, and frustrated when students are not cooperating as they are supposed to when I assign them an activity. However, I try not to show my irritation or anger because I don't want to show my true feelings to the students. (Ricardo)

Another teacher similarly comments:

> It's the occasion when the students are silent and refuse to say anything that really annoys me. Usually when students are doing a group activity I wander around and offer any help that they need. But some students just stare at me silently and say nothing when I try to interact with them. (Stefanie)

In fact, the students' silence may signal that they themselves are too shy to talk or don't have the language they need to say what they want to say, so they feel it's better just to remain silent and avoid losing face. Consequently, you may sometimes feel like an actor when you have to hide your emotions and act the way you are expected to act in front of your students, using gestures, facial expressions and tone of voice to hide your real feelings, as a teacher comments:

> No matter how I am actually feeling when I am teaching, I try to act cheerful, enthusiastic and positive in front of the students. (Gina)

Both teachers and students sometimes experience frustration during a language lesson. What are some of the causes for this in your experience? How do you respond to it?

Although teaching can sometimes result in feelings of frustration and anxiety, more commonly teaching is a source of positive emotions and experiences and these sustain our interest in and passion for teaching throughout our careers. Positive emotions may include the warmth and affection we receive through relationships with our students, seeing the progress they make, the positive student feedback we get on our teaching, the pleasure we get from helping learners find successful ways of learning and an awareness that we can help students build self-esteem and believe in themselves and their ability to learn. A student-teacher comments:

> I think I have a sense of joy from being a teacher. I really hope I can do more as their teacher. I want to help them improve their test results, and I also want to be their friend. I want to take care of them and support them. (Teresa)

Another teacher comments on a colleague whose class she has observed:

> I really saw the value of teacher enthusiasm when I observed Ms Lim's grammar lesson. I expected that the lesson was going to be rather boring. Seeing her lesson plan on paper is one thing, but she magically transformed that plan into a lively and enjoyable lesson with her bubbly personality. Watching her teach made me realize that the teacher is the real method when it comes to teaching and materials or even lesson plans mean nothing if we don't succeed in engaging our students and making them enjoy learning. (Sandra)

9.3 Emotions and learners

For learners, emotions have been described as the driving forces of motivation in second language learning (Dewaele, 2005).

> An affectively positive environment puts the brain in the optimal state for learning: minimal stress and maximum engagement with the material to be learned. (Arnold, 2009: 146)

Learner emotions include feelings about themselves, about their teachers, about their lessons, about other students, about using English in class, about the teachers' command of English, and about the instructional methods and teaching resources the teachers make use of. Until learners sense that they are making progress with learning English, their classroom experiences can often lead to negative emotions such as frustration, loss of face, lack of confidence in their ability and so on. Learners can experience a range of negative emotions in classroom-based language learning. These include embarrassment of being laughed at by their peers, frustration of not being able to express what they want to say, and boredom with the textbook and learning resources.

> *What can you do to lower learners' anxiety about speaking in front of others?*

Learning a new language can start out to be a very negative experience for a learner and negative emotions can arise in the very first English lesson he or she experiences, as these university students comment on the feelings they had during their first few lessons in a spoken English class:

> Some of my classmates are much better than me. I wonder if I am capable of ever reaching their level.

> I will have to ask for some help from my classmates with the homework because I really don't know how to do it. It makes me so frustrated.

Comparisons with their more proficient peers may not only make them feel sad and frightened, but also make them aware of the time and effort needed to be able to speak fluently:

> Well ... I have tried to do certain things so I can feel good about myself and do not feel sad or down because I see the advanced students. If they are more proficient it is because they have studied more and I do not have to feel bad about it. On the contrary, I have to make my best effort in my studies. Thanks to all these experiences in class I am more conscious of the need to invest more time in study at home ... I have been looking for web pages with free activities and contacts to chat with.

> *One way of developing learners' confidence is to provide opportunities for them to showcase what they have learned. What kinds of activities can be used in this way?*

Negative emotions can demotivate learners due to a sense of frustration and disappointment when learners fail to achieve their goals, losing confidence in their ability to succeed and discouraging them from investing further time and energy in language learning. Positive learner emotions, on the other hand, encourage curiosity, risk-taking, experimenting, and willingness to interact and communicate in the new language, and support autonomous learning. A successful language learner comments:

> I think the thing that accounts for my success as a language learner was the enjoyment I got out of learning English. When I had opportunities to try out my English I came to develop a sense of enjoyment in being able to use English, a realization that real communication in English was actually taking place and that I was an active participant in it. Today my satisfaction comes not so much from learning English as from being able to enjoy communicating in a foreign language. (Husai)

In order to help build up students' confidence, teachers sometimes use exaggerated displays of positive emotions in response to students' efforts, for example: "Wow, you guys really did well today. I am so proud of all of you."

And because of the need to encourage students to focus on the tasks they have been assigned, you probably feel that you always need to be bright and cheerful, even if inwardly you may be feeling quite different. If your emotions suggest to the students that you are tired, depressed, anxious or worried, you will not be able to instill a motivation to learn in your students. You can motivate learners when they have feelings of success and achievement; and you are able to enhance their sense of self-esteem, encouraging them to invest further in learning and to make use of the range of learning opportunities available through the media or the Internet to use their English out of class. Thus you can compare the different emotions that your learners may experience in relation to activities such as those involving using English with a native speaker vs. using English with a non-native speaker, getting feedback from the teacher or from other learners, or using English with classmates rather than online in a chat room. We soon get a sense of which activities are stressful for students and which ones students can perform without developing negative feelings. Every student should leave a language lesson feeling that he or she has been successful and that it was worth his or her while to come to class. Building a successful experience into a lesson means identifying some features of the lesson due to which students can perform successfully and avoiding spending too much time on activities that lead to feelings of annoyance and frustration. We therefore need to do everything we can to develop students' positive experiences as language learners. One teacher comments on the advice he gives to his students and describes how important it is to encourage students and develop their sense of self-confidence:

> I encourage them to try to move from being students of English to being users of English. I also try to help develop their confidence – to help them feel that they will be able to communicate in English and to understand it, as well. I want them to focus more on their success in communication, rather than worrying about things that didn't go so well. I also encourage them to surf the web, trying to do as many interesting and fun things as possible in English. They should feel like learning about in English whatever they like learning about in their own language. I am an active promoter of reading formal literature for pleasure on a daily basis, too. And, of course, I recommend singing along their favorite tunes in English, taking advantage of the great amount of music videos, with lyrics on screen, available on the Internet. (Husai)

> *Do you ever use music and singing in your lessons? What might be some benefits of doing so?*

9.4 Creating an emotionally managed classroom

An emotionally managed classroom is one in which you manage your emotions productively, recognize the emotions that learners may be experiencing and seek ways of enhancing positive emotions and minimizing negative emotions that can disrupt or hinder the achievement of a successful language lesson. Your emotional competence describes your ability to develop and maintain an emotionally managed classroom – one where there is neither too much nor too little emotion on either you or your students' part. A challenge is to find ways of creating an emotionally supported class – one where there is a climate of collaboration and sharing and where the learners in the class see themselves as a learning community.

The following are comments by learners on the strategies teachers use to manage the emotional climate in class:

> In this class, we all participated ... you cannot feel tension in the environment and everything just flowed. This teacher made everyone participate without showing you up when you made a mistake. (David)

> When teachers tell me something good about my performance, I feel really happy and I would like that all day in my classes. You feel good and motivated ... I feel like participating more because I know I am doing things right. (Teresa)

> Well ... this teacher gives you security, confidence ... and this has helped me a lot because I participate all the time in class ... the teacher always asks everyone in the group without making any exceptions. Whereas other teachers ... er ... this teacher gives you the confidence to participate without feeling you are being judged. (Jona)

A teacher describes how she creates a positive learning experience for her learners:

> My learners' interest level picks up when activities involve their personal thoughts and feelings, as well as when they share ideas and feelings with their peers. They enjoy collaborating and helping each other and, for this reason, groups of mixed ability levels work well. With mixed ability levels, the students create a community of trust and cooperation and enjoy learning from each other's differences. They share ideas and responsibilities, and I love to see this happening in my class. I can see that they often feel more comfortable about learning within a group than from teacher-directed teaching. So this requires a shift in my role as a teacher – more to that of a facilitator than a presenter. (Marie)

As this teacher demonstrates, an important part of our role as teachers is creating conditions for students to experience positive emotions and be willing to relax and take risks – or as Borg (2006) puts it, to develop the ability to communicate freely and to radiate positive feelings. The emotional climate of the classroom will depend on how you see your role in the classroom, how you interact with your students and build rapport and trust, the responsibilities students have during your lessons, the materials and resources that you make use of, and how you use groups and collaborative learning in your lessons. Effective use of groups can help develop a spirit of cohesion – an important feature of an emotionally supportive and managed classroom climate (Senior, 2001).

> *In your experience, what kinds of group activities provide fun and enjoyment for learners?*

9.5 Strategies to achieve an emotionally supportive classroom climate

You can use a number of strategies to help create a positive emotional climate in your lessons. For example, learn to recognize signs of negative emotions on the part of learners and use strategies to respond to negative emotions, such as moving to a different activity or using an activity to promote relaxation and enjoyment, e.g. a song or a game. Encourage collaboration rather than competition among learners and encourage them to try out their English without undue concerns for correct grammar or pronunciation.

I am always on the lookout for activities that students can enjoy and accomplish and which give feelings of success and satisfaction. This means the activities should not be too difficult; they should be fun and they should give students the sense that they are making progress. For example, my students enjoy playing charades, where you have to "act out" a phrase without speaking, while the other members of your team try to guess what the phrase is and the objective is for your team to guess the phrase as quickly as possible. (Brian)

What are some things students can do to "try out" their English, without worrying about incorrect grammar or other kinds of errors?

One example of getting support for an emotionally supportive classroom climate is through your use of humor. There are a number of benefits that can result from the appropriate use of humor during teaching. It can help students relax and be more willing to take part in lessons, giving them greater confidence and increasing their motivation. When learners respond enthusiastically to a teacher's style of teaching, the teacher feels encouraged and teaches in a more energetic, creative and engaging way.

Conclusion

Emotions are often a hidden dimension of teaching and learning, yet they have an important influence on the dynamics of the classroom and influence whether lessons are going to be positive or negative experiences for our learners. Developing emotional awareness and emotional competence is a necessity for us as teachers and something that can be a useful focus for conversations with colleagues: What kinds of emotions do they encounter in their teaching and how do they deal with situations that cause negative emotions? For learners, emotions can be brought into awareness through the use of activities that encourage them to reflect on the role emotions play in their own language learning and in their responses to the emotional demands of learning and using English.

Follow-up

Complete this table with examples from your and your students' positive and negative classroom experiences. Then compare with other teachers.

Examples of when I experience positive emotions in teaching	Examples of when my students experience positive emotions in learning
Examples of when I experience negative emotions in teaching	Examples of when my students experience negative emotions in learning

References and further reading

Arnold, J. (2009). Affect in L2 Learning and Teaching. *ELIA, 9*, 145–151.

Borg, S. (2006). The Distinctive Characteristics of Foreign Language Teachers. *Language Teaching Research, 10*(1), 3–31.

Dewaele, J.-M. (2005). Investigating the Psychological and Emotional Dimensions in Instructed Language Learning: Obstacles and Possibilities. *The Modern Language Journal, 89*(3), 367–380.

King, J. & Ng, K.-Y. S. (2018). Teacher Emotions and the Emotional Labour of Second Language Teaching. In S. Mercer & A. Kostoulas

(Eds.), *Language Teacher Psychology* (pp. 141–157). Bristol: Multilingual Matters.

Méndez López, M. G. (2011). The Motivational Properties of Emotions in Foreign Language Learning. *Colombian Applied Linguistics Journal, 13*(2), 43–59.

Richards, J. C. (2022). Exploring Emotions in Language Teaching. *RELC Journal, 53*(1), 225–239.

Senior, R. (2001). The Role of Humour in the Development and Maintenance of Class Cohesion. *Prospect, 16*(2), 45–54.

Teng, M. F. (2017). Emotional Development and Construction of Teacher Identity: Narrative Interactions about the Pre-Service Teachers' Practicum Experiences. *Australian Journal of Teacher Education, 42*(11), 117–134.

PART 5

FEATURES OF CLASSROOM ACTIVITIES

Chapter 10 Use skill-getting and skill-using activities

Introduction

In Chapter 6 we have discussed several different kinds of activities that are commonly used in language teaching, including mechanical, meaningful, and communicative activities and those that have the features of tasks. Teachers and material developers choose activities such as these for different purposes. Sometimes an activity might prepare students for the language they will need to use in carrying out a task, such as matching words with their definitions prior to completing a reading activity. Sometimes an activity might model the kind of skills students should use in a reading or listening task or might provide opportunities for further practice of language or skills presented in previous lessons. The kinds of activities that students take part in during a lesson are key to how effectively the lesson provides opportunities for learning. In this chapter we will look at activities in terms of the kinds of learning opportunities they provide.

10.1 The purpose of classroom activities

Experienced teachers draw on their pedagogical content knowledge in selecting or designing the kinds of activities they use in teaching. For example, Teacher Denis teaches an advanced reading course for international students in an Australian university. The goals of the course are to improve reading skills and strategies, to improve vocabulary, to increase reading speed and fluency and to provide practice in extensive reading. In his course, Denis makes use of two kinds of reading texts: one is a kind of vocabulary building text that contains different texts together with vocabulary building exercises. The other is a set of commercial reading materials from a reading program called the Science Research Associates (SRA) Reading Laboratory that contains multilevel individualized learning materials focusing on reading and study skills. During a typical lesson using this program students take part in four different kinds of activities:

1) Students work on the "Reading for Understanding" section of the SRA kit, focusing on inferring skills.
2) Students work with the rate-builder portion of the SRA kit to focus on reading fluency.
3) Students work on exercises from the vocabulary text.
4) Students practice extensive reading based on a text from a content textbook.

The decisions that Denis makes in his reading course are typical of how we often choose the activities we use in a lesson. Denis may have the activities in mind for several different purposes. Some activities clearly have an instructional aim as Denis does with the activities he uses as the basis for his course. At other times some activities in a lesson may have more of a supporting or facilitating function, helping create positive conditions for learning, for example by creating an emotionally supportive classroom climate. A quiz or a game would be an example of an activity of this kind.

As we've noted above, classroom activities may be chosen for different kinds of purposes; for example, to help learners acquire knowledge of aspects of the language system (e.g. words, grammar, and pronunciation), to prepare learners to perform a task (e.g. a test) or to prepare them for out-of-class language use (e.g. conversation strategies).

> *What are some other purposes for the activities we use in our lessons? Give examples of activities that you use and their purposes.*

In describing classroom activities we can distinguish between activities that have an *instructional focus* (such as developing skills in listening) and the ones (such as games and songs) that have more of a *supportive role* rather than a direct instructional focus. Activities that have an instructional focus may be of many different kinds such as multiple-choice exercises, cloze exercises, dialog practice, sentence-combining drills, substitution tables and role-plays. For students you teach or are familiar with, can you give examples of activities that you use for the following types of lessons?

Lesson types	Typical classroom activities
A speaking lesson	
A listening lesson	

(to be continued)

(*continued*)

Lesson types	Typical classroom activities
A reading lesson	
A grammar lesson	
A writing lesson	
A pronunciation lesson	

10.2 The role of noticing

When we review the kinds of activities that we commonly use in teaching they usually involve two phases. The first phase involves *noticing* some aspect of language use. This could be an aspect of pronunciation, grammar, vocabulary, speaking, or text structure. The second phase involves *practicing* some aspect of language use. "Noticing" and "practicing" play an important part in second language learning. Language teaching activities usually involve some form of practice, and we will explore different kinds of practice shortly. But before we do that, we need to examine what is meant by noticing and the important role it plays in language learning.

Learning how to use a new feature of language first requires awareness of it. If a student never notices that final consonants in English are usually pronounced, he or she is unlikely to produce this feature in his or her English. Similarly, if a learner is never aware of the conventions or formats used to organize different types of written texts such as cause and effect paragraphs or comparison/contrast paragraphs, it is unlikely that he or she will ever use them correctly in a writing assignment. And if a learner never notices that English uses the past tense to refer to past events or the "s" in third person present tense, he or she is not likely to learn to use them. Belief in the role of noticing in language learning is known as the *noticing hypothesis* and is based on an important distinction between *input* (what we see or hear) and *intake* (what we take in and use for learning). Schmidt (1990) has proposed that for learners to acquire new forms from input (i.e. from language they experience, hear or see) it is necessary to notice such forms in the input. Consciousness of features of the input can serve as a trigger that activates the first stage in the process of incorporating new linguistic features into our developing language competence; in this process *input* becomes what can be called *intake*. When we notice something about some aspect of language use, the information we remember can now be "worked" on and hopefully learned. The *input* we work on is now *intake*. Only *intake* can serve as the basis for language development. This explains why someone may "hear" hundreds of hours of a foreign language but fail to learn anything about the language in doing so, which is the case of many adults who have spent time in countries where a foreign language is spoken but never learned anything of the language. They never learned anything because they didn't notice anything about the language and were never able to connect the forms that they experienced to how those forms were used to communicate meaning. They may have received lots of input, but none of it became intake and could then be used to initiate learning.

> *Have you met people who have received a lot of input through living in a situation where many people speak Chinese but never learned any Chinese? For them, input did not lead to intake. Why do you think this happened?*

The extent to which a learner *notices* a new item of language in the input that then becomes intake for learning (for example, the use of the past perfect tense in a narrative) may depend upon how frequently the item is encountered, how salient or "noticeable" it is, whether the teacher has drawn attention to it and the nature of the activity the learner is taking part in. Once input becomes intake, another process is essential if the learner is to learn from the input he or she receives – *practice*! Without practice in using new items of language, little learning can take place.

10.3 The role of practicing

Language learning requires more than simply input, noticing, and intake. It also requires practice. Learning how to take part in conversation, to read with understanding and to write well in English requires extended practice. While many aspects of our understanding of second language learning have changed over the years, the notion of practice is still central to current understanding of language learning. But what do we mean by "practice"? Practice can be understood in terms of the theory of skill-based learning. Skills are sets of behaviors that are learned through practice. They are made up of individual components or subskills that may be learned separately and that come together as a whole to constitute skilled performance. Complex skills such as how to take part in conversation or how to read a newspaper can be broken down into individual component skills. These exist in a hierarchy from lower-level skills (e.g. reading a text or recognizing key words in a text) to higher-level skills (e.g. recognizing the writer's attitude to the topic of a text), and the lower-level skills need to be acquired before the higher-level skills can be used. Initially, skills are often consciously managed and directed by the learner. This is called *controlled processing* (Ellis, 1994). Over time, skills can become automatic and do not require conscious attention. This is called *automatic processing.* Learning involves development from controlled to automatic processing and use of skills.

What kinds of skills need to be practiced for the learners to be able to use English for conversation?

Skills such as these may first be practiced individually before they are used together to practice conversation. The initial practice stages may involve what we have called *mechanical practice* in Chapter 6 (such as completing words in a dialog), and then move to *meaningful practice* (such as adding real information to complete a dialog frame) before moving to *communicative practice* (such as a role-play).

Many aspects of second language learning can similarly be understood as skill-based learning, such as the ability to compose complex written texts, the ability to follow a lecture, and the ability to write a persuasive essay. Central to the notion of skill-based learning is the notion of practice. Practice refers to repeated opportunities to use language over time, allowing the learners to gradually improve their performance. Teachers have always believed in the power of practice, and they are right, though as we shall see below, practice can take many different forms. As learners practice different uses of language they become more skillful at language over time. They become more effective *users* of language and more skilled at using it for the variety of communicative purposes it serves. Many items of English take a long time to learn, hence the crucial role of practice for learners. An item that is not practiced will soon disappear from the learner's linguistic or communicative repertoire.

> *What kinds of skills can be practiced through role-play activities?*

The following examples show how teachers build practice opportunities into their lessons.

Example 1: Teacher Teresa developed a speaking lesson that focused on making recommendations. The topic she chose was "recommending places to visit in a city".

- For *input* she first provided students with a list of possible things of interest to see when people visited a city for the first time. Her students ranked them, added others of their own, and then compared their suggestions. Then the teacher provided examples of patterns that can be used to give suggestions for places to visit, for example, I would suggest seeing .../I think ... is a great place to visit.
- To provide opportunities for *noticing* she then played an audio clip of people giving recommendations for things to do and places to visit in Shanghai. (She had asked two

colleagues to have a brief discussion in English and to record their suggestions.) The students listened to the audio clip and noted how the speakers gave suggestions.

- For *practice* she first gave the students a model dialog to read and practice. She then had them role-play their own conversations in pairs, and later some students performed their role-play conversations in front of the class.

Example 2: Teacher Edward's writing lesson dealt with writing a paragraph describing a city.

- For *input* he gave examples of descriptions of cities from guidebooks and online sources. He asked the students to note the kind of information the descriptions typically included.
- For *noticing* he gave examples of well-written and poorly-written descriptions of cities and pointed out the typical format used in descriptive texts of this kind.
- For *practice* he first asked the students to rewrite the poorly-written descriptions in groups. He followed this with a pair writing task in which each pair of students chose a city or place of interest and prepared a short description of it.

> *Choose a topic for a writing lesson and suggest activities you could use for input, for noticing, and for practice.*

10.4 Skill-getting activities

One way of describing different kinds of classroom techniques is in terms of skill-getting and skill-using. Activities that focus on *skill-getting* develop such things as the ability to use the main sound features of English, to produce grammatically correct sentences, and to learn the different forms of tenses in English and other grammatical distinctions such as singular and plural nouns and subject and object pronouns. Exercise types include gap-filling, substitution drills, minimal pair drills, sentence completion, sentence combining, dialog writing and other exercises that are accuracy-focused and that seek to develop mastery of the building blocks of language and to develop accurate use of grammar, vocabulary, pronunciation, etc.

Here are some examples of skill-getting activities:
- completing verbs in sentences with the correct tense
- reordering sentences to make a dialog
- turning statements into questions
- a cloze activity
- completing a dialog with fillers and responses
- using conjunctions to create complex sentences
- minimal pair drills

Group activities can also be used for skill-getting practice. For example, students in a class are practicing dialogs; the dialogs contain examples of falling intonation in wh-questions; the class is organized in groups of three, two students practicing the dialogs, and the third playing the role of the monitor. The monitor checks that the others are using the correct intonation and corrects them when necessary. The students rotate their roles between those practicing the dialogs and those monitoring. The teacher moves around, listening to the groups and correcting their language when necessary.

Could you give examples of activities you make use of that involve skill-getting?

Some of the characteristics of skill-getting activities are that they reflect language use in the classroom, they focus on the formation of correct examples of language, they practice language out of context, they practice small samples of language, they may not require meaningful communication, and the choice of language is usually controlled.

10.5 Skill-using activities

We can compare *skill-getting activities* with *skill-using activities*, which involve meaningful communication and may draw on student-generated language or information. In skill-using activities students are required to activate and use linguistic and communicative skills which they may have practiced in skill-getting exercises for freer production. Examples of skill-using exercises are:

- answering questions in a class quiz
- interviewing someone about his or her vacation
- telling a real story
- reading a newspaper article for specific information
- reading instructions on how to assemble a product
- reading a text and making a summary of it
- extending a conversation with additional turns and real information
- giving an oral summary of a newspaper story
- watching a cooking demonstration and writing down the ingredients used and the steps involved
- writing a book review
- writing an account of a historical incident

Can you give examples of skill-using activities that you use in your speaking and writing lessons?

In comparison with skill-getting activities, skill-using activities have characteristics such as these: they practice the natural use of language in context, they involve meaningful and purposeful use of language, they usually make use of extended amounts of language input and output, they focus on achieving and maintaining communication rather than practicing language for its own sake, they draw on skills students have developed through skill-getting practice and they give students choice over language content and form.

Skill-using practice often involves interaction and communicative use of skills that are required in role-plays, information gap activities, games, problem-solving tasks, discussions, opinion-sharing activities, and other activities in which learners use their language resources to perform routines and tasks and engage in information sharing and information exchange. These activities provide opportunities both for noticing features of language and for practice in using and applying language skills and in developing fluency in language production. Many lessons contain both skill-getting activities and skill-using activities.

Here are examples of skill-using activities:

Example 1: A group of students with mixed levels of language ability carry out a role-play in which they have to adopt specified roles and personalities provided for them on cue cards. These roles involve the drivers, witnesses, and police officers at the site of a collision between two cars. The language is entirely improvised by the students, though they are heavily constrained by the specified situation and characters.

Example 2: The teacher and a student act out a dialog in which a customer returns a faulty object he or she has purchased to a department store. The clerk asks what the problem is and promises to get a refund for the customer or to replace the item. In groups students now try to recreate the dialog using language items of their choice. They are asked to recreate what has happened preserving the meaning but not necessarily the exact language. They later act out their dialogs in front of the class.

We can now compare skill-getting and skill-using activities in the four skills:

Skills	Skill-getting activities	Skill-using activities
listening	• recognizing stressed syllables in words • recognizing spoken forms of words in natural speech • recognizing final consonants • recognizing vowel contrasts	• following a lecture • watching a news broadcast • identifying a speaker's opinion in a debate • taking notes when watching a TV documentary
speaking	• practicing consonant clusters • using turn-taking expressions • using rising and falling intonation • learning expressions used in introducing people	• giving directions to a place • giving advice for a health problem • telling a story • complaining about a meal in a restaurant • interviewing someone

(to be continued)

(*continued*)

Skills	Skill-getting activities	Skill-using activities
writing	• comparing text structures • predicting topic sentences • choosing correct vocabulary in a cloze passage • learning descriptive adjectives	• writing a description of a building • summarizing a text • writing a review of a movie • writing a letter complaining about a purchase
reading	• identifying the main clause in a complex sentence • distinguishing between the main idea and supporting statements • predicting questions related to a topic	• reading a newspaper story for specific information • making inferences about a situation for clues in the text • reading a commentary and identifying the writer's opinion about the topic of it

Can you give other examples of skill-getting and skill-using activities?

Conclusion

While there are many different kinds of classroom activities that can be used in language teaching, it is important to understand what their purposes are as well as their advantages and limitations. There is a place in language teaching for both skill-getting and skill-using activities, for practice activities that are mechanical as well as those that are meaningful and communicative as we have discussed in Chapter 6, and also for activities that have the features of tasks. However, lessons that consist largely of skill-getting and mechanical activities and do not provide opportunities for meaningful and communicative language practice are unlikely to help learners develop their ability to communicate effectively in English, which requires practice involving meaningful communication and the use of English for authentic purposes.

Follow-up

Work with a colleague and choose a teaching item (e.g. an item of grammar or pronunciation, a function, etc.) that would be relevant to a group of learners you teach or are familiar with. Prepare activities and exercises that provide skill-getting/skill-using practice.

References and further reading

Bygate, M. (2005). Structuring Learning within the Flux of Communication: A Role for Constructive Repetition in Oral Language Pedagogy. In J. A. Foley (Ed.), *New Dimensions in the Teaching of Oral Communication* (pp. 70–90). Singapore: SEAMEO RELC.

DeKeyser, R. M. (Ed). (2007). *Practice in a Second Language: Perspectives from Applied Linguistics and Cognitive Psychology.* New York: Cambridge University Press.

Ellis, R. (1994). *The Study of Second Language Acquisition.* Oxford: Oxford University Press.

Lightbown, P. M. & Spada, N. (2006). *How Languages Are Learned* (3rd edition). Oxford: Oxford University Press.

Schmidt, R. W. (1990). The Role of Consciousness in Second Language Learning. *Applied Linguistics, 11*(2), 129–158.

Willis, D. & Willis, J. (2007). *Doing Task-Based Teaching*. Oxford: Oxford University Press.

Chapter 11 Showcase your creativity

Introduction

When we begin our careers as language teachers, we must quickly learn how to use many of the regular activities that we use when we teach English. For example, we soon develop procedures and techniques for using a reading text to develop reading skills, for organizing a discussion activity, and for making use of role-plays and information gap activities. We learn how to prepare students for a writing activity, how to use questions to guide and test students' understanding of a text, and how to use activities of choral repetition. Learning to use the procedures associated with commonly used teaching exercises and activities such as these involves the use of routines that become established through practice. This reduces some of the pressures associated with teaching. However, when we continually teach our lessons in the same way, students can find lessons predictable and neither challenging nor engaging. Similarly, we may find lessons less than engaging to teach if the textbook continually draws on the same bank of exercises and tasks. In too many English lessons, teaching is often book- and test-driven rather than learner-centered. One way to address this issue is to develop the ability to teach creatively. In this chapter we will explore what teaching creatively means, why it is important in teaching, and how we can make our teaching practices more creative.

Can you think of occupations that demand particular creative skills?

11.1 The nature of creativity

There are many ways of defining creativity, depending on whether we see it as a property of *people* (who we are), of *processes* (what we do) or of *products*. Creativity is usually defined as being able to solve problems in original and valuable ways that are relevant to our goals, being able to see new meanings and relationships in things and to make connections, having original and imaginative thoughts and ideas about something, and using our imagination and experience to create new learning possibilities. When creativity is viewed as a *product* the focus might be on a particular lesson, a task or an activity in a book, or a piece of student writing. What are the specific features of the lesson that enables us to say it is creative? When creativity is viewed as a *process* the focus is on the thinking processes and decisions that a person makes use of in producing something that we would describe as creative. But why is creativity important?

We can probably all recall teachers we know who were very creative in their approaches to teaching. Of course, we have all encountered teachers who made use of carefully developed lesson plans, who kept their lessons focused on accurate performance of tasks, or who were strict about getting homework in on time and returned it with detailed corrections and suggestions. Hopefully, however, we might also have powerful and fond memories of a teacher who sparked our imagination, who inspired us by his or her personal teaching style, or who motivated us to want to continue learning and perhaps to eventually decide to become an English teacher. What makes teachers like this different?

> *Do you sometimes draw on your ability to think creatively in your teaching? Can you give an example?*

Creativity depends upon the ability to analyze and evaluate situations and to identify novel ways of responding to them. Creative teaching can result in increased level of motivation and self-esteem on the part of learners and prepare them with the flexible skills they need for the future. In education creativity is emphasized and encouraged because it can improve academic attainment. Fisher (2004: 11) reports:

> Research ... shows that when students are assessed in ways that recognise and value their creative abilities, their academic performance improves. Creative activity can rekindle the interest of students who have been turned off by school, and teachers who may be turned off by teaching in a culture of control and compliance.

> *What kinds of thinking do you think creative people often make use of? How do people develop these skills?*

11.2 Creativity in language teaching

In language teaching, many of the language activities recommended in contemporary language teaching methods are believed to release creativity in learners – particularly those involving student-centered, interaction-based and open-ended elements, and are therefore in principle ideally suited to fostering creative thinking and behavior on the part of learners. Creative intelligence seems to be a factor that can facilitate language learning because it helps learners cope with novel and unpredictable experiences. Communicative teaching methods have a role to play here since they emphasize functional and situational language use and employ activities such as role-plays and simulations that require students to use their imagination and think creatively.

One important issue, however, is that creativity has to be used in a way that is purposeful in language teaching, rather than simply as a gimmick to entertain the students. Creative teachers have a solid knowledge base. They know their subject and they draw on their disciplinary knowledge and their pedagogical content knowledge in building creative lessons. A knowledge base is important because without knowledge, imagination cannot be productive. Creativity doesn't mean making unfocused and unprincipled actions. It doesn't mean making it up as you go.

Let me first give an example of creativity *without* a solid knowledge base – which I characterize as misplaced creativity. I once worked with a native-speaker teacher who had no formal education in TESOL but had taught for 8 years in an EFL context by virtue of the fact that he was a native speaker. He had developed a technique which he used as a feature of every class he taught. For example, he might take a word to begin a lesson: "English". He would ask students to come up with words starting with the letter E/N/G/L/I/S/H. Then he would take the ending *-ish* and ask for nationalities ending in *-ish*. Suddenly he was comparing "Finnish" – the nationality – with "to finish". Next, he was asking students if they knew what a finishing school was.

And so it went on. When I asked him to explain the theoretical rationale for this activity and what it was supposed to achieve, he could not come up with a convincing response.

Unlike this teacher, having a solid knowledge base means that the teacher has a rationale and purpose for the creative activities he or she uses. The activities have not been chosen merely for their novelty value but because they reflect the teacher's knowledge and understanding of teaching and learning. So what are some principles of creativity in language teaching? The following are some examples from teachers' practices.

11.3 Have confidence in your intuitions

Well-developed disciplinary knowledge and pedagogical content knowledge (which have been the focus of Chapter 2) can provide a sense of confidence that enables you to be original and creative. One feature of confidence is that it gives you a sense that *you* are in control of your classroom and that it is *you* – not the book or the curriculum – that can make a difference. Creative teachers see their input to the lesson as being decisive, and so they have a sense of personal responsibility for how well learners learn:

> At first, I used to worry about what my students thought about me: Did I know my subject? Did I know how to introduce the material? Was I in control of the class? ... and so on. Now that I am much more confident as a teacher, I am more willing to follow my intuitions, to try out new approaches and strategies, to take risks and to experiment. It makes teaching more enjoyable for me. I am always on the lookout for new and creative ways of using my teaching resources such as mobile phones. One thing I did recently was to ask my students to

work with a partner and video themselves recounting an unusual experience they had had recently and to bring their videos to the next lesson. Then in the lesson they shared their videos; everyone noted one interesting or unusual thing that he or she saw in his or her partner's video. Then we shared these with the class and used them to note the different ways in which they responded to each other's videos – with questions and expressions such as "really", "wow" and "fantastic". This led to practice using questions and backchanneling responses in conversation. (Andria)

> *What are some creative ways in which mobile phones can be used in the language classroom?*

11.4 Find original ways of doing things

One way of adding a creative dimension to your teaching is to look for original ways of using activities that reflect your own individual teaching style. Creative teachers are often very different from each other. Learning to be a creative teacher does not mean modeling or copying the practices of other creative teachers, but rather it means understanding and applying the principles that underlie creative teaching. Individual teachers will realize these principles in different ways. For example, below are five different ways of practicing the past tense. Rank them from most creative (1) to least creative (5):

Dialog completing: Students are given a dialog about a past event while all the past tense verbs have been deleted. They have to complete the missing verbs. _____

Charades: Students act out or mime an activity. Others describe what they did using the past tense. _____

Milestones: Students write about or discuss a milestone in their life and the events that led up to it. _____

Stories: Students are given phrases to start a story. Each member of a group develops the story by adding a sentence in the past tense. _____

News photos: Students are given a news picture and have to make up a story to go with it. _____

> *Can you think of creative ways of practicing the use of the past tense and the present perfect?*

11.5 Vary the way you do things

Learning to teach means mastering the formats of different kinds of lessons – reading lessons, conversation lessons, listening lessons and so on, which we have discussed in Chapter 6. As we have noted above, through delivering lessons over many years of experience, teachers develop routines and procedures that enable lessons to be carried out efficiently and effortlessly. But there is a tendency for teaching to become increasingly standardized – the "one size fits all" approach – particularly if you are working within a prescribed curriculum and teaching towards tests. This often results in a teacher working from pre-packed materials such as a textbook and "transmitting" them efficiently. This is perhaps appropriate at the beginning stages of a teacher's career but should not characterize the lessons of experienced teachers. Here are some comments by a teacher on how she seeks to introduce variety into familiar activities:

> I find that the easiest way to do something new in the lesson is to invite the learners to make decisions about different

aspects of the activities. There is no reason why the teacher has to decide which activities to focus on or in which order to complete them. There are also many possibilities for arranging the grouping of learners as they work on tasks, from individuals to pairs to small groups. I try and work through different aspects of lesson organization and systematically vary the following: the text type, audience, purpose, skill focus, and learning configuration (individuals, pairs, groups, and the whole class). I also routinely ask the learners to tell me how long they believe they will need to complete a particular activity. They have a much better idea than me and I always make sure I write some kind of "extension task" on the board while they are working, so that anyone who finishes early has something else to do. (Gina)

Finding different ways of using familiar teaching activities is a way of avoiding lessons becoming repetitive.

> *What are some creative ways of using dialogs in a speaking lesson?*

11.6 Don't be afraid to take risks

One of the characteristics of a creative teacher is a willingness to experiment, to innovate, and to take risks. If you are a risk-taker, you are the sort of teacher who is willing to try things out even if at times they may not work quite the way they are intended, as was the case with this teacher:

Last year I got students to try and keep a writing portfolio. The idea was to get them to reflect on their progress and motivate them by getting them to see evidence of their work. They hated it! They just thought it was more work and didn't help them with their exams. I really need to rethink this one.

So, this means that you are willing to rethink or revise, or if necessary, abandon your original plan and try something else. But this is seen as a learning moment and not an indication of failure:

Recently in my writing class I asked learners to find any website or blog that interested them and submit a question to that website or blog and see if they could get an answer. I was a bit nervous because learners might choose unsuitable sites but thought I'd give it a go anyway. As it happened only a few students completed the assignment, but one of them did report on a Tandem Language Learning website she had found that welcomed learners to join for free. She had been paired up with an Australian girl who was learning Spanish and they had already exchanged several emails and were planning to have a Skype meeting. Her report was completely unexpected but ended up motivating several other students to visit the same site and find their own partners. Whereas at first, I thought the activity had been unsuccessful because not everyone did it, in fact this one student's enthusiasm ended up influencing several others to follow her lead, which eventually provided lots of additional written communication practice in English. (Danial)

Can you recall trying out something with your students for the first time to see how well it worked? What was the response?

11.7 Use activities which have creative dimensions

Creative teaching can be supported with activities and tasks that require learners to think creatively. Tasks that promote creative thinking and responses from learners have features such as these:

Challenges: tasks in which learners solve problems, discover something, overcome obstacles, or find information

Novelty: aspects of an activity that are new or different or totally unexpected

Intrigue: tasks that concern ambiguous, problematic, paradoxical, controversial, contradictory or incongruous materials and that stimulate learners' curiosity

Connections: tasks that require students to make novel connections between things, such as between architecture and botany

Originality: tasks that require students to come up with original ideas

Imagination: activities in which students have to put themselves in imaginary situations

Fantasy: activities that invite learners to use their imagination, for example by creating make-believe stories or acting out imaginary situations

---

- *Can you think of examples of activities for each of the features above?*
- *What aspects of creativity are involved in the activities below?*

    Brainstorming*: Students are presented with a problem and have to come up with as many responses or solutions to the problem as they can.*

> ***Role-play****: Students take the roles of different people affected by an issue and discuss issues or events from the perspectives of those people.*
>
> ***Storytelling****: Students are given the beginning and an unusual conclusion to a story and have to create a main body that connects the two parts.*
>
> ***Reinventing****: Students are given a common item to discuss such as a toothbrush and have to come up with novel and unusual ways in which it could be used.*

The following are examples of teachers thinking creatively:

> Even though my students don't seem to like doing the writing exercises in our textbook in class, I realized that they do quite a bit of writing in their daily lives, in the form of tweets and Facebook updates, for example. I created a Twitter account and a Google+ page for our class and got students to start writing short messages in response to each other. Gradually I assigned them different roles and had everyone contribute different parts to a short story we wrote collaboratively. The students loved it as it made the activity more familiar to their out-of-class experiences. (Kumiko)

> In my business writing course we have to work with lots of very routine texts such as email messages, blog posts and business letters. To make it more interesting I ask students at the start of the semester to invent their own company, logo, staff list and products so that they can use this material when they are developing their own scenarios and situations throughout the semester rather than have to stick rigidly to examples in the

textbook. In this way, they create a kind of personal narrative throughout the semester, telling different stories about what has happened in the company and what they need to communicate about. (Sara)

One of my learners popped into my office the other day and asked me if I had a minute to read something written on his phone. I was intrigued. When I read it, I saw that it was the opening lines of a thriller, rich with description of place and person. Because he was in my research writing course, I had no idea he had such a lively imagination and an ability to write such a creative text, so I asked him how we could find a way of seeing more of his talent for words in his research writing. He took a risk in showing me that writing but I figured that he did so because he wanted me to know what he was capable of. Since that day I've encouraged him to be as creative as possible during our free writing sessions and to focus on personal links to the rather academic and serious topic that he is exploring in his research paper. (Steven)

As these examples illustrate, teachers draw on creativity in different ways, but always keep in mind how an activity with creative elements can help raise students' level of interest, engagement and motivation in learning.

11.8 Make creative use of technology

Creative use of technology in the classroom can support the development of imagination, problem-solving, risk-taking and divergent thinking on the part of teachers and students (see Chapter 15), as is seen in this example of how a teacher uses blogging as a resource:

A productive way of engaging my students and helping them to improve their writing skills is through creative non-fiction (CNF). CNF involves using creative literary techniques and devices when we write about non-fiction events, e.g. diaries, memoirs, autobiographies, essays, obituaries, journalism, and travel writing. I have incorporated a CNF strand into my writing course – blogging.

I begin by showcasing blogs to the class as a whole using the classroom computer and screen, e.g. a leading newspaper, *The Guardian*, ran a blogging competition and I bring up the winning sites, e.g. "Scaryduck: Not scary. Not a duck". The blogs express a particular point of view, and are funny and aimed at a younger adult audience, which reflects the age range and interests of my students. This particular blog is full of short, often witty pieces, about whatever interests the blogger. It is reader-friendly, consisting of short, lively texts liberally punctuated with photographs. I find that my students engage very quickly. I look in more detail at one of the blog's eliciting ways that the writing is creative, e.g. use of adjectives, irony, voice, register and metaphor. My students bring their tablets, laptops and smartphones to class and after the showcase I give them the web addresses for three other suitable blogs and ask the students to browse them and be prepared to comment.

I then set up their blogging task. Each student has to set up an online blog and then blog on five separate subject areas from a choice of eight subject areas: food, music, transport, sport, media, politics, religion, and fashion. Students are encouraged to read and interact with their fellow students' blogs. After each set of blogs I give a whole-class commentary on selected student blogs, highlighting areas of successful creative writing, e.g. alliteration, original use of adjectives, and realization of a distinctive voice. I also give personal, online feedback to my students about their blogs through one-to-one emails. The intrinsic interest of their chosen materials and freedom to express their own points of view have a highly motivating effect on my students and there is a crossover into their academic writing, which I foster in class and through individual feedback on their academic writing tasks.

(Dino)

What are some other possibilities of using blogging in teaching English?

11.9 Review how creative your teaching is

To review the extent to which you use creative thinking in your teaching, it is useful to step back from the daily routines and activities of teaching from time to time and to reflect on questions such as these: Do I vary the way I teach my lessons? Do I try out new activities and assess their roles in my lessons? Do I compare my teaching with the teaching of other teachers to find out creative solutions that they may have developed? Can I find ways of making my tasks more creative and hence more engaging for learners? One way of developing creative ways of planning lessons is through shared lesson planning, as this teacher comments:

At our institute we use a well-known series of commercial textbooks. The students enjoy them and I find the materials fairly easy to use. However, I am always looking for ways to make my teaching less book-centered. One activity we make

> use of is for those of us using a particular level in the series to
> meet regularly and to brainstorm different ways of teaching
> the units. It always amazes me to see how many interesting
> and different ways the group can come up with for presenting
> the different exercises in the book. Sharing our ideas in this
> way is fun and I think it results in classes that our students find
> engaging and useful. (Ken)

Journal writing is another way of reviewing how creative our teaching is:

> I keep a teaching journal in which I jot down thoughts and
> reflections on my teaching. I try to take 30 minutes or so, once
> a week, to look back at my teaching and reflect on things
> of interest, or issues which arose that I need to think more
> about. If I have tried out a creative new activity and it worked
> particularly well I may make a note of it for future reference. I
> find journal writing to be a useful consciousness-raising tool.
> It helps me focus on things that I may otherwise forget and
> helps me make better decisions about my future teaching. It's
> interesting to read things I wrote at different times to get a
> sense of how creative I am as a teacher. (Jose)

Conclusion

In this chapter the focus has been on just one aspect of teaching. There are many other important dimensions to effective teaching that we have explored in other chapters. But adding the concept of creative teaching to our understanding of what it means to be an effective language teacher has benefits for both teachers and learners. For learners, creative teaching helps them develop their capacities for original ideas and for creative thinking. It also improves the quality of the experiences learners receive, can help them develop increased level of motivation, and can lead to better learning outcomes. For you as a teacher, creative teaching provides a source of ongoing professional renewal and satisfaction – since when learners are engaged, motivated and successful, teaching is motivating for you too.

Follow-up

Review the textbook you are using or are contemplating using. How creative do you think the activities used throughout the book are? Choose two activities to which you think a more creative element could be added and revise the activities based on your suggestions.

References and further reading

Dörnyei, Z. (2001). *Motivational Strategies in the Language Classroom.* Cambridge: Cambridge University Press.

Fisher, R. (2004). What Is Creativity? In R. Fisher & M. Williams (Eds.), *Unlocking Creativity: Teaching across the Curriculum* (pp. 6–20). New York: Routledge.

Jones, R. H. & Richards, J. C. (Eds.). (2015). *Creativity in Language Teaching: Perspectives from Research and Practice.* New York: Routledge.

Maley, A. (1997). Creativity with a Small 'c'. In C. Coreil & M. Napoliello (Eds.), *The Journal of the Imagination in Language Learning* (Vol. 4) (pp. 8–16). Jersey City: The Center for the Imagination in Language Learning.

Starko, A. J. (2021). *Creativity in the Classroom: Schools of Curious Delight* (7th edition). New York: Routledge.

Tin, T. B. (2022). *Unpacking Creativity for Language Teaching.* London: Routledge.

PART 6

ACHIEVING FUNCTIONAL LANGUAGE DEVELOPMENT

Chapter 12 Focus on learning outcomes

Introduction

When we plan a lesson, we usually begin by considering what kind of lesson it is, such as a reading lesson, a speaking lesson or a writing lesson. We also consider the learners' proficiency level, such as whether their level of English is basic, intermediate or advanced. Following this we can make decisions about the content of the lesson. For example, a reading lesson might involve reading about a historical event, a speaking lesson might practice giving a short presentation, or the focus of a writing lesson might be writing an essay. Once the content of the lesson has been decided we can choose the activities to use in the lesson. If a reading lesson involves reading about a historical event, the activities might involve:

1) Students discuss what they know about a historical event.
2) Students read statements about the event and check whether they are true or false.
3) Students read a text and answer comprehension questions.

Or in the case of a speaking lesson the activities might involve:
1) The teacher talks about their weekend.
2) Students ask and answer questions about their recent activities.
3) Students complete a class survey to find out who did things that could be considered exciting, scary, unusual, funny and so on.

However, the activities we choose in a lesson are not an end in themselves. They are chosen according to the aims of the lesson and how well they help students develop different kinds of language knowledge, skills or abilities, that is, how well they help students develop their proficiency in English. The lesson may also require students to demonstrate something they have learned from it, such as whether they are able to use a particular sound contrast that has occurred in a dialog or drill, or how well they are able to use the grammar and sentence patterns that have been the focus of a writing activity. Demonstrations of the learning occurring in a lesson are known as the *learning outcomes* of the lesson. In this chapter we focus on the relationship between lesson aims, activities and learning outcomes, and their roles in planning an effective lesson.

What do you think your students' main aims in learning English are?

12.1 The nature of "general English"

English programs for secondary school learners in what Kachru has referred to as Outer Circle contexts (Chapter 1) address very general skills in English, since the amount of time available for English in the school curriculum may be limited and students' needs for English at this stage in their learning may not yet be clear or specific. The kind of English taught at this level is often referred to as *general English* (sometimes also referred to as *English for no obvious purpose*). Commenting on the teaching of English in China, Ye (2020: 1) states:

> English for general purposes (EGP) has been the mainstream practice under the guidance of the authoritative *College English Curriculum Requirements* (Ministry of Education, 2007, p. 1), which stipulates that English for undergraduate programs aims to develop students' listening, speaking, reading, and writing skills so that they will be able to "engage in effective communication in English" in the future study, work, and social interaction.

The aims of a course or lesson help decide on what kinds of activities to use in teaching, but these will depend upon the learners' proficiency level in English. As with course aims, the proficiency levels of general English courses have also been described in very general terms involving a progression from a *basic level* to the *intermediate level*, and to the *advanced level* of proficiency, and textbooks usually use these labels to identify the proficiency levels they address. Identifying what these levels refer to in practical terms, however, is quite complex and somewhat impressionistic, and is usually based on the knowledge and experience of language teachers and specialists in the development of language courses.

> *How is the proficiency level of students in your school or institution determined?*

12.2 Describing proficiency levels

The nature of different proficiency levels in language learning is based on identifying the specific kinds of language knowledge and skills needed at basic, intermediate or advanced level. These are usually described in terms of vocabulary, grammar and the four skills but may also include topics, functions, texts and pronunciation. For the choice of vocabulary, targets are often between 1,500 to 2,000 words to reach a basic level of proficiency, with higher vocabulary knowledge needed to reach the advanced level. O'Keeffe et al. (2007: 48–49) comment:

> A receptive vocabulary of some 5,000 to 6,000 words would appear to be a good threshold at which to consider learners to be at the top of the intermediate level and ready to take on an advanced level programme.

The choice of grammar to include in a general English course is usually based on the most frequent sentence patterns, tenses and other items of grammar used in spoken and written English as well as the kinds of grammar and syntax needed to use English at different proficiency levels. For example, the first 24 grammatical items in a basic-level English course are:

1. present tense verb *be*	12. adjectives
2. subject pronouns	13. *have/has got*
3. possessive adjectives	14. present simple tense
4. indefinite article: *a/an*	15. object pronouns
5. plural nouns: *-s, -ies, -es*	16. *Whose ...? How often ...?*
6. prepositions: *from, in, near, at, with*	17. *enough*
7. *there is/there are*	18. *can/cannot (can't)*
8. countable nouns with *some* and *any*	19. *like* + noun/*like* + gerund
	20. adverbs of frequency
9. definite article: *the*	21. *Do you like ...?*
10. plural nouns: irregular	22. *Would you like ...?*
11. demonstrative pronouns: *this/ that, these/those*	23. past tense verb *be*
	24. present continuous tense for present activities

What criteria do you think were used to determine the sequence of grammar items in the syllabus above?

In order to help plan courses and textbooks some language teaching organizations such as the ACTFL (American Council on the Teaching of Foreign Languages) have developed proficiency scales that give detailed descriptions of the language knowledge, skills and abilities involved at different proficiency levels. For example, the following is a description of the ability of a learner at the Intermediate High level for the skill of speaking in the proficiency guidelines of ACTFL (ACTFL, 2012):

> Intermediate High speakers are able to converse with ease and confidence when dealing with the routine tasks and social situations of the Intermediate level. They are able to handle successfully uncomplicated tasks and social situations requiring an exchange of basic information related to their work, school, recreation, particular interests, and areas of competence.
>
> Intermediate High speakers can handle a substantial number of tasks associated with the Advanced level, but they are unable to sustain performance of all of these tasks all of the time. Intermediate High speakers can narrate and describe in all major time frames using connected discourse of paragraph length, but not all the time. Typically, when Intermediate High speakers attempt to perform Advanced-level tasks, their speech exhibits one or more features of breakdown, such as the failure to carry out fully the narration or description in the appropriate major time frame, an inability to maintain paragraph-length discourse, or a reduction in breadth and appropriateness of vocabulary.

> Intermediate High speakers can generally be understood by native speakers unaccustomed to dealing with non-natives, although interference from another language may be evident (e.g., use of code-switching, false cognates, literal translations), and a pattern of gaps in communication may occur.

The Common European Framework of Reference for Languages (CEFR) is another widely used framework for describing learners' ability at different proficiency levels in each of the four skills. Six levels of achievement from lowest (A1) to highest (C2) are divided into three broad divisions and outline what a learner should be able to do in reading, listening, speaking and writing at each level:

Basic user – A1, A2

Independent user – B1, B2

Proficient user – C1, C2

For the skill of listening the knowledge and ability of a learner at the basic level (A1 and A2 of the framework) could be described as follows:

- Can understand phrases and expressions related to areas of immediate priority (e.g. very basic personal and family information, shopping, local geography, and employment), provided speech is clearly and slowly articulated. (A2)
- Can understand enough to be able to meet needs of a concrete type, provided speech is clearly and slowly articulated. (A2)
- Can follow speech which is very slow and carefully articulated. (A1)

> *Can you give examples of listening activities that could be used with students at A1/A2 level of listening ability?*

The ability of an advanced-level listener (C1 and C2 on the CEFR) could be described like this:

- Has no difficulty in understanding any kind of spoken language, whether live or broadcast, delivered at fast native speed. (C2)
- Can understand enough to follow extended speech on abstract and complex topics beyond his or her own field, though he or she may need to confirm occasional details, especially if the accent is unfamiliar. (C1)
- Can recognize a wide range of idiomatic expressions and colloquialisms, appreciating register shifts. (C1)
- Can follow extended speech even when it is not clearly structured and when relationships are only implied and not signaled explicitly. (C1)

> *What are some activities that could be used with students at C1/C2 level of listening ability?*

12.3 Developing a syllabus

The CEFR descriptors above reflect decisions that have been made both about the nature of different language knowledge and skills and the sequence in which they should be taught or included in a course. Sequencing the content of a course in terms of language, skills, abilities and other kinds of knowledge results in a syllabus – a plan or map of the content and sequence of learning items in a course. This approach to developing a course is described in Docking (1994: 10):

> The traditional approach to developing a syllabus involves using one's understanding of subject matter as the basis for syllabus planning. One starts with the field of knowledge that one is going to teach (e.g. contemporary European history, marketing, listening comprehension, or French literature) and then selects concepts, knowledge, and skills that constitute that field of knowledge. A syllabus and the course content are then developed around the subject. Objectives may also be specified, but these usually have little role in teaching or assessing of the subject. Assessment of students is usually based on norm referencing, that is, students will be graded on a single scale with the expectation that they spread across a wide range of scores or that they conform to a pre-set distribution.

Wiggins and McTighe (2005) give an illustration of this process with an example of the lesson plan that follows the steps above:

- The teacher chooses a topic for a lesson (e.g. racial prejudice).
- The teacher selects a resource (e.g. the American novel *To Kill a Mockingbird*).
- The teacher chooses instructional methods based on the resource and topic (e.g. a seminar to discuss the book and cooperative groups to analyze stereotypical images in films and on television).
- The teacher chooses essay questions to assess student understanding of the book.

What kind of syllabus is used in the textbook that you teach from?

In a general English course, the textbook is generally planned around an integrated syllabus that identifies the topics, skills, grammar, vocabulary, functions, pronunciation and other language features that the course covers. For example, a unit in *Interchange Intro* (Richards, 2017b) which is described as at A1 level on the CEFR contains the following syllabus items:

Topics	Sports/Abilities and talents
speaking	asking about free-time activities; asking for and giving information about abilities and talents
grammar	simple present wh-questions; *can* for ability; yes/no and wh-questions with *can*
pronunciation/ listening	pronunciation of *can* and *can't*; listening for people's favorite sports to watch or play; listening to people talk about their abilities
writing/reading	writing questions about sports; reading about fitness records from around the world
activity	finding about a classmate's hidden talents

A syllabus serves as a guide for the textbook writer or the teacher in selecting the kind of activities that will be used in lessons or materials.

What criteria could be used to arrange the sequence of lessons or units in a reading course?

12.4 Activities and aims

While we generally think about our lessons in terms of the activities we make use of during the lesson, activities are chosen as a means to an end rather than an end in themselves.

In other words, activities are not chosen at random based on their interest level or the ease with which they can be used but in terms of how well they address the aims of the lesson and the skills students need to master at a given proficiency level. For example, each of the activities below has a particular aim or purpose. Can you suggest an aim for each activity?

Activities	Aims
putting together a scrambled set of sentences to make a text	
practicing a dialog in pairs	
a group discussion activity in which students compare opinions about an issue	
a translation activity in which students translate a short text from Chinese to English	
an activity of free writing in which students have to write as much as they can about a topic in three minutes	

In using activities, as well as considering their aims, other decisions are also required. The teacher has to decide not only how an activity will lead to learning but also if the activity is of the right level for the class, how much preparation might be needed to complete it, and what resources need to be provided, such as handouts. And the students need to know what procedures they should use to carry out an activity, how much time they should spend on it, and what the teacher expects if the activity is to be carried out effectively.

How well the students perform in the different activities in the course is often what teachers have in mind when assessing the effectiveness of their teaching, as we see in these teachers' comments:

> I have a checklist I use to give feedback on students' pronunciation when they practice dialogs. Sometimes students take turns to listen to other students and use the checklist to grade each other's performance. (Rita)

> I make a lot of use of group-based activities. The thing I emphasize in group work is the extent to which all the members of a group participate in a group activity and how much talking each group member contributes. (Ann)

> I don't move on from a listening activity until the students have understood everything in the listening. If they misunderstood quite a lot of the passage I will play it again several times, and also give out the text of the listening for them to follow as they listen. (Karl)

12.5 Aims and objectives

Aims are very general statements of the goals of a course or lesson. For example, the aim of a course in business English might be: *to learn English for use in the hotel and tourism industry.*

However, the aim does not describe whether the course will include both spoken and written English, nor the kinds of situations that will be covered in the course. It is still too general to be used as the basis for developing a syllabus or teaching materials. For these purposes the aim needs to be broken down into smaller sets of related aims. These are referred to as *objectives*. An objective is a more precise description of the aim of a course. Examples of objectives related to the aim above could be:

- to learn how to write effective business letters for use in the hotel and tourism industry
- to learn how to take part in conversational interaction with hotel clients

The following are examples of aims and sample objectives for a listening course and a speaking course.

Example 1: academic listening course
Aim: Students will learn how to listen to lectures in English.
Objectives: Students will be able to recognize and follow the main topic, theme or argument of a lecture; students will learn how to recognize the following features of a lecture:

- main ideas and supporting details
- links between sections of a lecture
- the purpose of a lecture, such as whether it is to summarize, criticize or persuade

Example 2: spoken English for social communication
Aims:

- Students will learn to use English for social interaction with appropriate accuracy, fluency and intelligibility.
- They will learn how to initiate and maintain conversations on topics commonly used in social interaction.

Objectives: To develop skills in the following features of conversation:
- using greetings, introductions, openings and closings in short conversations
- making small talk as a part of social interaction
- introducing topics in small talk
- asking and answering simple questions about everyday matters
- using backchanneling and turn-taking to maintain interaction
- using clarification requests to maintain understanding
- using narratives and personal recounts to relate past incidents and events

Describing outcomes of a course or lesson in terms of objectives makes it possible to plan the different components of the course and to design materials for teaching and assessment.

Think of some objectives for these courses:
- *Topic of course: **job interviews***
  ***Aim**: to develop the skills to perform successfully during a job interview*
  ***Objectives**: _____*
- *Topic of course: **public speaking***
  ***Aim**: to learn how to present an effective oral presentation*
  ***Objectives**: _____*

12.6 Learning outcomes

In planning a course or lesson, in addition to considering the aims, objectives and activities of the lesson, it is also useful to consider what the learners will actually be able to *do* as a result of completing the activities in the lesson. What can the learners actually do as a demonstration of what they have learned? For example, if a student has completed a series of activities aimed at practicing the language and skills used in social conversation, at the end of the lesson can he or she perform a short two-minute exchange in front of the class that demonstrates how to *open an exchange with a greeting, make small talk*, and *end the interaction appropriately*? This would be a demonstration of a *learning outcome* of the lesson. One approach to the development of courses and lessons argues that planning should always *begin* with a description of the expected learning outcomes. This approach is known as *backward design* (Wiggins & McTighe, 2005).

Learning outcomes can often be described in terms of a "can-do" statement. For example,

Aim: Students will learn how to understand lectures given in English.

Objective: Students will be able to follow the argument, theme or thesis of a lecture and write key points in note form.

Learning outcome: Students can watch a ten-minute video talk and write accurately in note form the main points of the talk.

Mickan (2013: 46–47) clarifies the relation between learning outcomes and objectives:

> The outcomes are based on objectives. They specify learners' participation and progression in a structured programme – what language practices learners will be able to take part in by the end of a programme or unit of work. Outcomes provide

> teachers and students with measures of progress towards goals. For teachers they provide a standard for assessment or testing. For students they provide a map detailing interim progression, or milestones towards a goal, as well as a sense of making progress as they experience achievement through participation in practices.

Below are some further examples of objectives and the learning outcomes that relate to them for a course on spoken English.

Example 1:
    Objective: Students will learn how to present information, ideas and feelings clearly and coherently in spoken English.
    Sample learning outcome: Students can present a two-minute talk to the class, describing an interesting thing that they did over the weekend and how they felt about it.

Example 2:
    Objective: Students will learn how to participate in social communication with people and manage the opening and closing of a short exchange.
    Sample learning outcome: Students can take part in class role-play activities in which they greet foreign visitors, ask and answer polite questions, and wish them well.

Example 3:
    Objective: Students will learn how to describe a process involving a sequence of events.
    Sample learning outcome: Students can describe in five minutes how to prepare one of their favorite dishes, including the ingredients and equipment used and the steps involved in making the dish.

- *What is the possible learning outcome for this example?*
  Aim*: to develop the communication skills needed for front desk staff in a hotel*
  Objective*: to learn how to conduct arrival and check-in procedures with arriving hotel guests*
  Learning outcome*:* _____
- *Think of a course that you teach or are familiar with, for example an integrated course or a skill-based course such as a reading or speaking course. What learning outcomes do you hope your students will achieve at the end of the course? Describe some of the things they should be able to do.*

Conclusion

The ability to think about and plan lessons and materials in terms of aims, objectives, activities and learning outcomes is an essential skill no matter at what level you teach. It involves changing your thinking about a lesson from simply asking, "What am I going to teach today?" to the question "What are the students going to learn to *do* today?". What do they need to know in order to be able to do this? The learning outcomes should be brief and concise so that students themselves can assess how well the learning outcomes have been accomplished. For students, being able to come away from a lesson with a feeling that "now I can do something in English that I couldn't perform very well before the lesson" is motivating and helps develop a sense of confidence. For you as a teacher, a focus on learning outcomes can help you see the practical results of your teaching. This too is motivating and rewarding for you as a teacher. And no matter what basis is used for a course – whether it is language-based, skill-based, function-based or text-based for example, it is always possible for you to *add* precise learning outcomes to the course that describe practical communicative outcomes that students will learn from the course.

Follow-up

Work in groups and explain what you understand by aims, syllabuses, objectives, activities and learning outcomes. Give examples from a course you teach or are familiar with.

References and further reading

ACTFL. (2012). *ACTFL Proficiency Guidelines 2012.* https://www.actfl.org/uploads/files/general/ACTFLProficiencyGuidelines2012.pdf

Burns, A. & Richards, J. C. (Eds.). (2012). *The Cambridge Guide to Pedagogy and Practice in Second Language Teaching.* New York: Cambridge University Press.

Council of Europe. (2001). *Common European Framework of Reference for Languages: Learning, Teaching, Assessment.* Cambridge: Cambridge University Press.

Docking, R. (1994). Competency-Based Curricula: The Big Picture. *Prospect, 9*(2), 8–17.

Fujiwara, B. (1996). Planning an Advanced Listening Comprehension Elective for Japanese College Students. In K. Graves (Ed.), *Teachers as Course Developers* (pp. 151–175). New York: Cambridge University Press.

Mickan, P. (2013). *Language Curriculum Design and Socialisation.* Bristol: Multilingual Matters.

O'Keeffe, A., McCarthy, M. & Carter, R. (2007). *From Corpus to Classroom: Language Use and Language Teaching.* Cambridge: Cambridge University Press.

Richards, J. C. (2015). *Key Issues in Language Teaching*. Cambridge: Cambridge University Press.

Richards, J. C. (2017a). *Curriculum Development in Language Teaching* (2nd edition). Cambridge: Cambridge University Press.

Richards, J. C. (2017b). *Interchange Intro* (Teacher's edition, 5th edition). Cambridge: Cambridge University Press.

Wiggins, G & McTighe, J. (2005). *Understanding by Design* (2nd edition). Alexandria: Association for Supervision and Curriculum Development.

Ye, Y. (2020). EAP for Undergraduate Science and Engineering Students in an EFL Context: What Should We Teach? *Ampersand, 7*, Article 100065.

Chapter 13 Teach grammar as a communicative resource

Introduction

The history of language teaching reflects many changes that have been made in language teaching approaches and practices. These include the adoption of communicative and learner-centered approaches to teaching and proficiency-based frameworks for the curriculum, course design and assessment such as CEFR, and the use of English to teach content subjects as in English Medium Instruction. Despite the kinds of changes that language teaching regularly undergoes, the role of grammar in teaching English continues to be an issue for teachers and learners. Teachers often ask whether grammar should be a priority in teaching, whether it should be taught directly or be acquired by learners naturally as their language proficiency develops, and whether they should correct students' errors.

> *What other questions does the issue of grammar pose for you?*

Cullen (2012: 258) comments that beliefs about the status of grammar in teaching English tend to be of two kinds: one is the view that "the most effective form of grammar instruction was no overt instruction: learners would acquire the grammar of the language implicitly through exposure to comprehensible input roughly tuned to their level and engagement in meaning-focused tasks", and the other is the belief that some kind of focus on form "in the language classroom is necessary both to accelerate the processes of grammar acquisition and raise ultimate levels of attainment".

However, the practical problem that you may face is that students often have issues with grammar in their written or spoken English – issues that require a response. Grammar may also be a feature in English tests that students are required to take. So, grammar is sometimes viewed as "the elephant in the room" – a problem which is obviously present but that many people would prefer to ignore. In this chapter we will explore the nature of this problem and suggest what we might refer to as a communicative approach to the teaching of grammar.

13.1 Understanding grammar vs. using grammar

To understand the issues grammar poses in teaching and learning we need to distinguish between two kinds of grammatical knowledge: in written and spoken communication, one is *knowing about* grammar, and the other is *knowing how to use* grammar. These are two quite different things. We sometimes meet people who know a lot about English grammar. They may have studied English linguistics or philology at university and can explain the differences between the different ways of expressing the present and the past in English or the meanings of the English article system, yet they may have very limited ability to write or speak in English. They have grammatical *knowledge* but no grammatical *ability*. On the other hand, the typical native speakers of English who have not studied linguistics may not be able to say anything about the differences between the different ways of expressing time in English, although they know how to use the language effectively. They have grammatical *ability* but no grammatical *knowledge*.

Grammatical *knowledge* refers to knowledge of the rules that account for the grammatically correct formation of language. Its unit of focus is typically the sentence. In traditional approaches to language teaching, it is typically viewed as the foundation of language ability and assessed through tests on the mastery of different grammatical items. Correct language use is achieved through a drill-and-practice methodology and through controlled speaking and writing exercises that seek to prevent or minimize opportunities for errors – the approach used in the Audiolingual Method referred to in Chapter 4.

What techniques do your students make use of to develop grammatical knowledge of English?

Grammatical *ability* by comparison refers to the ability to use grammar as a communicative resource in spoken and written discourse, and requires a different pedagogical approach. Its unit of focus is the *text*. As Cullen (2012: 259) puts it:

> The grammatical choices that speakers or writers make – for example, whether to use an active or passive verb form, or whether to use the modal *can* or *could* when making a request – are not made in a vacuum, but in a context of language use. They are thus text-based, not sentence-level, choices made in the act of participating in a communicative event, whether it be a conversation with friends or writing an e-mail to a colleague. In each situation there is a "text" being created and an audience.

"Text" here is used to refer to structured and conventional sequences of language that are used in different contexts in specific ways such as interviews, requests, reports, news broadcasts, essays and reports. Each of these uses of language involves the use of texts, that is, stretches of language that constitute a unified whole with a beginning, a middle and an end, which conform to norms of organization and content, and which draw on appropriate grammar and vocabulary. Grammatical ability involves using grammar as a resource to create different kinds of spoken and written texts for use in specific contexts. Students often develop a good understanding of grammatical knowledge through traditional teaching methods that focus on grammar as a somewhat isolated collection of rules that exist independently of their use in the production of authentic written or spoken language. They may have spent many hours practicing the rules for making grammatically correct sentences but cannot use grammar as a resource in communication.

> *Do you think grammar translation develops grammatical knowledge or grammatical ability?*

In the rest of this chapter, we will describe strategies for the teaching of grammar as a resource, that is, as a skill that can be used in communication.

13.2 Teach awareness of the nature of texts

A starting point is to help students understand the difference between a sentence and a text. While students are generally familiar with the role of grammar at the level of sentences, they may not have thought about how grammar is used at the level of texts. The key feature of texts is the use of recognizable patterns of organization. For a longer, written expository text, the reader generally expects to see the text organized into paragraphs and, within paragraphs, to find main ideas and supporting details – features that contribute to the coherence of a text.

There are several ways in which you can introduce your students to the concept of "text", to the ways in which texts work, and to how grammar functions in texts. For example:

- Have students read two texts with the same content and identify what makes one an effective text and the other not effective.
- Have students compare written and spoken texts on the same topic (e.g. a news event) to find out how they are organized and how the grammar of the texts differs.
- Have students listen to or read examples of transactions such as requests made in different contexts (e.g. among friends vs. with a boss) and see how features such as modals and pronouns work together to create politeness.
- In more advanced academic contexts, give students examples or model texts of different types of writing and have them analyze how each text is put together, i.e. have them study the different "moves" or sections that make up a text, and use the information to inform their writing. Students focus on questions such as: How does a text begin? Where is the main idea introduced? How is an idea developed?

Lock (1995: 129–133) shows how by comparing texts, students can learn the difference between ergative and non-ergative verbs and the restrictions on passive voice in descriptions of processes. The procedures (in shortened form) are:

1) The teacher prepares two short texts, one describing a manufacturing process (e.g. the manufacture of olive oil) and one describing a natural process (e.g. the rain cycle).
2) Students compare the two texts and discuss why a different verb form is used in each text: verbs in one text imply a "doer" or "causer" but not in the text describing a natural process.
3) Students create their own texts on topics of their choice.

As a follow-up activity, you can source authentic texts, delete the verb forms, and have students complete them and compare in groups.

> *What kind of written texts do your students need to be able to write?*

13.3 Develop awareness of differences between spoken and written language

An important feature of texts is the way they reflect differences between spoken and written grammar. One of these differences is the use of clausal and non-clausal units. A clausal unit is defined as a structure "consisting of an independent clause together with any dependent clauses embedded within it", while a non-clausal unit "cannot be analysed in terms of clause structure, and … is not analysable as part of any neighbouring clause" (Hewings & Hewings, 2005: 8, citing Biber et al., 1999). Students can explore examples of spoken texts to find examples of clausal and non-clausal units such as in the following conversation between two friends in Japan who meet in a shopping mall. Students could then turn the conversation into a written text (e.g. in the form of a blog to a friend or a recount) and compare the language of the two types of text:

> A: Hi.
>
> B: Oh hi, how's it going?
>
> A: Good, good, fine.
>
> B: Are you, er, doing some shopping?
>
> A: Yeah, just a few things really, you know.
>
> B: Yeah.
>
> A: Yeah ... actually, I've been looking for a present, for Hiroko, but it's difficult to ... you know ...
>
> B: Yeah, umm, what kind of thing?
>
> A: Oh, something like, umm, a present ... something like, it's her birthday tomorrow actually. [laughs]
>
> B: Tomorrow?
>
> A: Yeah, tomorrow. So I've looked in Hamaya, like at the make-up and stuff, but it's not very exciting.
>
> B: Tomorrow? How about Amu Plaza ... they've got Tower Records and some kind of new shops.
>
> A: Yeah. OK, great, Tower Records might be good. I might give that a go. I've got to go over to the station, anyway. So, anyway, good to see you, and thanks for the tip.
>
> B: That's fine. Say "happy birthday" to Hiroko from me.
>
> A: OK, I will. Bye.
>
> B: Yeah, bye.
>
> A: Bye.
>
> (Hinkel, 2016: 155)

What features of spoken language are illustrated in this text?

By comparing examples of spoken and written texts, students can become aware that spoken and written grammar would often make use of different grammatical resources.

13.4 Use corpora to explore texts

A corpus is a large collection of samples of spoken or written language that can be used to study how grammar is used in authentic spoken or written texts. There are several online corpora such as MICASE (https://quod.lib.umich.edu/cgi/c/corpus/corpus?c=micase;page=simple), MICUSP (https://micusp.elicorpora.info/main) or COCA (https://www.english-corpora.org/coca/) that can provide teachers and students with examples of different kinds of texts or highlight differences between spoken and written language. MICUSP is composed of over 800 papers (over 2 million words) with a grade of A written by upper-level college students across 16 different disciplines. The website is designed to allow for user-friendly searches of not only vocabulary, but also across different types of papers (e.g. argumentative essays, research papers, and reports). An example of a classroom application of MICUSP would be where students in an academic writing class explore which verbs are used to refer to figures or charts, or what verb tenses are used in abstracts of academic articles. A corpus can be used to help identify the vocabulary that is commonly used with different text types such as *procedures*, *information texts*, *persuasive texts* and *story texts*. It can also help students become aware of the verbs that most frequently occur in the passive and of which prepositions frequently go with some of the passive forms, thus assisting students in mastering some of the more difficult aspects of English.

What kind of texts are likely to contain examples of the passive?

13.5 Use deductive and inductive approaches

Learners may have different preferences when it comes to the learning of grammar. Some students like explanations and are uncomfortable when they do not have a clear understanding of something. They like to find logical relationships, rules and structure. Others are more tolerant of ambiguity and do not feel the need for detailed explanations. Therefore, at times it may be appropriate to present grammar explicitly using a deductive or rule-driven approach (Thornbury, 1999): the lesson may start with the teacher presenting information about the role a particular grammatical feature plays in texts, and then the class can examine one or more texts to see how a text reflects this grammatical feature. Students may also be introduced to the terminology needed to identify and discuss grammatical features, such as *defining* and *non-defining relative clauses*, or *finite* and *non-finite verbs*. A deductive approach can also be used within a problem-solving collaborative format. For example, to teach the differences between the use of the simple past and the present perfect, the class could be arranged into sets of pairs and given an information gap task. Half of the sets of pairs receive a summary of rules for the use of the simple past. The other half receive a summary for the use of the present perfect. Next, they all receive a partially completed text in which there are many instances involving a choice between the simple past and the present perfect. The students use their grammar summaries to complete those sentences where rules apply. Following this the pairs are regrouped so that each pair consists of one student who received rules for the simple past and one who received rules for the present perfect. They then examine the text again and share their ideas on how it can be completed, justifying their choices using the information from their summaries.

What are some other activities that make use of a deductive approach to teaching grammar?

At other times the teacher may prefer to use an inductive approach, providing examples of texts that include particular grammatical items and inviting the students to examine their grammatical features. One way in which this can be achieved is through activities in which students compare two texts on the same topic or situation, but which differ in their use of grammatical features. Students can consider differences that may be reflected in the *mode* (e.g. spoken or written), *purpose* (e.g. to persuade or to describe) or *genre* (e.g. a newspaper report or an encyclopedia entry). For example, you might give your students an extract from a travel guide that offers suggestions and advice on things to do and see in a city, and have them compare this with a blog entry or an email message from a friend on the same topic. In comparing the two texts, they could consider how obligation is expressed in each text through choices related to modality.

Can you give examples of other activities that make use of an inductive approach?

13.6 Provide opportunities for guided noticing

Consciousness plays an important role in language learning, and in particular in the form of *noticing* as we have discussed in Chapter 10. Consciousness of features of language can serve as a trigger which activates the first stage in learning grammar. An example of a guided noticing activity is for you to give out extracts from texts (e.g. magazine or newspaper articles) and to ask students to see how many examples they can find of a particular form or grammatical pattern. These are then examined more closely to observe the functions they perform at both the sentence and the text level. An example of taking a noticing activity outside the classroom is when students act as "language detectives": they can be asked to notice and observe target forms in use in the "real world", such as by watching interviews and other speech events on the Internet or on television and documenting the use of specific grammatical features they have been asked to focus on. This can serve to reinforce vocabulary or grammar, but it can also be used to help more advanced students become aware of how grammar works together at a textual level instead of focusing only on vocabulary or on sentence-level structures.

Textual enhancement (e.g. by underlining, using boldface, italicizing, capitalizing or color-coding) can also be used to help students notice forms or features they may not be aware of. The procedures involve:

1) Select a particular grammar feature that you think the learners need to attend to.
2) Highlight that feature in the text using one of the textual enhancement techniques or their combination.

3) Make sure that you do not highlight many different forms as it may distract the learners' attention from meaning.

4) Use strategies to keep the learners' attention on meaning.

5) Do not provide any additional metalinguistic explanation.

Can you suggest noticing activities that make use of watching television?

13.7 Provide opportunities for meaningful communicative practice

In Chapter 6 we have compared *mechanical, meaningful* and *communicative practice. Communicative practice* refers to activities where practice in using language within a real communicative context is the focus, where real information is exchanged, and where the language used is not totally predictable. Communicative practice implies practicing the use of language with a focus on form, meaning, and most importantly, context. Contextualized practice involves using grammar in the context of spoken or written communication. It also means ensuring that contexts for spoken or written practice are authentic and that the grammar of spoken or informal language is not practiced in a formal written context just to provide additional practice. Meaningful practice means that when the teacher overtly teaches a form or focuses on accuracy, practice moves from controlled practice to open-ended or free practice. Once students can control the form, they then need opportunities to practice using it in a variety of ways and in tasks that move from sentence to text, i.e. from skill-getting to skill-using. Communicative practice often involves collaboration on tasks, and this can be included at all levels of instruction. For example, in beginning-level classes, students can be given strips of texts, either sentences or paragraphs that have been cut apart, and then in pairs reconstruct the sentences and/or paragraphs. This task can raise awareness as to how texts, even at a sentence or paragraph level, can be reordered to create different effects. At a more advanced level, students can participate in group-editing tasks that might include guidelines or ideas for beginning discussion of a text. Tapping into expertise that students have is another way to increase collaboration and the co-construction of texts. If some students are very good at synthesis, they could be responsible for combining information that others have gathered and presented in the form of notes from the specific reading that individuals have done on particular topics relevant to the task.

Do you sometimes make use of peer editing of texts? If so, when and how do you use it?

13.8 Provide opportunities for students to produce stretched output

An important aspect of language learning is the complexity of the learner's language – in the case of grammar, the range of grammatical resources the learner can use. For the learner's language to complexify, new linguistic forms have to be acquired and added to the learner's productive linguistic repertoire. This is referred to as *restructuring*. For restructuring to occur two things seem to be required: noticing features of language that the learner has not yet acquired (referred to as "noticing the gap"), and using tasks that require the learner to use new and more complex grammar, i.e. tasks that require the learner to use certain target language forms which "stretch" the learner's language knowledge, thus requiring a "restructuring" of that knowledge. For example, a task may be completed orally, may be recorded, or may require writing. In each case, different opportunities for language awareness and production are involved. Jones and Lock (2011) recommend "elaborating" as a means of helping learners expand their grammatical resources. This refers to activities in which students add to and expand the information contained in a text, and in the process, need to use more sophisticated grammatical features. "Elaborating activities can help to dramatise for them the fact that learning grammar is not just about 'correctness' but that it is first and foremost about gaining control over resources for making communication more effective." (Jones & Lock, 2011: 73) Jones and Lock (2011: 74) describe the general procedures used in elaborating:

1. Present the students with a simple text.
2. Create a situation in which certain questions are asked about the text in a way that students **notice** both that additional information would make the text better and that this new information is typically associated with certain grammatical features.
3. **Explore** with students why certain kinds of additions in the text require certain grammatical features and others require different ones.
4. Have students **practise** by continuing to elaborate on the same text or elaborating on a similar text.

Dictogloss (an activity in which you read a short text at normal speed while students jot down key words and phrases and later work in groups to reconstruct the original text) can also be used to facilitate restructuring.

Can you suggest other activities that require students to "stretch" their language resources?

13.9 Make links between grammar and vocabulary

Although grammar and vocabulary are often presented separately, the boundary between them is not rigid. In fact, it is sometimes difficult to separate the two. There are several ways in which the connections between grammar and vocabulary can be highlighted and developed. A simple activity that helps strengthen knowledge of connections between grammar and vocabulary is gap-filling. Jones and Lock (2011: 43–44) comment:

> Having learners either listen for the missing 'bits' in the transcript of a spoken text, or try to work out from the context what is missing in a written text can be good ways of drawing their attention to the use of particular forms in particular contexts, and can provide a starting point for exploration of their functions. Also, having them compare ways that they have filled in blanks with the original version of a text or conversation can help them notice where they are having difficulties producing appropriate forms and to explore why certain forms are appropriate and certain forms are not.

Jones and Lock (2011: 44) recommend the following procedures:

1. Find, adapt or write a text containing occurrences of a particular feature you would like your students to work on.
2. Prepare a version of the text with some or all the occurrences of this feature blanked out. They may be single

words or longer stretches of text like phrases or clauses.

3. Have the students fill in as many gaps as they can, either based on some limited exposure to the original text (listening to it or reading through it once) or based on their own contextual or grammatical knowledge.

4. Present the original text to the students (either in spoken or written form) and have them compare the ways they filled in the gaps with the occurrences of the feature in the original text and **notice** the kinds of forms that are used and where their answers are different from the original.

5. Have students **explore** the reasons why certain forms are appropriate or inappropriate by trying to either justify what they wrote or explain why it should be changed.

6. Have students **practise** producing the feature in an appropriate way in similar conversations or texts.

> *Prepare a gap-filling exercise that you could use with your students, and if possible, try it out to see how useful the students find it.*

13.10 Use student errors to inform instruction

Problems which students experience in using grammar can be a useful source for teaching. Students' errors might be both at the level of the sentence and the text, and teaching activities can be developed both around a collection of typical errors students have made in the past and through addressing errors that arise in ongoing classroom work. These patterns of errors can then be used to inform instruction.

An example of a sentence-level error is from a class where

students were struggling with *result* + preposition and using *result of* and *result in* interchangeably. Let's see how the teacher addressed it. The teacher noticed this error pattern and created an activity that led students through a guided noticing activity to help them understand that *of* is used when *result* is a noun (e.g. *The result of heavy rain is often flooding.*) and *in* is used when *result* is a verb (e.g. *Heavy rain can result in flooding.*):

1) Fill in the blanks with either *in* or *of*. Check your answers with a classmate.

   a. Failure to do so may result _____ an "F" for your final grade.

   b. Five unexcused absences will result _____ a failure in this class.

   c. You should become better writers as a result _____ this course.

   d. The result _____ this exercise will be a carefully organized essay.

   e. Excessive absences may result _____ a failing grade.

2) Look at the sentences and answer the two questions below:

   What part of speech (noun or verb) is *result* when used with *in?* _____

   What part of speech (noun or verb) is *result* when used with *of?* _____

The teacher then gave students several short texts based on extracts from students' writing which contained examples of incorrect uses of *result in/of*, and asked them to work in pairs and correct the texts.

An example of an activity that draws on students' errors at the level of text is one that addresses problems with the active/passive distinction. This distinction can only be understood in the context of an extended text since the correct voice depends on the context of the text and its communicative purpose. Students can be given examples of texts containing clauses that can be completed in the active or passive voice, or containing clauses with an incorrect voice, together with guiding questions that prompt them to think about the contexts of the texts and the information focus, and then to use this information to make the choice between the active voice and the passive voice. Using error patterns from student texts in this way is an efficient way to inform instruction.

Can you suggest other activities that make use of student errors as a source of learning?

13.11 Integrate grammar with the four skills

Grammar does not exist in isolation as lists of rules for forming sentences but is an essential part of the structure of texts. It can be thought of as the "glue" that holds words and sentences together to create written and spoken texts. Grammar is not an end in itself but a means to an end, so it is essential that grammar is taught and practiced across all skills and in a manner that moves from part to whole, or from sentences to entire texts. In many cases the appropriate place for grammar in the curriculum is as a component of skill-based courses in reading, writing, listening or speaking or as part of an integrated approach which includes all skills such as content-based instruction, rather than as a stand-alone course on grammar. Much of what is often taught in traditional grammar courses that focus on sentence-based practice (i.e. skill-getting activities) can be assigned for self-study, using the resources that technology provides for practice activities of this sort (see below).

13.11.1 Grammar and reading

There are many ways in which grammar can be included in a reading activity. For example, a reading text may contain "while-reading" tasks that occur alongside the text to guide the reader through it and through the reading process. Guiding or focusing questions can be used in this way and can be used to draw attention to grammatical choices made by the writer. The type of the while-reading activity will depend upon the type of the text. If the text is a narrative, students might number the sequence of events in the narrative on a list or chart, and later write their own version of the narrative using the information in the list/chart.

Here is another example of an activity that links reading and grammar:

1) The teacher prepares (or chooses) a text that can be divided into three sections (e.g. a descriptive text, an expository text, or a narrative) and that includes several examples of a grammar feature that will be the focus of the activity.
2) Students receive the beginning and final sections of the text but not the middle section. They examine the sections and the teacher draws their attention to the grammar feature in focus (e.g. tenses, conjunctions or adjectives depending on the content of the text). They also discuss the discourse features of the sections that enable them to be read as a beginning section and a final section.
3) Students work in pairs or groups to try to construct the middle section of the text.
4) They compare their efforts with others and make any needed changes, paying attention to the grammar feature that has been used.

5) Students then receive the original middle section of the text and compare their texts with the original.

13.11.2 Grammar and writing

Writing classes are often the most obvious place to link grammar as a resource that is used in the creation of texts, while oral interviews can be used as a springboard for practicing creating texts that contain various time frames (and tense uses) and following the conventions of English written discourse. Students are first assigned a topic, and then they interview a number of people to collect information for use in a written report.

13.11.3 Grammar and speaking

In speaking classes, grammatical choices and features can be a focus at different stages of a lesson. For example, prior to a speaking activity focusing on casual conversation, students might be given a handout containing a transcript of a conversation to consider the use of discourse markers, the choice of tenses, and the differences between spoken and written grammar as seen in ellipsis. (See the transcript of the conversation in 13.3.) Students might then practice writing their own dialog using the same grammatical features, and later enact and compare it with those produced by other students. Noticing activities can also be a useful feature of speaking activities. Students can observe examples of different oral activities on video or on the Internet and be given tasks that involve tracking the use of different features of grammar. They can then replicate some of the examples they have observed in dialog development and role-plays.

Gap-filling (discussed above) can also be used with conversations and other spoken texts, in which students are given examples of spoken texts from which key grammatical features or items have been deleted, and they need to complete these blanks in pairs or groups.

13.11.4 Grammar and listening

In a listening lesson, post-listening activities can be found that involve returning to the listening texts that serve as the basis for comprehension activities and using them to raise language awareness. For example, students can again listen to a recording or view a video to identify differences between what they have heard and a printed version of the text, to complete a cloze version of the text, to complete parts of sentences taken from the text, or to check off from a list forms that have occurred in the text.

Restructuring activities are oral or written tasks that involve productive use of selected items from a listening text. Such activities could include written sentence-completion tasks requiring use of grammar that has occurred in the listening text, and dialog practice based on dialogs that incorporate grammatical features from the text or role-plays in which students are required to use key language features from the text.

> *What are some ways in which you include a focus on grammar in listening, speaking, reading or writing activities?*

13.12 Use the resources of the Internet and technology

Both the Internet and technology or TLLT (technology for

language learning and teaching) can offer useful tools to help learners expand their grammatical resources (see Chapter 15). The Internet and technology can bring many types of language use into the classroom, allowing students to be exposed to and interact with a variety of spoken and written texts. At an advanced level, in content or ESP (English for special purposes) classes students can use the Internet to find authentic examples of content-related texts. These can then be used in class to explore structures such as the use of transitions, or to see how features work together to create a particular type of text. For example, students can identify which features are used to signal contrast in persuasive texts, or which grammatical resources are used to package information in scientific reports.

The Internet can also be used to provide a real audience for student writing. Students can submit movie or book reviews to online sites, expanding the audience beyond the classroom teacher. This can be a powerful motivator for students to produce accurate texts, since now the task is a real-world one and goes beyond simply writing a class assignment that only the teacher will read.

Technology also offers a wide range of resources to support the learning of grammar (Erben et al., 2009). Software programs that focus on the role of grammar in spoken and written English have become increasingly sophisticated and have moved well beyond the error-correction features of earlier programs. Modern programs provide interactivity with learners as they guide them through the processes of decision-making, monitoring and evaluation that are involved in the use of grammar.

> *What kinds of apps do your students use to help develop their ability in using English grammar? How useful do they find them?*

Conclusion

It is important to remember that learning to use grammar involves learning how grammatical choices reflect their roles in texts and how texts reflect both their functions and the contexts in which they are used. Teaching of grammar aims to develop learners' awareness of the nature of texts and the functions of grammar within them, and to expand the grammatical resources learners make use of when they engage in the production of spoken and written texts. In this way the teaching of grammar can move beyond sentence-level grammar and incorporate a focus on grammar as an essential communicative resource, i.e. from skill-getting to skill-using.

Follow-up

Review a practical grammar practice book for students. Does it provide activities both for grammatical knowledge and grammatical ability?

References and further reading

* This chapter draws on suggestions in Richards and Reppen (2014) below.

Biber, D., Johansson, S., Leech, G., Conrad, S. & Finegan, E. (1999). *Longman Grammar of Spoken and Written English*. Harlow: Pearson Education Limited.

Cullen, R. (2012). Grammar Instruction. In A. Burns & J. C. Richards (Eds.), *The Cambridge Guide to Pedagogy and Practice in Second Language Teaching* (pp. 258–266). New York: Cambridge University Press.

Erben, T., Ban, R. & Castañeda, M. (2009). *Teaching English Language Learners through Technology.* New York: Routledge.

Hewings, A. & Hewings, M. (2005). *Grammar and Context: An Advanced Resource Book.* London: Routledge.

Hinkel, E. (2016). *Teaching English Grammar to Speakers of Other Languages.* New York: Routledge.

Jones, R. H. & Lock, G. (2011). *Functional Grammar in the ESL Classroom: Noticing, Exploring and Practising.* New York: Palgrave Macmillan.

Jones, W. (2012). Assessing Students' Grammatical Ability. In C. Coombe, P. Davidson, B. O'Sullivan & S. Stoynoff (Eds.), *The Cambridge Guide to Second Language Assessment* (pp. 247–256). New York: Cambridge University Press.

Lock, G. (1995). Doers and Causers. In M. C. Pennington (Ed.), *New Ways in Teaching Grammar* (pp. 129–133). Alexandria: TESOL.

McAndrew, J. (2007). Responding to Learners' Language Needs in an Oral EFL Class. In A. Burns & H. de Silva Joyce (Eds.), *Planning and Teaching Creatively within a Required Curriculum for Adult Learners* (pp. 189–204). Alexandria: TESOL.

Richards, J. C. & Reppen, R. (2014). Towards a Pedagogy of Grammar Instruction. *RELC Journal, 45*(1), 5–25.

Thornbury, S. (1999). *How to Teach Grammar.* Harlow: Pearson Education Limited.

PART 7

CREATIVE PRACTICE IN TEACHING

Chapter 14 Use your textbook as a sourcebook

Introduction

Textbooks play an important role in language teaching. Despite advances in technology, the role of the Internet and the media, and the availability of a wide variety of other educational resources, textbooks continue to provide important support for teachers and learners. In many schools a textbook series provides the framework for the curriculum, establishing the goals and content of the English course as well as a teaching methodology for teachers to use. In some contexts, the use of textbooks may be a requirement, and schools may be provided with books developed by the ministry of education. This may be to standardize teaching, to ensure that all students receive well-prepared textbooks at no or little cost, and to provide teachers with books that have been developed by experts in material design and are published to high production standards.

Today's educational materials are very different from those seen in schools a generation ago. They reflect the same standards of design and illustration that students are used to seeing in magazines and advertisements, and on the Internet. In fact, today's textbooks often do not even look like textbooks. The titles of the books do not indicate that they are textbooks, and are suggestive of journeys, destinations, or interaction between people, such as *Streamline*, *Person to Person*, *In Touch* and *Interchange*. Textbook design, however, is not merely decoration. It plays a key role in making the materials easy to navigate, and can help promote learners' engagement with the materials. In this chapter we will examine the role of textbooks and how you can use them to support rather than restrict creative teaching.

14.1 Functions of textbooks

If you use textbooks, you may use them for a variety of purposes. These may include providing a map that outlines the content and structure of lessons, ensuring a balance of skills that learners need to acquire, or preparing students for high-stake tests.

> *What other functions can textbooks be used for? What is the function of textbooks for you?*

Teachers describe the role of textbooks in different ways as seen in these teachers' comments:

> I couldn't teach without a textbook. I have too many hours to teach so I regard my textbook as a collection of tried-and-tested lesson plans. Of course I also add activities of my own, but I find my textbook works pretty well for my learners. (Chris)

> For me a textbook would be a straightjacket. I teach adult students and their needs and concerns change from week to week. I am always on the lookout for things I can bring to class (magazines, pictures, advertisements, etc.) that I can use as a springboard for discussion and practice. I don't want to be

restricted to what is in the book. (Sunny)

For me the textbook saves time, gives direction to my lessons, guides the students in reading and discussion activities, makes teaching easier, faster, and better organized, and above all, gives me confidence and security. (Won Gyu)

I am fairly new to teaching and I need the support of the textbook and the teacher's manual. The manual has lots of great ideas and teaching tips so I am using it together with the textbook as a resource to help me develop my skills as a teacher. (Astrid)

I have a group of adult learners who meet just once a week for a three-hour session. Obviously I can't teach a lot since I only meet them once a week. But the textbook has an excellent workbook and online supplementary exercises so it provides good extra support for self-study for my students. (Carmen)

I am trying to make less use of my textbook because I think it hinders my ability to be creative. Each unit in the book has the same kind of exercises but it is very easy to use. So I worry that it is making me a bit lazy and overdependent on the book rather than on my own ideas and skills. (Fiona)

> *What do you think are the advantages of teaching from a textbook? What are some limitations?*

14.2 Teachers and textbooks

McGrath (2002: 8) lists a number of metaphors teachers use to describe how they view the role of a textbook: "recipe", "springboard", "straightjacket", "supermarket", "holy book", "compass", "survival kit", and "crutch". As these metaphors suggest, some teachers use the textbook as their primary teaching resource. The materials provide the basis for the content of lessons, the balance of skills taught and the kinds of language practice students take part in. In other situations, the textbook may serve primarily to supplement the teacher's instruction. For many inexperienced teachers, the textbook, together with the teacher's book, may be an important source of on-the-job training. For learners, apart from hearing English from their teacher, the textbook and its audio, video and digital components may provide a major source of the English language input they receive, serving as the basis for in-class use as well as for self-study, both before and after lessons. The textbook can give learners a sense of independence, which teacher-prepared lesson handouts do not provide.

Which metaphor would you use to describe textbooks? And what metaphor do you think your students would choose to describe their textbook?

When teachers use the textbook, they expect it to do many of the things a teacher normally does when teaching. For example, the textbook should provide content that reflects the students' interests, give authentic examples of how English is used, and enable students to check their progress. At the same time teachers expect the textbook to be easy to use with clear guidelines in the teacher's manual on how best to use it as a teaching resource. The activities must be clearly presented and easy for the teacher and students to use. However, because textbooks are usually designed for use in many different contexts they invariably need to be adapted or supplemented to match the needs of a specific teaching situation. To do this you will need to draw on your knowledge of your learners' individual interests, needs and difficulties, as is described later in this chapter.

> *What features of a textbook are most important for you and for your learners?*

14.3 Limitations of textbooks

In some teaching institutions such as private institutes, the use of commercial textbooks may be discouraged on the grounds that teacher-made materials are more relevant to the learners' needs. The content of international textbooks may be too generic (e.g. fashion, celebrities, shopping and travel) and not of interest or relevance to the learners, so teachers may be encouraged to use authentic materials in their classes (i.e. materials that were not developed for teaching purposes). The lack of authenticity in textbook language is also a criticism that is sometimes made. One reason is that dialogs, texts and other sources of language input in textbooks are often specially written to ensure that they contain language at a suitable level for learners, and provide vocabulary and grammar that students need to make use of in activities. As a consequence the language input provided as part of the presentation phase of a lesson may be unnatural and contrived, as can be seen in the following textbook dialog that introduces different forms of the verb *sing*:

A: When did you learn to sing?

B: Well, I started singing when I was ten years old, and I've been singing every day since then.

A: I wish I could sing like you. I've never really sung well.

B: Don't worry. If you start singing today, you'll be able to sing in no time.

A: Thank you. But isn't singing very hard?

B: I don't think so. After you learn to sing, you'll be a great singer.

Issues such as those above have prompted a teacher to carry out research on textbook language:

> I decided to look at the role of modal verbs in school textbooks. What I found was that many of the scripted language models and dialogs were unnatural and inappropriate for language learning. Many of the textbooks depicted unrealistic views of real-life situations and oversimplified the language, neglecting important information on the semantic and syntactic aspects of modals. In addition, the frequency with which different modal verbs were presented in the textbooks did not match what I found in information about native-speaker English; some that were not common received a lot of attention in the coursebooks; other much more common ones, very little at all. As teachers, we have to become aware of the limitations of textbooks. Corpora can be a great help in giving us insight into native-speaker use of the target language, and we can draw on them in our own teaching and even show our learners how to use them by themselves. That way, we can become less dependent on textbooks. (Edda)

> *What can you do to supplement a textbook if you feel it does not provide enough input of authentic language?*

However, for those responsible for the development of textbooks the issue of the authenticity of textbook language is usually a priority and is addressed in several ways. For example, instead of a script being used, audio and video materials may be partially scripted or not scripted at all. The speakers, who are often professional actors, are encouraged to speak naturally and to use features of spoken language such as false starts, repeats and clarification questions. With reading materials it may not be possible to find texts that are the right length or level of difficulty, that reflect the reading or listening skills that are being addressed, or that are relevant to the unit topic. In this case, the writer may adapt or create a text, but making sure that it requires the use of the processes the text is intended to practice, such as reading to make inferences or reading to identify cause and effect.

The developments in textbook publishing in the last few decades have also mirrored developments in language teaching more generally, with an increased focus on authenticity of language content on the one hand, and through links to international benchmarks and standards on the other hand. For example, the impact of corpus research on features of spoken interaction is seen in courses such as *Touchstone* (McCarthy et al., 2005), an American English integrated course, which includes a comprehensive syllabus of conversation strategies based on corpus research. The need for textbooks to be referenced to standards is seen in the use of the benchmarks of the Common European Framework of Reference for Languages (see Chapter

12) in courses such as *Four Corners* (Richards & Bohlke, 2011), where each lesson is linked to an outcome or a "can-do" statement in the CEFR.

Do you supplement your textbook with authentic materials? If so, what kind of materials?

14.4 Choosing textbooks

Do you have a choice over which textbook you will use for a course in your school? Sometimes decisions may be made by a group of teachers who share their ideas on what they look for in a textbook. In considering the choice of a textbook, or in evaluating a textbook that you have been assigned to use, the starting point is to look through the book and ask questions about the textbook's aims, target audience, level, organization and resources.

What other issues are important in evaluating a textbook?

You might also need to consider the methodology that the textbook is based on and how appropriate the methodology is for your teaching context. For example, does it reflect the principles of Communicative Language Teaching or of learner-centered teaching? Does it make use of group-work activities and collaborative learning? What approach to reading and listening skills does it reflect? Does it contain a balance of skill-getting and skill-using activities? Is the methodology of the book pedagogically sound?

> • *Which aspects of a textbook are most important to you in deciding whether or how to use it?*
> • *When you were learning English as a student, was there a particular textbook that you liked? What did you like about it?*

14.5 How teachers use textbooks

No matter how well-developed or "complete" a textbook may appear to be, teachers usually seek to personalize the textbook in some way. It is always interesting for me to visit a school where teachers are using an assigned textbook or a textbook series and to compare how they use it. Often the same book may have very different functions in the hands of different teachers as you can see in the following examples.

Teacher Andrew studies the textbook and the teaching manual closely prior to every lesson he teaches and makes every effort to teach lessons exactly as prescribed in the manual. His lessons are an impressive reflection of techniques recommended in the teacher's manual. For him the textbook is a *coursebook* – something that prescribes what should be taught and how to teach it. However, using a textbook in this way can sometimes lead to what is termed "deskilling". He hasn't used the creative techniques and strategies the teacher was introduced to and encouraged to use during his initial teacher training; many of these skills have been forgotten and are not used due to the teacher's sense that he must teach to the book. The teacher now uses a restricted repertoire of techniques and activities which over time become predictable for his learners and do not succeed in generating engagement and enthusiasm for the way he teaches. In a sense the teacher has reduced the art of teaching to "presenting the material in the book".

For Teacher Betty on the other hand, the textbook is a *source-book*. Rather than use the book to prescribe how to teach, she looks for opportunities to adapt the book to her learners' needs and interests. Her lessons often have an unpredictable element since every lesson is different, just as every class is different. Sometimes she improvises around an unexpected opportunity or issue that arises during a lesson. In order for her to be able to do this she assigns some exercises from the book as self-study, giving her time to add activities that connect to the students' lives and interests to the lesson.

Which of the two teachers above are you more like?

14.6 Using a textbook as a sourcebook rather than a coursebook

When you use a textbook as a sourcebook rather than a coursebook you look for ways of personalizing the content to make it connect more closely with your learners, you look for creative, novel and engaging ways of presenting and using activities, and you look for additional resources and activities that you can use to complement the book. Here are some of the ways.

Localizing the content of the lesson. Textbooks are developed to be used in many different kinds of teaching situations, and textbook topics as a consequence are often predictable and may not be of interest to your learners. And topics that work well with one group of learners may not be effective with a different group of learners. Topics and activities may be more effective if you can modify them to reflect local issues and content. Content may also need to be changed if it does not suit the target learners' demographics, e.g. their age, gender, occupation details or cultural backgrounds. Localization also involves adapting or supplementing content to address the specific language learning needs of a group of learners. For example, pronunciation problems relating to a specific group of learners based on their language backgrounds may need to be addressed.

> In using international textbooks, some of the topics included can be problematic for both students and teachers. For example, when asked who John Lennon or Nelson Mandela was, my students had absolutely no idea, let alone how to use the information about these people in the book to practice specific rules of grammar and discourse. For various reasons, my students have very limited knowledge of famous people and places outside of their country. Therefore, trying to introduce new language and unfamiliar content at the same time creates an unnecessary learning burden for my students. I generally localize the content of the lesson by using names of people and other information that my students are familiar with, which helps them connect learning of English with their own knowledge and interests. (Theara)

Personalizing the content in the textbook. Learners are more engaged in learning when an activity makes a connection to their own lives, i.e. when the content is personalized. Here are the examples.

As far as I can, I try to personalize my lessons. I involve my students in developing the content of lessons. For example, if I am teaching students to write narratives, while the textbook provides examples of what narratives and their features are, as soon as possible I shift the lesson focus to sharing personal stories. When students share accounts of their childhoods and write about important events or experiences in their lives, they become much more involved in their writing. (Fiona)

I ask my students to collect examples of interesting texts they encounter out of class and bring these to class. I use these as the basis for teaching them about different text types and styles. The texts they bring to class are often more interesting than the ones in the book because these are the texts that THEY are interested in. (Jose)

Increasing the interest level of an activity. Teachers often sense that the way an exercise in the book has been presented can be adapted to make it more interesting, as this teacher describes:

When I teach, I may not have a detailed lesson plan, but I keep my goals firmly in mind and I know what I am trying to teach, whether it is a reading lesson or a speaking lesson and so on. And if I decide to do something that I haven't planned it's because I suddenly thought of a more interesting and engaging way of practicing something. So I may put down the textbook and follow where I think we need to go. For example, the other day we were studying narratives and were looking at a text in the book when it occurred to me that it would be fun if students created a jigsaw narrative in groups. Each group would prepare the opening section of a narrative, and then

> pass it around so that each group added the next section to the story. It turned out to be a good way of reinforcing what we had been studying, about the features of narrative texts – you know, about setting, characters, events, problems and resolution. (Sara)

Reorganizing. Sometimes you may decide to reorganize the syllabus of the book and arrange the units in what you consider to be a more suitable order. Or, within a unit, you may decide not to follow the sequence of activities in the unit, but to reorganize them for a particular reason. Or some exercises within a sequence may be dropped or taught in a different order to avoid repetition.

> I have been using the same textbook for over five years, along with lots of other teachers in my school. Each time I teach from it I try to do different things with it, to use it in ways that are a little bit different from the ways my colleagues use it. They tend to stick to the book a lot of the time. I find it much more interesting to try to find different ways of teaching it, sometimes reversing the order of exercises in a unit, sometimes having students rewrite some of the reading texts, sometimes having students teach the book themselves. It becomes more interesting for me as well as more fun for the learners. I try to challenge myself by not repeating things too many times. (Michael)

Correcting information in the textbook. Information in a textbook sometimes reflects things that may be true in the textbook writer's culture but may not be true elsewhere, as this teacher describes:

One of the things that my students seem to find interesting and even amusing is when I present a different point of view from an idea presented in the textbook. I guess this is just a matter of confidence but I feel it is good for learners to see that ideas in print can be challenged. The most obvious example of this is when texts we are reading have been written by someone writing in a different cultural context. For instance, the other day we were reading a text, written in the USA, about taking part in a job interview. The text said very clearly that the interviewee should call any male interviewers "sir" and any females "ma'am". So I explained that in the country I come from, that would be completely inappropriate because those terms of address are not familiar. This opened up a very interesting discussion about terms of address, formality and respect. My intention was to highlight for the learners that such matters are defined very differently in different cultural contexts and it is important to be sensitive to the context. The same issues of formality and informality occur in writing of course, so I was able to refer to this conversation later when we started working on letter writing. (Stefan)

Modifying tasks. You may find that some exercises and activities in the textbook need to be changed or replaced to give them an additional focus. For example, a listening activity may focus only on listening for information, so you may need to adapt it so that students listen a second or third time for a different purpose. As noted above, sometimes an activity may be extended to provide opportunities for more personalized practice.

Even though my students don't seem to like doing the writing exercises in our textbook in class, I realized that they do quite

> a bit of writing in their daily lives, in the form of tweets and
> Facebook updates, for example. I created a Twitter account
> and a Google+ page for our class and got students to start
> writing short messages in response to each other. Gradually
> I assigned them different roles and had everyone contribute
> different parts to a short story we wrote collaboratively. The
> students loved it as it made the activity more familiar to their
> out-of-class experiences. (Kumiko)

Providing additional practice. A textbook unit has a limited
number of pages, and at times you may need to add additional
practice of grammar, vocabulary or skills. Perhaps the book
deals well with skill-getting practice but the students need more
skill-using practice, so you may need to use additional material
to supplement the book.

Addressing testing requirements. Sometimes supplementary
material may be needed to address the demands of a specific
institutional or other exam. For example, the reading component
of an institutional test may make use of multiple-choice
questions rather than the kinds of comprehension tasks found in
a textbook, so extra material to practice using multiple-choice
questions may be required.

> *If you use a textbook, do you usually have to adapt it to
> make it more suitable for your students? In what ways?*

14.7 Teachers as developers of materials: a case study

Sometimes teachers find that no published coursebooks are

suitable for a particular group of learners and they will need to develop their own course materials. For example, an institute was asked to design a course for groups of company employees who were planning to visit several manufacturing centers in Canada and the US. For the teachers who were given this assignment they first had to understand the context of the course and the kind of teaching materials that would be needed. Questions they asked were:

- Who is the course for?
- Who are the learners?
- What are the aims of the course and its duration?
- What kind of content and skills will the course cover?
- What resources will be used, such as videos, the Internet, audio recordings and realia?

Once the parameters of the course were known, the aims and objectives of the course could be developed (see Chapter 12) and the role and nature of the teaching materials and resources needed could be decided. This involved consultation with the client company and conduction of background research on the Internet. The teachers decided to develop four sets of materials, each one organized as a unit and related to one of the course aims, such as *giving an oral presentation about their company's products* and *listening to descriptions of manufacturing processes*. In thinking about the kind of course materials they would use the teachers made use of their disciplinary knowledge (their understanding of listening skills in a second language) and their pedagogical content knowledge (how to teach listening skills).

The next planning stage involved choosing a topic or theme for each set of materials and mapping out, in precise details, exactly what the learners should be able to do at the end of each unit. During the planning and development process the teachers selected the kinds of listening texts and video resources they wanted the students to be able to understand, the listening skills the materials would practice, and the kinds of activities that would be used in the course and materials. They also considered the features of a successful unit in the materials, keeping these criteria in mind as they worked as a team on developing the course materials:

Length: Sufficient, but not too many, materials are included.

Development: One activity leads effectively into the next; the unit does not consist of a random sequence of activities.

Coherence: The unit has an overall sense of unity.

Pacing: Each activity within the unit moves at a reasonable pace. For example, if there are five sections in the unit, one does not require five times as much time as the others to complete.

Challenge: Activities are at a level that presents a reasonable challenge, but does not lead to frustration on the part of the learners.

Interest level: The content of the unit is likely to arouse the learners' interest.

Outcome: At the end of the unit, learners are able to demonstrate a set of learning outcomes.

Once the course was developed, experienced teachers were allocated to teach the course during an initial trial of the materials with the first group of clients. The teachers made weekly notes regarding the usefulness of the materials. These were reviewed by the course manager who discussed with the teachers any problems with the materials. For the second cycle the teachers filled in gaps or replaced any materials and activities that had been tried and proven unsuccessful.

Do you sometimes make use of teaching materials you have designed yourself? What challenges did you experience in designing them?

Conclusion

Depending on the textbook you teach from, a textbook can either be a hindrance to providing effective and engaging lessons or it can provide opportunities to support learners' enthusiasm and motivation for learning. A textbook can become a hindrance when the activities in the book do not interest or engage the students and when you are not able to adapt it for your classroom context. Sometimes the challenge in teaching is "getting through the lesson materials" rather than providing experiences that you and your students have positive feelings about. A textbook becomes a welcome support for you and your learners when it provides a springboard for creative teaching through the way you use it as a source of language input and learning activities and when it allows you to adapt and supplement the materials in ways that reflect your own teaching style.

Follow-up

Choose a recently published textbook or textbook series that you might consider using. Choose criteria to review the book (series) and evaluate it in terms of its suitability for your teaching context.

References and further reading

Garton, S. & Graves, K. (Eds.). (2014). *International Perspectives on Materials in ELT.* Basingstoke: Palgrave Macmillan.

Gray, J. (Ed.). (2013). *Critical Perspectives on Language Teaching Materials*. Basingstoke: Palgrave Macmillan.

Harwood, N. (Ed.). (2010). *English Language Teaching Materials: Theory and Practice*. New York: Cambridge University Press.

Harwood, N. (Ed.). (2014). *English Language Teaching Textbooks: Content, Consumption, Production*. Basingstoke: Palgrave Macmillan.

McCarthy, M., McCarten, J. & Sandiford, H. (2005). *Touchstone*. New York: Cambridge University Press.

McGrath, I. (2002). *Materials Evaluation and Design for Language Teaching*. Edinburgh: Edinburgh University Press.

Richards, J. C. (2015). *Key Issues in Language Teaching*. Cambridge: Cambridge University Press.

Richards, J. C. & Bohlke, D. (2011). *Four Corners*. New York: Cambridge University Press.

Tomlinson, B. (Ed.). (2003). *Developing Materials for Language Teaching*. London: Continuum.

Chapter 15 Use the resources of technology

Introduction

Today's English teachers face a very different reality from the classrooms in which their parents studied. While only a few years ago the primary resources teachers used were textbooks and the tape recorder or video player, today's learners inhabit a different world. Interactive whiteboards, mobile devices, computers and the Internet are increasingly viewed as an integral and necessary component of the teaching and learning process, and teachers are challenged to discover effective ways of integrating technology into their lessons. And for many learners the classroom might constitute only a small segment of their learning environment, since they conduct much of their learning outside of the classroom – at home or in a media lab watching English television broadcasts or movies with subtitles in their language, or on the train or bus using mobile devices to watch. The classroom has been "flipped" in many cases and may serve not as the primary learning site but just one of many, and often as a place to prepare for and review out-of-class learning. For teachers and students, technology is now mobile, and laptop computers, tablet devices and smartphones are a normal part of the teaching and learning context in many schools. More and more teachers and school administrators accept the role that digital resources and the Internet can play in raising learners' levels of motivation and engagement, supporting learners with different learning styles, and helping improve the quality of teaching and learning. In this chapter we explore the role of technology in language teaching, and the support technology can provide for you and your students.

What kinds of technology do you make use of in your daily life? What do you use them for? How do you think your use of technology may differ from that of your students?

15.1 Teachers and technology

Teachers today are expected to be technologically literate, as seen in a summary of the National Educational Technology Standards (NETS) for Teachers created by the International Society for Technology in Education:

1) Teachers demonstrate a sound understanding of technology operations and concepts.
2) Teachers plan and design effective learning environments and experiences supported by technology.
3) Teachers implement curriculum plans that include methods and strategies for applying technology to maximize student learning.
4) Teachers apply technology to facilitate a variety of effective assessment and evaluation strategies.
5) Teachers use technology to enhance their productivity and professional practice.
6) Teachers understand the social, ethical, legal, and human issues surrounding the use of technology in PK-12 schools and apply that understanding in practice.

How confident are you with the use of technology in teaching? Have you had a chance to attend a workshop or had special training in the use of technology?

TESOL has developed technology standards for both learners and teachers, consisting of both goals and standards. These give a useful overview of the kind of skills with technology that we are expected to have today. The goal that describes teachers' use of technology states: "Language teachers integrate pedagogical knowledge and skills with technology to enhance language teaching and learning." (TESOL, 2008) And then four standards for this goal follow (TESOL, 2008):

> Standard 1: Language teachers identify and evaluate technological resources and environments for suitability to their teaching context.
>
> Standard 2: Language teachers coherently integrate technology into their pedagogical approaches.
>
> Standard 3: Language teachers design and manage language learning activities and tasks using technology appropriately to meet curricular goals and objectives.
>
> Standard 4: Language teachers use relevant research findings to inform the planning of language learning activities and tasks that involve technology.

What use do you make of technology in your teaching? What benefits does it provide for you? What are the benefits for your students?

15.2 Support for learners

For learners, technology can offer a wide variety of benefits both in the classroom and beyond. Some of the potential benefits are:

- It provides a wider exposure to English. The Internet increases opportunities for authentic interaction with other learners either nationally or worldwide.
- It enables flexible learning – students choose when and where to learn.

A teacher gives this example:

> On top of all of the benefits the aspect I consider the most relevant is that the Internet has become my best tool to promote learners' autonomy. Not only do I teach the lesson, but I also teach the strategies that my students can use to take advantage of the Internet without the need of a teacher, and that is the kind of learning that really helps a person move from being a student to being a user of English.
>
> It supports different ways of learning such as through written, visual or auditory means.
>
> It can be used to support different skills, allowing students to focus on a particular skill such as reading or listening.
>
> It is suitable for learners of different proficiency levels.
>
> It encourages more active learning since students are more in control of the process and the outcomes.
>
> For some learners it provides a less stressful learning environment than classroom learning.
>
> It provides a social context for learning, allowing learners to interact socially with other learners.
>
> It can increase motivation and allows access to engaging materials such as digital games and movies.
>
> (Jose)

A student comments:

> I get much better opportunities to practice my English from some of the great apps that are available, which make learning much more interesting than the kinds of things we do in class. (Simon)

What the three most important benefits from the list above for your learners? Are there other benefits?

15.3 Supporting learning beyond the classroom

One thing that characterizes successful language learners is that they look for and make use of opportunities for learning English beyond the classroom. The Internet, technology and the media, and the use of English in face-to-face as well as virtual social networks provide greater opportunities for meaningful and authentic language use than what is available in the classroom. There are many websites or apps that provide support for learning English, for example:

- BBC Learning English
- Duolingo
- Babbel
- Learn English Online | British Council
- FluentU
- Livemocha
- EnglishCentral
- PhraseMix

The following are some examples of how technology provides new opportunities for teaching and learning English.

15.3.1 Chat rooms

One of the easiest ways for learners to engage in real communication out of class is through an online chat room. Chat rooms enable people with similar interests to interact, either through written text-based messages or in the spoken medium. Chat rooms are organized by topics and there are literally thousands of them on the Internet. Some are intended specifically for language learners at different levels of proficiency and enable them to use their English language resources to engage in real-time communication and interaction with other language learners as well as with native speakers. Whereas for some of your learners, classroom-based communication in English may be stressful, making them unwilling to communicate, the chat room is a stress-free context for the use of English. The participants are not handicapped by their limited English proficiency or their fear of making mistakes in front of peers. Consequently, chat-room interaction often results in more successful comprehension as well as a greater amount of target language production than classroom-based communication. Here are some chat rooms that you can invite students to try out:

- Speaky
- LingoGlobe

> *Do your students participate in chat rooms that function in English? Are there any chat rooms that you can recommend to them?*

15.3.2 Digital games

Most students play digital games and these offer possibilities both for entertainment and for language learning. Chik (2015) describes how digital gameplay can contribute to second language learning, particularly in developing familiarity with topics and vocabulary that may not be included in a regular language course. Chik followed a learner who wanted to move beyond the language of academic discourse (the focus of his university English program) in order to become familiar with the vocabulary and expressions needed to talk about topics such as sports – a topic that he wanted to be able to talk about in casual conversation. Chik comments:

> Taking the advice from a gaming friend, Edmond started playing digital basketball games on his PC. He enjoyed the in-game audio commentaries and jokes and read all the instructions dutifully. Transferring the learning strategies acquired from school, Edmond used an electronic dictionary and kept a vocabulary book. Even though the audio commentaries and on-screen texts were repetitive, he worked hard to memorize the terminology. He also thought the repetition necessary for learning the basketball vocabulary and names of basketball players. At the same time, he searched for gaming strategies from online discussion forums. He found a number of Chinese and English forums and blogs discussing different sports games, but the more popular Chinese forums specialized in football game series. As Edmond combed through online communities, he connected with other gamers using sports games to learn English to better enjoy live sports TV programs. After playing digital basketball games for more than six months, Edmond found it a lot easier to understand the conversation with his international team players. (Chik, 2015: 76)

15.3.3 Online resources

The Internet is a major source of different kinds of spoken and written texts. Coxhead and Bytheway (2015) describe the potential of an online source known as TED Talks for developing different language skills (https://www.ted.com/talks). There are high-interest talks on almost every topic on the site, with different lengths, difficulty levels and genres. They may include transcripts as well as translations into different languages and people can share their reactions to the talks with others by posting messages. Some of the talks available on TED Talks have received over 12 million views and the site is regularly updated with new talks of different lengths and difficulty levels, many of which are of high interest. Although the site is not designed for second language learners it has great potential as a learning resource. Coxhead and Bytheway (2015: 67) observe:

> ... learners can listen before or after reading a transcript in English or perhaps their first language or choose short talks on familiar topics before moving on to more difficult topics. ... This means when learners don't have much time for independent listening practice, they could just focus on short talks that are not so conceptually challenging, such as Ric Elias talking about "three things I learned while my plane crashed."

15.3.4 Email-mediated tandem learning

Sasaki (2015) describes how he linked teenage language learners learning each other's language through email-mediated tandem learning – a web-based language learning activity in which two learners with a different native language (L1) use an L2 (the partner's L1) to exchange emails. During their exchanges they talk about topics of mutual interest such as school life and cultural activities; they may pose questions, give clarification, ask for suggestions and so on, and they may also give feedback to each other on the appropriateness of their language use. Sasaki linked Japanese learners of English in Japan with American learners of Japanese in California. The students communicated with each other out of class over an eight-week period using personal computers at home and/or in the school's Computer-Assisted Language Learning (CALL) lab. Throughout the process the learners kept a journal that was shared with the teacher, in which they wrote about their partners' language use, as well as reflecting on the process of tandem learning.

15.3.5 Television and movies

Many young people (and teachers as well) like to watch TV dramas, soap operas and comedies as well as international movies with subtitles – a source of authentic input of everyday English, and students often attribute their mastery of English to watching movies and television in English. They may watch movies at home or in the cinema and with the advent of Internet television (television delivered on any Internet-enabled devices such as smartphones, tablets and personal computers using video streaming), learners can take movies and television with them wherever they go, accessing their favorite programs with just a few clicks. They can spend "dead time" on the subway, on the bus or at the bus stop, watching television programs and movies in English. However, it is worth remembering that in order to be able to watch TV programs and movies in English with subtitles, they need a vocabulary of at least 2,000 words.

Do your students improve their knowledge of English through watching television and movies in English? How do they say it helps them?

15.4 Support for teachers

There are many ways in which technology can be integrated with teaching, learning and assessment, and new possibilities become available almost weekly. For example:

- project-based learning using technology
- use of mobile devices in the classroom
- electronic portfolio assessment
- PowerPoint presentations
- learning with mobile and hand-held devices such as cell phones, MP3 players and tablets
- creative uses of interactive whiteboards
- video-based final assessment
- web-based projects and collaborative online research
- student-created media such as podcasts, videos and slide shows
- collaborative online tools such as wikis or Google Docs
- use of social media

> *Which of the above resources do/would you use? Are there others that you make use of?*

Technology can add another dimension to teaching, including modeling language, assisting with classroom management, and teaching specific skills or grammar as these teachers comment:

> Technology helps my shy students speak up. To boost students' confidence in using English, I use software that allows my students to record videos of themselves reading and speaking. (Patricia)

> My coursebook includes videos that accompany each unit and are designed as models for students to create their own videos using a phone or another device. They can share their videos with students in other countries who are using the same book. (Brian)

> I load all my students' attendance and test scores onto our school's learning management system and I get alerted automatically by email if a student's attendance or performance drops. (Hidalgo)

> I let my students bring their mobile phones to class. For some activities, they use their mobile phones to text answers to grammar exercises from the textbook. Every answer appears without a name on it, on a wall-mounted interactive whiteboard for everyone to see. This takes the boredom out of doing grammar exercises. (Vivienne)

> I sometimes use poetry in my class of young adult learners in Mexico. To present a poem, I often use a podcast of someone reading the poem, since there are usually many examples available online. One of the sites I regularly use includes a reading of the poem, a short text about the poem and some illustrations. I use these as a warm-up to the lesson. (Donna)

As the examples above illustrate, technology-supported teaching potentially enhances teaching in several ways:
- It enables more learner-centered teaching.
- It provides support for teaching mixed-level classes.
- It expands the classroom to the real world.

Just as this teacher reports:

To help develop the use of English as a communicative tool, we try to build bridges between students' families and youth cultures and the academic texts we want them to study. We don't use textbooks, and instead study music, films and documentaries from around the world, read stories and poetry, play games, and do work online. We use Facebook groups to communicate and to do writing, and each student has his or her own blog. This year we joined QuadBlogging to collaborate on blogging with three classrooms around the world. I learn about the conflicts students face in their lives, and that they use English as a way to learn about themselves and to learn to solve problems in their communities.

It gives teachers a much wider range of strategies to use in teaching.

It provides new roles for teachers from a transmitter of knowledge to a facilitator who supports and guides student learning.

It provides opportunities for teachers to take greater individual responsibility for their courses.

It creates a better learning environment where students are engaged in interaction and communication among themselves.

It offers greater opportunities for monitoring learning through Learning Management Systems (LMSs) as well as many CALL materials.

It provides practical support simplifying administration and assessment through CALL and LMSs.

(Belinda)

Sometimes teachers complain that they encounter technical problems when they try to use technology. Is this your experience? How can these sometimes be avoided?

15.5 Support for the four skills

Creative users of technology are also finding many possibilities to help with the learning of the four skills.

15.5.1 Speaking and pronunciation skills

Computer-mediated communication. Synchronous (real-time) computer-mediated communication (such as chat rooms as we have noted above) and some other forms of near-instantaneous interaction (for example, microblogs) share many of the characteristics of spoken language, offering practice of conversational skills and an environment that many learners experience as non-threatening. A teacher comments:

> Real-time, online communication gives the conversation-club activities a whole new meaning. It is the most rewarding experience for my students to see that they are able to have a conversation with real native speakers over the Internet; they get a chance to discuss current topics of mutual interest, and the cost for the institution and for me as a private tutor is [very] affordable. (Simon)

Spoken interaction. Programs such as Skype allow two or more participants to interact. The inclusion of video in many of these programs can be very helpful for learners, as the added visual information helps them understand the message.

Observing how interaction takes place. The students may watch video clips of real or simulated interaction (e.g. checking into a hotel), and then play the part of either of the participants in it. A teacher gives another example:

> The Internet and multimedia technology provide a chance to bring the world into my classroom. Whatever the topic and/or language item I am working with, I always expand my lesson with a real-life, multicultural and multimedia experience. My students really enjoy the different accents and cultural contexts in which the target structure or function we are studying comes alive through the videos on the Internet. (Fiona)

Comparing spoken texts. Some websites allow students to record a spoken text, such as a story, a conversation or an oral presentation. They can then compare their production with the speech of a native speaker.

> *What are some ways in which smartphones can be used in a speaking class?*

15.5.2 Listening skills

Listening resources for L2 learners. Materials specially designed for L2 learners are available on some websites, offering a variety of graded listening texts, with aids such as subtitles, glossaries, captions, transcripts and comprehension quizzes.

Authentic materials with learner support. Several websites provide access to a variety of listening text types (advertisements, movie clips, etc.), accompanied by tasks of listening comprehension.

Authentic materials without learner support. Teachers can make use of authentic listening materials in the form of news broadcasts, interviews and TV shows, which can be input for different kinds of activities.

15.5.3 Reading skills

Fluency development. Support is available for speed-reading practice, with texts that progress in length and difficulty.

Sentence and text awareness. Activities are available that develop awareness of the grammatical and discourse organization of texts.

Test preparation. Activities to prepare students for the reading component of standardized tests can include timed components, immediate or delayed feedback and model answers.

Practice in reading skills. There are opportunities to practice a range of skills, such as skimming, scanning, inferencing and summarizing, with some software highlighting key parts of the text, accompanied by explanations.

Vocabulary building. Text-completion tasks are available where students see a text, guess missing words and get feedback on their choices.

> *Do your students use technology to help with reading in English? What resources do they find useful?*

15.5.4 Writing skills

Learner support. Web-based writing labs are available to help students with assignments.

Sharing and showcasing work. Students can share their compositions through desktop publishing or through sharing via a blog or web publishing.

Computer-mediated peer review. Students can share drafts of written work, for example, in the form of blog posts that other students can comment on.

Collaborative writing. Collaborative online tools such as wikis make the process of generating ideas, and drafting and revising a piece of writing more interactive.

Personal writing. Blogging provides learners with an opportunity to write online and for others to respond to and post their own comments, as is described in this example:

> In our school, journal writing has long been an activity utilized in the primary classroom. Journal writing allows students to reflect on what they are learning and how they are learning. This traditional, notebook-and-pencil activity can become digital when word processing software is used. Or it can go online as a blog. A blog (a short form of "weblog") is a personal journal website on which a user can type an entry, adding images, videos and links to other websites. Readers of a blog usually can post comments. For primary school students, the use of blogs has been found to be an engaging and effective way to promote writing skills, particularly when student peers provide feedback to the blog's writer. It is exactly this feedback and sharing mechanism that makes the blog different to the traditional journal. In the notebook-and-pencil version, the contents of the journal are private to the student, apart from the teacher and whomever the student decides to share the journal with. With the blog, access can be provided to the teacher, the class, the student's parents and the world. (Agnes)

Editing tools. These include online dictionaries, spelling checkers and model texts to assist learners as they write.

15.6 Creative uses of technology

The possibilities above can support learning in different ways through the development of imagination, problem-solving, risk-taking and divergent thinking on the part of teachers and students. The following are examples of teachers' creative uses of technology in their teaching.

15.6.1 Blogging

Social media plays an important role in the daily lives of most people including language learners, and can also be used to support language development. Do Carmo Righini (2015) describes how social media can be used to develop skills needed to read authentic texts and news articles from the electronic media. According to do Carmo Righini (2015), news articles on topics of interest were taken from different news sites and assigned at the end of each lesson as self-study. Students were asked to choose one article a week and teachers were encouraged to create a blog where students would upload comments on the chosen articles while commenting on their peers' posts at the same time. To promote student participation teachers employed different forms of interaction with students on the blogs, and also different social media tools, such as microblogging.

15.6.2 Using VoiceThread

Pontes and Shimazumi (2015) describe how they used an online program to improve their learners' speaking skills in preparation for the Cambridge Certificate of Proficiency in English (CPE) exam. They made use of the online program VoiceThread to enable learners to improve their speaking performance. Learners were assigned a topic, and then asked to prepare a short recording on the topic (approximately two minutes) and upload it to their restricted area on VoiceThread. Once all the recordings had been uploaded, teachers and learners would listen to them and record their comments, impressions and general feedback. Learners would then listen to the comments made on their production, and record and re-upload an improved version, incorporating aspects they considered relevant from their peers' or teachers' feedback, either in terms of grammar (accuracy), vocabulary (lexical appropriacy) or pronunciation (prosodic features), which led to their linguistic development.

15.6.3 Using a video documentary

Miller and Hafner (2015: 213) in Hong Kong, China describe how students in an ESP course collaborated out of class to produce a video:

> [In this project] university students invest their time beyond the classroom when asked to create a digital video project, which documents a simple scientific investigation. This digital video project is part of a credit-bearing EAP course all science students have to take in order to complete their programme in an English medium university in Hong Kong. The project is structured as an integral part of the course and students work in groups outside of class time to create their own scientific documentary which they then up-load onto YouTube. During the course, the students are introduced to the concept of how scientific texts can be presented using different genres: the scientific documentary vs the lab report. They are also introduced to some simple technology which they can use when making a digital video. Then, the students are given

freedom to decide on the type of documentary (observational, expository, participatory); write their own script; prepare a storyboard; record the video footage; and present their scientific findings in as creative a fashion as they like. The results show that when given responsibility for creating a scientific documentary these students invest a large amount of their own time out of class and develop a number of skills: cooperative learning, learner autonomy, and language skills. They invest their time for a number of reasons: they are aware of a potentially large authentic Internet audience who may view their work; they want to present their oral skills well on video; they enjoy the process of being creative and want to showcase their work to the best of their ability.

What are some other ways that producing videos can be used in teaching?

15.6.4 Using a video in the form of a public service announcement

One creative teacher asked students to prepare a video on a social issue of their choice in the form of a public service announcement that would later be included in their final class presentation.

Since we had an Apple lab in the school, I thought it would be exciting for us to learn to use the iMovie software installed in the Apple computers (they were all PC users). First, I produced a two-minute video myself over the weekend. When they saw how I could create a video out of a short recording made with my cheap Nokia phone, they were keen. In our introductory lab session, they came up with some video recordings shot with their iPhones so that they could "fiddle" with the different functions and effects available in the software. I walked them through the basic steps of importing the recordings, cutting up segments, inserting transitions, and adding visual and sound effects. But quite quickly, they took over the learning themselves in their groups. And then they were left to make their videos in their own time. They were basically in their element, and the mode used for the task was something they were cognitively linked to. This is the generation of "digital natives", and when we deliberately plan for language learning to take place in a multimodal setting, one they feel comfortable in, we stand a good chance of engaging them instantly. (Susanna)

Conclusion

Today technology changes at a pace that is sometimes difficult to follow, and today's innovations sometimes turn out to be tomorrow's memories. However, technology is here to stay, and teachers and schools are accumulating growing experience and expertise in the use of technology in language teaching. In the process, teachers are finding creative ways of using technology to enhance both their own teaching and, as well, learning opportunities provided for their learners. In doing so, they are finding ways of using technology not as a gimmick or novelty but as a resource that can support the teaching of all aspects of language as well as assessment and evaluation. Online and technology-supported learning provides limitless opportunities for new modes of learning – learning that draws on multiple modalities and takes learners out of the classroom and into a world without walls. Changes in the ways people learn also provide opportunities for new ways of teaching, enabling creative teachers to develop innovative and creative approaches to using technology in language teaching.

Follow-up

What are some ways in which watching videos, television or movies can be used to help students improve their English? Work with a colleague and suggest activities that can be used for the following skills:

- to learn conversational expressions and phrases
- to develop awareness of different varieties of English

References and further reading

Chik, A. (2015). "I Don't Know How to Talk Basketball before Playing NBA 2K10": Using Digital Games for Out-of-Class Language Learning. In D. Nunan & J. C. Richards (Eds.), *Language Learning beyond the Classroom* (pp. 75–84). New York: Routledge.

Coxhead, A. & Bytheway, J. (2015). Learning Vocabulary Using Two Massive Online Resources: You Will Not Blink. In D. Nunan & J. C. Richards (Eds.), *Language Learning beyond the Classroom* (pp. 65–74). New York: Routledge.

do Carmo Righini, M. (2015). The Use of Social Media Resources in Advanced Level Classes. In D. Nunan & J. C. Richards (Eds.), *Language Learning beyond the Classroom* (pp. 85–94). New York: Routledge.

Miller, L. & Hafner, C. A. (2015). Taking Control: A Digital Video Project for English for Science Students. In D. Nunan & J. C. Richards (Eds.), *Language Learning beyond the Classroom* (pp. 212–222). New York: Routledge.

Pontes, C. & Shimazumi, M. (2015). Learning-to-Learn with Ourselves and with Our Peers through Technology. In D. Nunan & J. C.

Richards (Eds.), *Language Learning beyond the Classroom* (pp. 180–188). New York: Routledge.

Sasaki, A. (2015). E-Mail Tandem Language Learning. In D. Nunan & J. C. Richards (Eds.), *Language Learning beyond the Classroom* (pp. 115–126). New York: Routledge.

TESOL. (2008). *TESOL Technology Standards Framework.* Retrieved from https://www.tesol.org

Ziegler, N. & González-Lloret, M. (2022). *The Routledge Handbook of Second Language Acquisition and Technology.* New York: Routledge.

PART 8

THE NATURE OF TEACHER CHANGE

Chapter 16 Explore your teacher identity

Introduction

While the ability to teach well is usually viewed in terms of the teacher's professional knowledge, knowledge of English and the skills with which the teacher guides and manages student learning – issues which we have explored throughout this book – there are many other less visible aspects of teaching that influence the way we think about and carry out our teaching. One of these is the roles that our teacher identity plays in teaching. Identity is how we understand and express who we are, and how we position ourselves in relation to others in different situations. Identity is also identified with those aspects of oneself that we choose to express in an act of interaction. At the same time, identity is dynamic and shaped by the context of an act of interaction and the people and activities that occur in a situation, expressed through language and the way language is used. Identity is also multifaceted and shaped by experience, beliefs, and personal attributes.

In this chapter we will explore the notion of teacher identity, how it helps us understand the nature of what it means to be a language teacher, and the roles that identity plays in our teaching.

16.1 The nature of teacher identity

When we start our language teaching career we become engaged in many different dimensions of learning. There are issues related to mastery of the subject matter of language teaching. There are issues that involve managing teaching and learning in the classroom. But there are also less visible issues to do with what being a teacher of English means to us and how we develop an understanding of ourselves as teachers. In this process, identity represents a core component of teacher learning. Learning to teach is hence a struggle not only around methods and content knowledge, but essentially about who we are as "teachers". This means considering the following questions: What does it mean to be a teacher? What does my teacher identity consist of? Where do the values and beliefs I hold about second language teaching come from? How does my identity in the classroom influence my interaction with students?

To explore and understand the roles of identity in teaching we need to consider two aspects of identity: our personal identities which define and reflect who we are, and our teacher identity.

> *Think about two very different kinds of people that you know. What are some ways in which you think the identities which they realize in social interaction are different?*

16.2 Personal identity and teacher identity

Our *personal identities* refer to the unique sets of characteristics that define us as particular persons and that we realize through the way we express ourselves and interact with others. Our personal identities are the sense we have of ourselves as individuals, including our self-images and self-awareness which may be reflected in what aspects of ourselves we choose to reveal to others, the stories which we tell about ourselves and how we are understood by others. These features of our inner selves reflect differences among people which play a role in our interaction with each other. They include physical characteristics, abilities and skills (e.g. personality characteristics, special abilities or talents); societal positions (e.g. professional or socio-economic status); and connections we have with other groups (e.g. friends, family and colleagues). Our personal identities also reflect the contexts or activities in which we are participating. For example, we take on the identity of a teacher once entering the classroom, adopt the identity of a colleague in the teachers' common room, and perhaps take on the identity of a parent or partner once returning home. Throughout our lives, as we widen our social networks and the contexts in which we live and work, we continue to construct and to modify our identities over time in relation to the new individuals and groups we interact with and in relation to the new roles we take on in new situations. A personal identity can therefore be understood as not only something that one "has", but something that one "does" in a given situation.

> *How would you describe some of the features of your personal identity? Which features of your identity do you think these people notice: your family; your colleagues; your students?*

Our *teacher identity* may reflect features of our personal

identities, but is primarily identified with features that derive from the nature of teaching itself. Teacher identity has been defined as "the beliefs, values, and commitments an individual holds toward being a teacher (as distinct from another professional) and being a particular type of teacher (e.g. an urban teacher, a beginning teacher, a good teacher, an English teacher, etc.)" (Hsieh, 2010: Abstract). However, like a personal identity, our teacher identity is not fixed. It reflects the contexts in which we work. We may have different identity features when teaching adults compared to teaching young learners and when teaching the whole class compared to teaching small groups of learners.

What are some aspects of your teacher identity that you express when you teach?

16.3 Identity and the teacher's roles in the classroom

One way in which our identity is realized in the classroom is through how we see our roles in our teaching. As language teachers we have different kinds of roles in the classroom. These can include:

A model: providing examples of how language is used and giving feedback on students' language use

A planner: selecting and organizing learning materials for lessons

A resource: providing information about English

A performer: creating lessons that reflect careful planning and execution

A manager: controlling and managing learner behavior to maximize learning opportunities and to minimize disruptions

A motivator: providing experiences that motivate and engage learners

An inquirer: learning more about the nature of second language learning through teaching different kinds of learners and reflecting on the observations

A mentor: guiding learners towards successful learning strategies and approaches

A learner: learning more about teaching through the experience of teaching

A theorizer: developing a deeper understanding of language teaching by developing explanations and theories to account for things observed in the classroom

> *Choose four of the roles above that reflect your teacher identity. How do they influence the way you teach?*

16.4 Characteristics of identity

Just as we realize aspects of our personal identities in teaching, leading to differences in the way we teach compared to other teachers, other identity characteristics are more closely linked to our sense of ourselves as teachers and the distinctive attributes that define us as teachers. These include factors of commitment, self-esteem, agency and self-efficacy.

Commitment refers to how personally we are engaged with teaching, i.e. the extent to which we have a sense of vocation, to which we identify with and support the school's goals and practices, and to which we are willing to invest our personal resources of time and energy in order to achieve excellence in teaching. This is powerfully expressed by Hsieh (2010: 1), a teacher and researcher:

> I am a teacher. But, I am not simply a teacher. I am an English, social studies and math teacher, a teacher of teachers, a student of teachers, who believes in and is committed to a just society, equity of outcomes, ongoing dialogue with students, professionalism and professional competency, inquiry-based communities, high expectations, and thoughtful practice.

Self-esteem refers to attitudes towards ourselves and the extent to which we believe ourselves to be successful, competent and of value to others. Positive self-esteem contributes to what we call our *social competence*, enabling us to communicate effectively with our students and colleagues, and to play a part in resolving conflicts and critical incidents in teaching. It can provide emotional support and job satisfaction, equipping us with feelings of confidence as well as strong coping skills. Self-esteem also relates to the value, status and importance we attribute to language teaching as a profession:

> Whenever I have a conversation with someone, the peak of my pride and honor is when I introduce myself as a teacher. Unfortunately many people take teachers for granted and don't value teaching as a profession. So I try to be a positive representative of my profession. (Hamed)

Agency refers to the extent to which we can actively contribute to and manage change in our own teaching and professional development. Rather than being the recipient of decisions and changes initiated by others, teacher agency is seen in our ability to take charge of our own learning and to set goals, develop the curriculum, embark on changes and make decisions that affect our work and our working conditions.

> I like to try out new things in my teaching. To do so, I take charge of my own learning and try to learn a new language using my own tips and techniques. This is a very good way to experience what my learners go through in their journeys of language learning. Besides, by using this strategy, I get a lot of ideas of what works best for me as a basis for my future plans. (Efren)

Self-efficacy refers to how we view our own effectiveness, i.e. the ability to perform well as a teacher of English, to achieve goals and potential, to maintain commitment to teaching in spite of difficulties we may encounter, and to provide support for students' learning. Self-efficacy has been linked to our teaching experience, to the extent of our professional knowledge as well as to our command of English. Positive experiences of teaching practices, such as observation of students' progress and feedback from students and others, contribute to the sense of identity as a competent and successful teacher, which in turn contributes to our sense of agency as well as our commitment to teaching.

> I believe that in order to be effective I have to inspire my students with the idea that their success in learning English will prepare them well for the future. More independent learning will also be required to achieve their goal. So, putting the students on the right path is the key for my effectiveness and success as a teacher. (Virak)

In the following example the teacher describes how she sees her role as to providing an example of how to become a successful language learner, i.e. being both a model and a motivator:

> I am a highly motivated teacher with a passion for the English language and culture. Having had to learn the language myself has always provided me with that extra inside knowledge of how best to help and encourage my students to master the intricacies of the language ...
>
> Two key elements I tried to put forward were passion and hard work. I used the image of the language student as a sponge, not missing any chance to learn and practice the target language. Another important message I tried to convey was that there is never an end to language learning. It is the labor of a lifetime, more so as language is a living thing which changes, evolves and grows with every passing day.
>
> I used every opportunity to draw from my own experience as a learner, in order to make my students realize that if I had managed to reach a fairly acceptable level of proficiency in English, it was within their reach to do so, too.
>
> (Theara)

The factors above play a role in influencing how we respond to issues we encounter in teaching and in our professional development. They also suggest the complex and subtle ways in which our teacher identity contributes to our classroom practices. In addition to how we see our roles in the classroom, our teacher identity may influence how we understand good teaching and the qualities of a good teacher, how we see our goals and purposes in teaching (e.g. to empower, encourage or develop autonomous learners), and the extent to which we seek to initiate change and take responsibility for it.

> *What are some ways in which your teacher identity influences your understanding of and approach to teaching?*

16.5 The sources of our teacher identity

The sense of identity as a language teacher is influenced by several factors. Here are some examples.

Past experience. One source of what we believe it means to be a teacher is our past experience as learners – our experience of formal schooling, and of teachers we have observed and lessons we have participated in. Many of us teach the way we were taught. We all have memories of ourselves as students and of teachers who may have inspired us. Negative experiences may remind us of the kind of teaching we seek to avoid, while positive experiences may shape our image of the nature of teaching and of the kind of teacher we aspire to be. As one teacher comments:

> People learn through modeling behaviors. If we see another teacher, especially one we respect, doing something successful in the classroom, it's easy for us to be on board and want to replicate that success in our own classrooms. That's why videos of best practices from other teachers' classrooms are so powerful. (Anna)

Teacher education. Another source of our teacher identity is the extent of our professional education. During our teacher training we will have acquired a core set of knowledge, principles, beliefs and practices that will inform our understanding of language teaching and of our identity and roles as language teachers. Our professional knowledge base may be solidified and maintained throughout our careers, or modified and sometimes replaced by subsequent experiences and professional development opportunities. An English teacher is also expected to be knowledgeable about English, and inadequate professional knowledge is sometimes a cause of stress. "Identity stress" can happen when we feel unsure about our teacher identity, which may be the result of negative feedback from a supervisor or from our students, as seen in these comments from a supervisor:

> An example of identity stress occurred in a class I observed of a student teacher (native speaker), who when asked what "several" meant, stumbled for a few seconds and then said "it means seven". When questioned later by the practicum supervisor as to why he gave this answer he said: "Oh I couldn't think of an answer and didn't want the students to think I was stupid, so I just said the first thing that came into my head." (Ivy)

Language proficiency. For English teachers, English is the means of teaching as well as the object of learning, and our proficiency in English has traditionally been viewed as a core element of our sense of professional identity as discussed in Chapter 3.

> To be admired by my students, I believe I must demonstrate an excellent nativelike accent when speaking. (Lim)

An interesting question is: How do so-called native-speaker teachers of English view themselves and how are they viewed by their learners compared to teachers for whom English is a second or other language? For example, native-speaker teachers are often attributed with an identity they may not have – experts, and are often privileged in schools and institutes compared to colleagues who may be much better qualified but are viewed differently by their employers, their learners and their colleagues. Language proficiency is often seen by teachers as an important component of their professional identity as teachers, hence teachers with limited English language proficiency are often conscious of how it affects their professional identity.

Teachers who have limited proficiency in English but are still excellent teachers are sometimes conscious of their "non-native" status and feel concerned about their language proficiency. They may see improvement in their language proficiency as central to their professional development and to their identity as knowledgeable professionals. However, a strong focus on the students and strong preparation for and involvement in lessons can override this factor so that the teacher can develop a confident classroom identity, as this teacher has discovered:

> As a non-native English speaker I was worried about my language skills at first when I started to teach English. ... As the lessons progressed, I became more confident in my teaching and I actually forgot that I was a non-native speaker of English while I was teaching because I became so engrossed and interested in delivering my lessons. (Soo Jin)

Experience with teaching can help create an "insider" identity as a language teacher; the same is true for non-native English-speaking teachers such as this one:

> Since I have been in teaching practice and inside teaching a real class with real ESL students, I no longer feel an outsider in this profession even though I am a non-native speaker of English. Now that I have had a chance to prove myself as a teacher in front of these students and shown them that I know many different techniques as well as skills in using English (yes,

> and even if I still have a bit of an accent), they have begun to accept me as their teacher and I am beginning to feel more like a teacher of English. (Paul)

However, recognition of the role of English as an international language as well as criticism of the philosophy of "native-speakerism" has led many English teachers to question the importance of a native-speaker target and to prefer to position their identity as *multi-competent language users* rather than as second language users (Chapter 3).

> *What are some of the factors above that you think have had a great impact on the development of your language teacher identity?*

16.6 Other aspects of teacher identity

16.6.1 Appropriate teacher behavior

A self-image and sense of identity are also based on values and beliefs one has about how he or she should conduct his or her life and behave in front of others. We conduct our lives according to our understanding of "good" and "proper" or "appropriate" behavior-guiding actions. The roles of a teacher assume several features of teacher professional identity that are prescribed by the teaching profession. For example, as English teachers we are expected to know the subject well, to have good teaching and classroom management skills, and not to show negative emotions such as anger or frustration while we teach. This means that we sometimes monitor and assess our own behavior and performance in terms of the goals we set for good behavior, as we see in these comments from a teacher:

> Ideally I see my roles in the classroom as those of a mentor, a
> facilitator and a motivator. However, when I looked at a video
> I made of one of my lessons recently I came across as more of
> a manager and organizer. (Sam)

Have you ever watched a video of yourself teaching? Was there anything about the way you taught that surprised you? Teachers like the one above are often surprised when they see video recordings of themselves that perhaps reveal different aspects of teacher identity than the one they assume they are enacting while teaching.

16.6.2 Cultural differences

Differences in teacher identity can also reflect the understanding of good teaching in a particular culture. This is seen in the very different teaching philosophies and approaches of two secondary school English teachers observed by Tsui (1995) in Hong Kong, China – one labeled "Chinese", called May Ling, and the other labeled a "Westerner", called George. May Ling had a strong focus on organization and discipline, achieving learning outcomes that Tsui has attributed to the influence of "Chinese culture":

> May Ling had been brought up in the Chinese culture ... She
> had been educated in a system that viewed teachers as
> people with knowledge and wisdom, and in a society that held
> teachers in great respect. In this culture, the teacher's role
> was to impart knowledge, the students' role was to receive
> knowledge, and the relationship between students and
> teachers was formal. (Tsui, 1995: 358)

This teacher's behavior is contrasted with the "Western" teacher, George, who established more informal classroom structure and relationships with students. Tsui has attributed this to the influence of "Western culture":

> George, on the other hand, had been brought up in the Western culture and had gone through a Western education system, in which more emphasis was placed on the individual, most classrooms had done away with the traditional protocol, and the relationship between students and teachers was much less formal. These differences in cultural and educational backgrounds seemed to permeate the practical theories underlying the two teachers' classroom practices. (Tsui, 1995: 359)

Whether or not the differences observed by Tsui would be characteristic of all or most Chinese and all or most Westerners, the contrasts described represent quite different aspects of teaching culture and teacher identity which may or may not be effective when transported to new contexts.

16.6.3 Aspirations for the future

Your view of yourself as a teacher may also include your view of the kind of teacher you would like to become in the future, that is, your "aspirational identity". For example, perhaps in the future you see yourself as becoming a teacher trainer, or a specialist in testing or curriculum and material design. For many teachers their focus on their future identities provides the motivation to learn more about applied linguistics or to take further language or professional development courses (see Chapter 17).

Conclusion

Our sense of identity as teachers has an important influence on how we teach, on the kinds of interaction we have with our students and colleagues as well as on how we are understood and perceived by them. The ways in which we realize our teacher identity in classes and schools help us understand who we are as teachers, how identity influences our interaction with others as well as how other people understand us. Understanding the roles and power of identity in the contexts in which we work adds another dimension to what we understand about the nature of language teaching, language learning and teacher development.

Follow-up

Do you keep a teaching portfolio? A portfolio is a collection of items that you assemble to present an overview of your thinking and practice. The portfolio contains items that reflect your knowledge, skills and achievements as a teacher. An important item in the portfolio is a description of your philosophy of teaching. This consists of a brief account of your approach to teaching, the beliefs and principles you bring to teaching, how you describe your teaching identity and how it influences the kind of learning you try to encourage and develop in your learners. Preparing such a description is the suggested follow-up to this chapter.

References and further reading

Danielewicz, J. (2001). *Teaching Selves: Identity, Pedagogy, and Teacher Education.* New York: State University of New York Press.

Dörnyei, Z. & Ushioda, E. (Eds.). (2009). *Motivation, Language Identity and the L2 Self.* Bristol: Multilingual Matters.

Hsieh, B. Y.-C. (2010). *Exploring the Complexity of Teacher Professional Identity* (PhD dissertation). University of California, Berkeley.

Martel, J. & Wang, A. (2015). Language Teacher Identity. In M. Bigelow & J. Ennser-Kananen (Eds.), *The Routledge Handbook of Educational Linguistics* (pp. 289–300). New York: Routledge.

Norton, B. (2013). *Identity and Language Learning: Extending the Conversation* (2nd edition). Bristol: Multilingual Matters.

Pennington, M. C. & Richards, J. C. (2016). Teacher Identity in Language Teaching: Integrating Personal, Contextual, and Professional Factors. *RELC Journal, 47*(1), 5–23.

Prabjandee, D. (2019). Becoming English Teachers in Thailand: Student Teacher Identity Development during Teaching Practicum. *Issues in Educational Research, 29*(4), 1277–1294.

Richards, J. C. (2021). Teacher, Learner and Student-Teacher Identity in TESOL. *RELC Journal,* 1–15.

Tsui, A. B. M. (1995). Exploring Collaborative Supervision in In-Service Teacher Education. *Journal of Curriculum and Supervision, 10*(4), 346–371.

Chapter 17 Plan your professional development

Introduction

For most language teachers, teaching is long-term professional commitment. However, our professional journeys can be more productive and rewarding if they take us to destinations that we want to reach. These can be to become a subject specialist, a teacher trainer, a curriculum specialist or a textbook writer. Important transitions in our careers may happen by chance, or of course they may not. A key to long-term professional development is the ability to reflect on our teaching experience, and then to use this critical reflection to help decide where we currently are in our careers and where we would like our careers to take us. Reflection means asking questions about what kind of teacher we are, our strengths and limitations, and how we see and plan for what lies ahead of us in our careers. In this chapter we consider several initiatives that you can take to be in charge of your own professional development. These initiatives involve: 1) reviewing your professional development; 2) developing a professional development plan; 3) deciding how to implement your plan.

17.1 Reviewing your professional development

In thinking about your professional development, a starting point is to reflect on how you may have changed as a teacher over time. Change is something we all experience in our teaching careers. Over time we become more confident, we acquire new knowledge and skills, and we develop a deeper understanding of ourselves and of our learners. Some changes may take a long period of time, while others may happen relatively quickly. However, change does not necessarily mean doing something differently: it can mean a change in awareness, it can be an affirmation of current practice or belief, and it is not necessarily immediate or complete.

> *Think about some of the ways you may have changed since you started your career as a teacher. How have changes you have made affected your teaching practice?*

Here, a teacher describes how he has developed since he first started teaching:

> I think I have changed in two important ways. First, I have moved away from textbook-dependent teaching to context-dependent teaching. For instance, I have become independent in terms of deciding the needs of a particular group of students and of the programs they enroll in. As a teacher, I have harmonized the mismatch between the goals of the textbook [and] the needs of the programs and the students, and I do this with my ability to adapt the textbook, to use local authentic materials and to develop new ones. The second way I have changed is that I have started to concentrate more on students' learning than on my own teaching. During the last four or five years of teaching, I have tried to make sure students have the skills in doing independent learning, and

they do it beyond the boundary of the classroom schedule. For instance, I have raised awareness among my students about learning strategies and given students projects that they need to do individually or in small groups after class hours. These important changes in my ways of teaching probably come from two sources. One is my pursuing of graduate studies. Of course, during my graduate studies, I took many courses and exchanged thoughts with many lecturers and professors. The most important source of these changes is probably my own professional development. I have read a large amount of literature in ELT, and also have tested and retested ideas in my own classes every year. (Husai)

17.1.1 Causes of change

As the comments above suggest, change can result from different causes. It might be initiated by self-discovery, by feedback from students or from a supervisor or a peer, or by observing other teachers, through collaborating with other teachers, attending a workshop, or learning something from reading or researching your own classes, or from dissatisfaction with certain aspect of your teaching. Here is what one teacher comments:

Learning through trial and error is on the top of my list rather than simply following the book. When I plan my lessons, I often try to do things a little differently from the book, to make these lessons more interesting. The things I try don't always work as well as I have planned, but at least I get to find out what works well and what doesn't, and I add the successful ones to my teaching repertoire. (Hamed)

Here are some other comments by teachers on things that prompted changes in their beliefs and practices:

For me the in-service courses I have taken have had a huge impact on me, particularly the one on collaborative learning that I took recently. (Sue)

Feedback from students has been very important for me. I got the message that my teaching was not really very engaging a lot of the time. So I have moved towards a much greater use of group work and projects, and I give students a lot more opportunities to choose the kinds of activities they like to work on in class. (Kim)

I have been using team teaching with a colleague recently and watching her teach made me realize that my teaching was too much book-driven. These days I make much less use of the textbook in class. (Efron)

Watching my students learn has really changed my understanding of my role as a teacher. I used to think that the success of my learners depended on me. Now I think more about how I can be more of a facilitator and encourage more independent learning from my students. (Patrick)

> *Think about one way in which you have changed as a teacher since you first started teaching. What do you think was the main cause of the change?*

17.1.2 Compiling a teacher portfolio

We have noted in Chapter 16 that one way of reflecting on your past and present accomplishments as a teacher is with a teaching portfolio. A portfolio consists of a set of different types of documents and other items that have been selected on a principled basis and are organized to tell a story. The collection is updated and revised when needed and is accompanied by your account of the rationale behind the collection. The portfolio can serve several purposes. It provides a demonstration of how you approach your work and presents an account of your thinking, creativity, resourcefulness and effectiveness. It also serves as a source of review and reflection. And the process of compiling the portfolio can prompt you to engage in a comprehensive self-assessment of different aspects of your work.

Different kinds of things can be included in such a portfolio. For example:
- a description of your philosophy of teaching and of the principles you try to realize when you teach
- evidence of your understanding of the subject matter and current developments in language teaching (e.g. book reviews, reviews of materials, essays, and lists of courses taken or workshops attended)
- evidence of your skills as a teacher (e.g. student evaluations, examples of students' work, videos of lessons, comments by observers, and lesson plans and materials you have developed)
- an account of your approach to classroom management and organization (e.g. a report on how you deal with management and classroom problems, and comments on your teaching by coordinators or colleagues)
- documents showing your commitment to professional development (e.g. a professional development plan for yourself, a list of courses you have taken or a list of books you have read recently)

> *What are five things you could include in your portfolio that would provide a good understanding of you as a teacher?*

17.2 Developing a professional development plan

In thinking about professional development, a useful activity is to prepare a one-page statement of the kind that you could include in a job application about your experience and expertise as a teacher. What has worked well for you? What hasn't worked so well? What have been your most important learning opportunities in your career so far? Then, if possible, compare your statement with colleagues and discuss. How similar are you and your colleagues? Such a statement can help you see where you are at present in your professional development. Research on teacher development suggests that it constitutes a kind of life cycle. Teachers' professional lives tend to move in four stages, and the goals a teacher sets may vary depending on the stage the teacher has reached (Garton & Richards, 2008):

1) starting out
2) becoming experienced
3) new horizons: professional development
4) passing on the knowledge

You might like to plot yourself onto either of these stages – where are you currently situated? How soon will it be before you are ready to move on? The implication is that if your goal is simply to survive from one lesson to the next, then you may not be giving much thought to professional development. Nevertheless, even novice teachers probably don't plan to tread water forever. Professional development has a lot to do with transitioning from one stage to the next, and you may have both short-term and longer-term goals for it. For example, these goals could include getting up to date on current issues and developments in language teaching, learning how to become a teacher trainer, or studying for a higher degree or a qualification in a specialized area such as Educational Leadership.

What are the three most important priorities for you in terms of your professional development?

It is also useful to review the kinds of professional development activities you make use of. To what extent do you read books and magazines, write for publication, design instructional materials, attend workshops and conferences, research your teaching, or take part in online forums? Do you belong to a teachers' group or to a professional organization? Activities such as these are important ways to keep yourself informed of developments in language teaching and to reflect the fact that the knowledge base of language teaching is constantly changing. When teachers compare their professional development, I also find that they learn a lot from other activities they are involved in within their schools, such as organizing a conversation club or helping a student teacher with lesson planning. These can be valuable learning experiences, too.

What are some of the ways in which collaboration with colleagues can support professional development?

17.2.1 Bringing about change
In planning for change you also need to consider how to make it

happen:

> Although I have several years' experience of teaching in an institute, I don't have a formal qualification. I want to take a certificate course next year, and to be able to register for a course I first need to take the IELTS test. I have begun studying for the test on my own and will also take an IELTS preparation course in a couple of months. (Anna)

Here a teacher describes how he and his colleagues planned for change:

> As teachers, we are always looking for ways to motivate our students. But we also need to be motivated at times. Recently, the teachers in our school learned about a scholarship that was available for English teachers to spend six weeks on a cultural study program in an English-speaking country. One of the requirements was a high score on the TOEFL examination. All the 15 teachers in our English department decided to enter the competition. We committed ourselves to sharing the costs of buying books and test-preparation materials and to devoting two hours each day to preparing for the exam. And we agreed that the teachers who got the best grades on the exam would be given the chance to apply for the scholarship. We also agreed that even if none of us were successful, we had nothing to lose, since the opportunity to improve our TOEFL scores was well worthwhile anyway. (Jose)

While professional development involves looking forward, it also involves looking back and reviewing what you have achieved so far and whether there are aspects of your professional knowledge and skill base that you may want to develop further. As in the example above, this means you can start by looking at your current qualifications, whether they be a certificate- or diploma-level qualification in TESOL or a degree or other qualifications in the field.

> *What kinds of professional development activities have you taken part in? How useful were they?*

17.2.2 Acquiring a professional qualification

As the example above illustrates, teachers sometimes feel the need to take an additional qualification. Many different qualifications are available ranging from short certificate-level courses to undergraduate and graduate courses. There is also a growing demand for online professional development courses as a kind of response to the rising need worldwide for qualified English teachers. If that is your goal, a good place to start is by talking to someone who already has that qualification – perhaps a colleague or a teacher you can talk to online and ask how useful the qualification is, how difficult it was to obtain, whether it is best to study for it full-time, part-time, face-to-face or online, and what advice he or she would give you. Or rather than pursue an additional qualification you might consider some areas of TESOL that you would like to become more familiar with, such as testing and assessment, classroom research or the use of technology. What activities do you think could best help you develop expertise in each area? For example, you might be able to take a course, go online, use team teaching, do independent reading, observe another teacher, or attend a workshop.

Have you considered professional qualifications that are delivered online? What are some advantages and disadvantages of these ways of obtaining qualifications?

17.2.3 Expanding your professional responsibilities

Another area for professional growth is in terms of your responsibilities in your school or institution. These could include the classroom teacher, material designer, curriculum designer, test designer, mentor, teacher trainer, supervisor of other teachers or program coordinator. Are there responsibilities you would like to focus more on in the future and what steps can you take to achieve them? You may also realize that your current knowledge and skill set do not equip you for changes in your school or institution. For example, as a result of staff changes, you may have to take on new tasks and responsibilities for which you have not received any formal training, such as the preparation and supervision of entrance tests; or a key staff member has left, and you may have to take over some of the staff member's classes and responsibilities and teach courses that are not in your specialization.

Is there a new or different role or responsibility you would like to have in your institution in the future? What steps would you need to take to achieve it?

17.2.4 Thinking about your "future self"

Another way of thinking about professional development is by visualizing your ideal "teacher self": an important aspect of goal setting is having a clear "image" of who you want to be, professionally speaking, in the not-too-distant future. The theory of what is called "the motivational self-system" proposes that we are motivated when we have a clear idea of who we would like to become (the "ideal self") and the steps that need to be taken to bridge the gap between the actual self and this ideal one (Dörnyei & Ushioda, 2009). It works best if this ideal self can be very clearly visualized. In order to do this, you might want to think about your "ideal professional self" in, say, five years' time. Which of these possible selves below – if any – does it resemble?

- running your own language school
- becoming the head of an English department
- training new teachers
- teaching academic writing skills to students preparing for university study abroad
- writing textbooks for use in the primary sector
- giving presentations at regional and national conferences

17.3 Deciding how to implement your plan

The third step in your professional development involves thinking about how you can bring about the changes you would like to achieve.

17.3.1 Expanding your teaching skills

Many teachers would like to expand both the breadth and the depth of their teaching skills. In addition to teaching spoken English to adults, perhaps you may wish to develop experience in teaching EAP (English for academic purposes) courses. Or you may want to become familiar with approaches to teaching English to young learners. A teacher with a broad repertoire of teaching skills is likely to have better employment prospects, to be a more creative teacher, and to enjoy a more stimulating teaching career. Here are some ways to develop wider teaching skills.

Teach classes of different levels. If you are familiar with teaching older learners, try teaching younger learners. This may prompt you to rethink some of your assumptions about teaching.

Experiment. Do things differently from time to time. For example, try different ways of using a reading passage, or try using authentic reading texts rather than the ones in the text-book, and reflect on the issues that arise.

Teach different kinds of lessons. Teach a lesson in an area you have never taught before (e.g. a pronunciation lesson), and find out what works with this kind of lesson.

Attend a workshop. Watch out for opportunities to attend workshops on teaching approaches you may be unfamiliar with.

> *If you had the opportunity to participate in a workshop, what kind of workshop topics would you like to explore?*

17.3.2 Learning through collaboration with other teachers

One of the greatest resources in your school are the teachers who work there. In every school, there are teachers with varied experience, knowledge and skills, and both the school and the teachers who work there can benefit by learning from each other and collaborating in different ways. The following are examples.

Peer observation. This is useful to gain an understanding of different aspects of teaching, learning or classroom interaction. It provides an opportunity for you to see how someone else deals with a lesson and copes with common issues and problems in teaching. As an observer you may discover that a colleague has effective teaching strategies that you have never tried out. Observing another teacher can also trigger reflections about your own teaching. For the teacher being observed, you can provide an "objective" view of the lesson and collect information about the lesson that the teacher who is teaching may not be able to collect otherwise. For both teachers, peer observation also has social benefits. It brings teachers together who might not normally have a chance to interact and provides an opportunity for the sharing of ideas and expertise as well as for a chance to discuss problems and concerns. Although it may be difficult, at times, to arrange because of timetabling concerns, it has much to recommend. However, observation should not be confused with evaluation. The purpose of peer observation, as is discussed here, is for the observer to help explore one's own teaching by collecting different kinds of information about the lesson. The following procedures can be used with peer observation:

Select a colleague to work with. This may be a teacher who is teaching the same course or using the same textbook as you, or you could observe a different kind of lesson, depending on mutual interest. The two teachers take turns to teach and observe, as follows:

1) Arrange for a pre-observation orientation session. Before each observation, meet to discuss the nature of the lesson to be observed, the kind of materials being taught, the teacher's approach to teaching, the kind of students in the class, typical patterns of interaction and class participation, and any

problems expected. The teacher who is teaching the lesson should identify a focus for the observation at this stage and set a task for the observer to carry out. The observer's role is to collect information for the teacher that he or she would not normally be able to collect alone. It is important to stress that this task should not involve any form of evaluation. For example, the observer might collect information on how students carry out tasks, the kind of language they use, how much talking they do, etc. Decide on the observation procedures to be used (e.g. checklists, observation forms, and seating plans), and arrange a schedule for the observation.

2) Complete the observation, using the procedures agreed upon.

3) Arrange a follow-up conversation to share and discuss the information collected.

4) The teacher and the observer change roles and plan the next observation.

If you had the opportunity to arrange peer observation with a colleague, what would you hope to learn from it?

Shared lesson planning. Another example of learning through collaboration is with the lesson study approach. This involves several teachers cooperating to plan a lesson that focuses on a particular piece of content or unit of study. Throughout the planning process, the members draw on outside resources, including textbooks, research and teaching theories, and engage in extended conversations while focusing on student learning and the development of specific outcomes. Once the plan has been developed, one member of the team volunteers to teach it, while the others observe. (Sometimes outsiders are also invited to observe.) After the lesson, the group discuss their findings in a colloquium or panel discussion. Typically, the teachers focus on their rationale for how they planned the lesson and their evaluation of how it went, particularly regarding student learning. The planning group then reconvene to review the lesson and revise it, and a different teacher then teaches it to a different class. The cycle culminates in the team publishing a report that includes lesson plans, observed student behavior, teacher reflections and a summary of the group discussions. These are then made available to others.

What are some aspects of pedagogical content knowledge that can result from shared lesson planning?

Team teaching. This involves two or more teachers sharing the responsibility for teaching a class and, when circumstance permits, is an excellent form of collaborative learning. The teachers share the responsibility of planning the lesson or the course, for teaching it and for any follow-up work associated with it, such as evaluation and assessment. Team teaching, then, involves a cycle of team planning, team teaching and team follow-up. Both teachers generally take equal responsibility for the different stages of the teaching process. When these two teachers teach a class, they can learn from each other's strengths and weaknesses. Each teacher will have different ideas on how to deal with any difficulties in the lesson, as well as a different body of experience to draw on. The shared planning, decision-making and review serve as a powerful medium of collaborative learning. Team teaching, in addition, promotes collegiality among teachers in a school. Learners also benefit from having two teachers present in the class. They hear two different models of language, and they experience two different styles of teaching. Furthermore, there are more opportunities for individualized instruction because team teaching creates more interaction between teachers and learners.

> *If a supervisor did not believe in the value of team teaching, how would you convince him or her of its usefulness?*

Support groups. A support group is a group of teachers who meet to discuss goals, concerns, problems and experiences. Such a group can consist of teachers meeting together face-to-face or online. The online or virtual group consists of language teachers who communicate and interact on the Internet. Support groups provide a safe place where teachers can take part in discussing teaching issues, planning lessons collaboratively, reviewing activities, or describing innovations they may be implementing in their classes.

> *Look online for virtual support groups for English teachers. Are there any that you think would be beneficial to take part in?*

Conclusion

Professional development involves taking part in activities that review where we are in the process of professional development, self-reflect on our beliefs and understanding of language teaching and of ourselves as teachers, add to our knowledge and skills, acquire information about new trends and directions in language teaching, take on new roles and responsibilities, and develop collaborative relationships with other teachers. While all teachers are busy professionals and we do not always have time to stop and review where we are in our professional journeys, the process of doing so can help develop an awareness of our individual qualities and strengths as teachers, and better prepare us for both challenges and opportunities in the future.

Follow-up

What do you think institutions can do to support professional development for teachers? Prepare some suggestions and guidelines for institutions that wish to encourage professional development for teachers.

References and further reading

Bailey, K. M. (1992). The Processes of Innovation in Language Teacher Development: What, Why and How Teachers Change. In J. Flowerdew, M. Brock & S. Hsia (Eds.), *Perspectives on Second Language Teacher Education* (pp. 253–282). Hong Kong: City Polytechnic of Hong Kong.

Dörnyei, Z. & Ushioda, E. (Eds.). (2009). *Motivation, Language Identity and the L2 Self*. Bristol: Multilingual Matters.

Freeman, D. (1989). Teacher Training, Development, and Decision Making: A Model of Teaching and Related Strategies for Language Teacher Education. *TESOL Quarterly, 23*(1), 27–45.

Garton, S. & Richards, K. (Eds.). (2008). *Professional Encounters in TESOL: Discourses of Teachers in Teaching*. Basingstoke: Palgrave Macmillan.

Huberman, M. (1989). The Professional Life Cycle of Teachers. *Teachers College Record, 91*(1), 31–57.

Richards, J. C. (2017). *Jack C Richards' 50 Tips for Teacher Development.* Cambridge: Cambridge University Press.

Richards, J. C., Gallo, P. B. & Renandya, W. A. (2001). Exploring Teachers' Beliefs and the Processes of Change. *PAC Journal, 1*(1), 41–64.

Glossary

action zone the pattern of teacher–student interaction in a lesson as is reflected by those students the teacher actively communicates and interacts with

approach the principles and theoretical framework supporting a language teaching design

backchanneling in conversation, the use of expressions such as "really", "yeah" etc. to respond to what the speaker is saying

backward design an approach to course development that begins with a specification of learning outcomes as the basis for planning a course

CEFR the Common European Framework of Reference for Languages

classroom climate the atmosphere of the classroom, resulting from the relationships and communication between the teacher and the students

communicative approach a teaching approach that emphasizes learning through communication and the development of communicative competence

communicative competence a person's knowledge of how to use language appropriately as a communicative resource

competence/competency the knowledge and skills needed to carry out a real-world task

critical incident an unplanned and unanticipated event that occurs during a lesson and that triggers insight into some aspect of teaching and learning

emotional competence the teaching skills needed to manage the emotional aspects of classroom teaching and learning

fluency the extent to which language production is continuous, without causing comprehension difficulties or breakdowns of communication

function an act of communication that is realized in conversation, such as an offer, a request, or a complaint

input language that a learner hears or receives and from which he or she can learn

intercultural competence the ability to communicate effectively with people from different cultures

Kachru's three circles the Inner Circle – countries where English is a first language; the Outer Circle – countries where English is regarded as a second language because it has become established as a legacy of colonialism; the Expanding Circle – countries where English is a foreign language

learning outcome something that a learner is able to do as a result of learning, such as writing a 200-word essay

lingua franca a language that is used for communication between different groups of people, each group speaking a different language

linguistic competence a person's knowledge of how to use language that is grammatically correct

method a teaching design that reflects a specific theory of language and learning and that supports the use of specific teaching techniques

noticing conscious awareness of an aspect of language input

objective a statement that describes the outcomes of learning

pedagogical content knowledge specialized knowledge of a teaching subject that teachers make use of when they teach it

principle one of teachers' beliefs and theories about effective teaching that provide the basis for their teaching practices

scaffolding the support that a learner receives from others in understanding or using language

skill-getting activities activities that develop the ability to use correct features of language, such as grammar

skill-using activities activities that develop the ability to use language as a means of communication

syllabus a description of the content of a course and the order in which its items will be taught

task an activity in which learners use their language and communicative resources to achieve non-linguistic outcomes, such as solving a puzzle or following instructions to assemble a product

text a unit of communication that people use in spoken or written discourse, such as a narrative, a description, or a report

translanguaging another term for code-switching